THE COSTS OF ACCIDENTS

A Legal and Economic Analysis

THE COSTS OF
ACCIDENTS

A Legal and Economic Analysis

GUIDO CALABRESI

New Haven and London, Yale University Press

Published with assistance from the foundation
established in memory of William McKean Brown.

Copyright © 1970 by Yale University.
Fourth Printing, 1975.

Library of Congress catalog card number: 79-81414
ISBN: 0-300-01114-8 (cloth),
0-300-0115-6 (paper)
Designed by John O. C. McCrillis,
set in Garamond type,
and printed in the United States of America by
The Colonial Press Inc., Clinton, Mass.

Published in Great Britain, Europe, and Africa by
Yale University Press, Ltd., London.
Distributed in Latin America by Kaiman & Polon,
Inc., New York City; in Australasia and Southeast
Asia by John Wiley & Sons Australasia Pty. Ltd.,
Sydney; in India by UBS Publishers' Distributors Pvt.,
Ltd., Delhi; in Japan by John Weatherhill, Inc., Tokyo.

To Anne

Contents

Preface

Many of my colleagues read and criticized various parts of this book; others listened patiently and made valuable suggestions as I attempted to work out particular sections. I cannot list all those who helped me; I can, however, note my particular gratitude to Alexander M. Bickel, Ward S. Bowman, Ralph S. Brown, Jan G. Deutsch, Ronald M. Dworkin, Leon Lipson, and Harry H. Wellington. I would single out Fleming James, Jr., and Friedrich Kessler for special thanks not only for their encouragement and help but also for their teaching and writings, which first introduced me to the problems with which this book deals.

I am grateful also to the Walter E. Meyer Research Institute of Law, Inc., whose generous support enabled me to find the time necessary to write this book; to Dean Louis H. Pollak of the Yale Law School, whose guidance and understanding I appreciated as much as his unstinting material support; and to Professor Mauro Cappelletti, Director of the Istituto di Diritto Comparato of the University of Florence, who, with the support of the Fondazione G. Agnelli, extended me hospitality and made clerical assistance available in the period when the edited manuscript and proofs were being corrected.

Arthur A. Charpentier, the Librarian of the Yale Law School, and his whole staff were of great assistance to me; as were Isabelle Malone, the Registrar of the Yale Law School, and her staff, and Miss Roberta Rawle, my secretary when I was in Florence. The patience, dedication, and generosity of Mrs. Bernice Parent, my secretary at the Yale Law School, deserve particular recognition.

Many students at the Yale Law School helped me in the writing of this book, some by their participation in seminars and courses, others as research assistants. I am very grateful to Mary-Michelle Hirschoff and Dean Pope, but most of all to Jon T. Hirschoff, whose help over a four-year period amounted in many instances to coauthorship; without his devotion and insight this book might well not have been written.

Finally, I thank the editors of the *Journal of Law and Economics,* the *Harvard Law Review,* the *Law Forum of the University of Illinois, Law and Contemporary Problems,* and the *Yale Law Journal* for their permission to include, in somewhat different form, portions of articles that I first published in their journals.

Florence
April 1969

GUIDO CALABRESI

PART I

Introduction: The Need for a Theoretical Foundation of Accident Law

CHAPTER 1

The Renaissance of Accident Law Plans

The last few years have seen a rebirth of interest in accident law.[1]
Popular reaction to the increasing number of automobile accidents and rising automobile insurance rates, as well as to attempts
by some insurance companies to deal only with preferred risks,
has made automobile accidents and insurance controversial political issues. At the same time, the continued trends toward nonfault

1. This is not the place for a bibliography of the field. The classic
writings of Albert A. Ehrenzweig, W. G. Friedmann, Charles O. Gregory,
Leon Green, Louis L. Jaffe, Fleming James, Clarence Morris, and William L.
Prosser among others, who reawakened this interest in the United States, are
well known and are in any event collected in the extensive bibliography found
in Charles O. Gregory and Harry Kalven, Jr., *Cases and Materials on Torts*
(2d ed. Boston, Little, Brown, 1969), liii-lxii.

This interest has by no means been limited to the United States. Among the
most provocative of the recent books published abroad are, in England: H. L.
A. Hart and A. M. Honorè, *Causation in the Law* (Oxford, Clarendon Press,
1962); P. S. Atiyah, *Vicarious Liability in the Law of Torts* (London, Butterworths, 1967) (Mr. Atiyah is scheduled to publish a more general work on
torts in 1970, *Accidents, Compensation and the Law* [London, Weidenfeld
and Nicholson, 1970]); John G. Fleming, *An Introduction to the Law of
Torts* (Oxford, Clarendon Press, 1967); and Derek William Elliott and Harry
Street, *Road Accidents* (London, Allen Lane, Penguin Press, 1968); in France:
André Tunc, *La Sécurité Routière* (Paris, Librairie Dalloz, 1966); in Germany:
Eike von Hippel, *Schadensausgleich Bei Verkehrsunfällen* (Berlin, Walter
De Gruyter, 1968), which unfortunately reached me too late to be used in the
preparation of this book; in Italy: Stefano Rodotà, *Il Problema della Respon-
sabilità Civile* (Milano, Giuffrè, 1964); Marco Comporti, *Esposizione al Pericolo e Responsabilità Civile* (Napoli, Morano, 1965); and especially Pietro
Trimarchi, *Rischio e Responsabilità Oggetiva,* (Milano, Giuffrè, 1961), and
Causalità e Danno (Milano, Giuffrè, 1967), two remarkable books which are
virtually unknown in the United States and which, like Comporti's work, did
not come to my attention until this work was finished. In these books Trimarchi develops an approach to accidents closely analogous to that which I
developed independently in various articles published virtually contempo-

4 *Introduction*

liability in the courts for accidents in general and toward increasingly broad systems of general welfare legislation have caused commentators to ask how far the nonfault trend should go and whether nonjudicial systems of compensation would be more efficient.[2]

---

raneously with his works. His treatment of what I call the market or general deterrence method of accident control contains some notable differences in approach and conclusions from mine. But the similarities are striking, especially in view of the totally different legal environment from which his and my works spring.

Two Scandinavian and two English articles also must be mentioned: Jan Hellner, "Tort Liability and Liability Insurance," 6 *Scandinavian Studies in Law* 129 (1962); Stig Jørgensen, "Towards Strict Liability in Tort," 7 *Scandinavian Studies in Law* 25 (1963); J. A. Jolowicz, "Liability for Accidents," 26 *Cambridge L. J.* 50 (1968); and Jolowicz, "The Protection of the Consumer and Purchaser of Goods under English Law," 32 *Mod. L.Rev.* 1 (1969). Writings in Australia and Canada include Abraham Harari, *The Place of Negligence in The Law of Torts* (Melbourne, Law Book Co., 1962) (Mr. Harari's interesting and as yet unpublished review of Fleming's book is on file in the Yale Law Library); Allen M. Linden, *The Report of the Osgoode Hall Study on Compensation for Victims of Automobile Accidents* (Toronto, Ryerson Press, 1965); Linden, "A Century of Tort Law in Canada: Whither Unusual Dangers, Products Liability and Automobile Accident Compensation?" 45 *Canadian Bar Review* 831 (1967); and Paul C. Weiler, "Defamation, Enterprise Liability and Freedom of Speech," 17 *U. Toronto L.J.* 278 (1967). More generally 19 *Rev. Int. Droit Comparé* 757 (1967) contains an issue dedicated to the legal developments in the field in many countries. And Tunc's introduction to the issue is not only valuable in itself but contains an admirable survey of the literature. Perhaps the most up-to-date international bibliography of articles as well as books in the field can be found in von Hippel's book, supra this note at 125–36.

After this book was written, Roland McKean delivered an as yet unpublished paper, "Products Liability: Trends and Implications," to a meeting of the joint committee of the American Economic Association and the American Association of Law Schools on March 18, 1969. The general framework of that paper is parallel in many respects to that used in parts of this book. There are some differences in terminology, see, e.g., infra note 1, Chapter 7, and many differences in conclusions. It is one of the unfortunate effects of the time lag between writing and publication that his paper and my book were written totally independently of each other, so that I could not benefit from his insights. McKean's paper is on file in the Yale Law Library.

2. See Alfred F. Conard, et al., *Automobile Accident Costs and Payments: Studies in the Economics of Injury Reparation* (Ann Arbor, University of Michigan Press, 1964) (cited hereafter as *AACP*), which evaluates the present

Concurrently, there has been a realization on the part of theoretically inclined writers that the analyses that had seemed to support the trend toward nonfault liability are woefully unsophisticated. Some of these theorists have concluded that the bases of nonfault liability are so weak that fault looks good in comparison.[3] Others have sought instead to develop more satisfactory theoretical bases for what once seemed to be an inexorable trend.[4] As a result of these studies, such phrases as "distribute the risk" and "let the party who benefits from a cost bear it" can no longer be accepted as sufficing to determine who ought to bear accident costs. Such catch phrases of the nonfault trend have become nearly as suspect among scholars as the "justice" of the fault system became fifty years ago. And not surprisingly, in light of this development, there are even those who ask if, after all, the fault system is not indeed the most just.[5]

Despite this state of general uncertainty about the theoretical bases of accident law, plans and suggestions for reform abound, varying as much as their authors both in terms of what they propose and in the degree of theoretical justification they offer. They have, however, one thing in common: they cannot be evaluated properly given the current state of knowledge and analysis of the bases of accident law. A short discussion of a few of the suggested reforms should make this clear. I shall consider five categories of plans: (1) the social insurance and welfare legislation plans; (2)

system in the United States and contains valuable articles by Harry Street, Jan Hellner, Danièle Durin, and Herbert Bernstein summarizing reparations systems in England, Sweden, France, and West Germany.

3. See Walter J. Blum and Harry Kalven, Jr., *Public Law Perspectives on a Private Law Problem: Auto Compensation Plans* (Boston, Little, Brown, 1965) (cited hereafter as Blum and Kalven, *Public Law Perspectives*).

4. See, e.g., Guido Calabresi, "The Decision for Accidents: An Approach to Nonfault Allocation of Costs," 78 *Harv. L. Rev.* 713 (1965) (cited hereafter as Calabresi, "The Decision for Accidents"); and Calabresi, "Some Thoughts on Risk Distribution and the Law of Torts," 70 *Yale L.J.* 499 (1961) (cited hereafter as Calabresi, "Risk Distribution").

5. See, e.g., Blum and Kalven, "The Empty Cabinet of Dr. Calabresi: Auto Accidents and General Deterrence," 34 *U. Chi. L. Rev.* 239, 264–66 (1967) (cited hereafter as Blum and Kalven, "The Empty Cabinet").

the first-party motorist insurance plans, which include among others the Keeton-O'Connell plan, the Insurance Company of North America proposal, and the report of the Special Committee of the American Insurance Association; (3) the Defense Research Institute approach; (4) the Blum and Kalven "stopgap" plan; and (5) judicial moves toward nonfault liability, characterized by the rapid changes in products liability law.

SOCIAL INSURANCE AND WELFARE LEGISLATION PLANS

The most dramatic reform of accident law would abolish the field altogether. Proponents assert that the problem is how to compensate victims adequately and inexpensively and claim this can be best accomplished by generalized social insurance paid by the state out of tax revenues.[6] This, they argue, would effectively eliminate the cost to the victim of insufficient compensation as well as the cost to society of inadequate rehabilitation, obviously desirable goals. The problems arise when one asks who should pay the taxes to fund the program; how much compensation is fair; and whether the plan should be limited to automobile accident victims, or extended to all accident victims, or even to victims of serious illnesses, or become part of a broader negative income tax or income maintenance program. Discussion of any one of these problems reveals the need for more theoretical analysis.

Some proponents suggest that general tax revenues should be the source of the funding; this is inexpensive and held to be fair, as the rich would pay the highest taxes.[7] Others propose that at least part should be raised by direct taxes on the activities that "cause" the accidents;[8] "justice" is marshaled in support of this approach

6. See Fowler V. Harper and Fleming James, Jr., *The Law of Torts,* : (Boston, Little, Brown, 1956), at 759–63; cf. Conard, "The Economic Treat ment of Automobile Injuries," 63 *Mich. L. Rev.* 279, 289–91, 294–306 (1964 (cited hereafter as Conard, "Automobile Injuries").

7. Cf. Harper and James, *The Law of Torts,* 2 at 760 n.4.

8. I am using "cause" here and throughout this book as a "weasel" word I do not propose to consider the question of what, if anything, we mean when we say that specific activities "cause," in some metaphysical sense, a given acci

as is the notion that this is economically correct.[9] The first method is certainly inexpensive, but it fails to deal satisfactorily with the effect a general-tax based compensation system might have on the number of accidents unless it were supplemented by substantial criminal and safety legislation. It also fails to examine when and to what extent such criminal legislation is likely to be effective or desirable in controlling accidents.

The second method appears to deal with the problem of deterring accidents by taxing "accident-causing" activities, but it does not adequately answer the immensely difficult question of which activity "causes" the accident. Is it, for instance, the one in which the victim was engaged or the one in which the injurer was engaged? Nor does it fully examine the question of how specifically we should define the activities or individuals to be taxed. Should pedestrians be treated as a group or should there be subcategories of pedestrians according to age; and why one rather than the other? All these questions depend for their answers on a general theory of accident law, and since such a theory does not exist the plans cannot give fully satisfactory solutions.

FIRST-PARTY MOTORIST INSURANCE PLANS
(KEETON-O'CONNELL, ETC.)

The second category of proposals deals specifically with automobile accidents. It encompasses a whole group of admirable plans (there is a new one each month) which have in common an idea derived from their most recent and closely worked out progenitor, the justly celebrated proposal of Robert Keeton and Jeffrey O'Connell.[10] The theme is that, to a greater or lesser ex-

---

lent; in fact, when we identify an act or activity as a "cause," we may be expressing any of a number of ideas. See infra pp. 131–97 for some specific ideas I express by the word.

9. See, e.g., Marc A. Franklin, "Replacing the Negligence Lottery: Compensation and Selective Reimbursement," 53 *U. Va. L. Rev.* 774, 795–812 1967); see also Calabresi, "The Decision for Accidents," at 739–42.

10. See generally, Robert E. Keeton and Jeffrey O'Connell, *Basic Protection for the Traffic Victim* (Boston, Little, Brown, 1965) (hereafter cited as

tent, fault liability should be removed from automobile accident law and a system of first-party insurance should be substituted in its place. This would require each car owner to protect himself, his family, his passengers, and third parties such as pedestrians (unless they are also car owners and therefore self-insured) from losses due to accidents involving his car.

The differences among these plans are by no means insignificant. For example, some would retain the fault system as an appendage while others would not; some would subtract from the victim's recoveries any benefits due him from collateral sources (such as payments from Blue Cross, or employee wage security plans) while others would let the victim collect his full economic loss from the insured regardless of the existence of such collateral sources; and finally, some would do away with "pain and suffering" recoveries while others would retain them at least partially.[11] These differences raise signficant theoretical issues regarding the goals of each plan, but I will not examine them here. Instead I will consider the common denominator of these plans because this will indicate clearly the need for a basic reconsideration of accident law.

Each plan attempts to diminish or eliminate the importance of fault as a criterion for the allocation of accident damages, and each substitutes first-party insurance for the current system, under which the victim collects, if at all, from the party that injures him. Critics such as Walter J. Blum and Harry Kalven, Jr., claim that these plans give no adequate justification for placing accident costs

Keeton-O'Connell). A good précis of various plans of this type, as well as a particularly attractive new version, can be found in the *Report of Special Committee to Study and Evaluate The Keeton-O'Connell Basic Protection Plan and Automobile Accident Reparations* (New York, American Insurance Association, 1968) (hereafter cited as *AIA Report*). The report, which was adopted by the executive committee of the association, also contains a précis of totally different plans and a study of insurance costs under various plans.

11. Compare Keeton-O'Connell at 305–07, 310–11, and 358–62; the proposal recently made public by the Insurance Company of North America, see *AIA Report* at 2–3; and the American Insurance Association plan, id. at 5–7.

on driving rather than on passengerism or pedestrianism.[12] But whatever one may think of the justification given for placing such costs on driving, which at least has the merit of being in accord with the views of the majority of scholars in the field,[13] it is clear that no sufficient one is given for the almost total shift from third- to first-party insurance It is claimed that administrative cost savings will accrue. This may well be the case, but it is not the only thing that will occur, and we must ask whether the cost savings are purchased at too high a price or conversely whether other benefits besides administrative cost savings will result from the change.

If a person insures himself, his family, and his passengers, the cost of owning a car will depend on the probable number and frailty of his passengers, as well as on how well suited his car is to protect the passengers if an accident occurs. Under the current system, driving costs depend much more on the likelihood of imposing injuries on third parties, such as pedestrians, other drivers, and their passengers. Thus one might expect that adoption of one of these plans would substantially lessen driving costs to the young, who tend to drive alone and who, if injured, are more resilient and less prone to permanent injury, and increase driving costs for middle-aged men with large families. Similarly, insurance would be cheaper for owners of the Juggernaut Eight, which is likely to crush all that comes in contact with it but leave its passengers unhurt, or owners of the Safety Six, which has many expensive devices to protect the riders, and more expensive for owners of the Foreign Fly, which barely scratches what it hits but is likely to collapse on contact with a Juggernaut.

In effect, these plans propose that accident costs be placed not only on driving, but also on certain categories of car ownership. They may well be right, but they certainly give no adequate reason

12. See, e.g., Blum and Kalven, "A Stopgap Plan for Compensating Auto Accident Victims," *Ins. L.J.* 661 (August 1968) (cited hereafter as Blum and Kalven, "Stopgap").

13. See Blum and Kalven, *Public Law Perspectives,* at 3–6.

for the decision. Nor can they in the absence of a theory of accident law.

THE DEFENSE RESEARCH INSTITUTE APPROACH

The above plans can be contrasted with the position taken by the Defense Research Institute, an organization dedicated to the worthy purpose of increasing the "Professional Skill and . . . Knowledge of the [tort] Defense Lawyer."[14] This group is opposed equally to the suggestion that accident victims be compensated out of general tax revenues and to plans like Keeton-O'Connell which place automobile accident costs on driving.[15] Perhaps surprisingly, for a group so dedicated to free enterprise, they make suggestions which call for a plethora of direct government rules and regulations governing who may drive and requiring periodic or spot safety checks on cars.[16] These suggestions are sometimes coupled with attacks on recovery by victims from the faulty injurer's insurance company to the extent that collateral sources are available to them.[17] But as an insurance company

14. See, e.g., "A Program For Highway Accident Prevention," 9 *For the Defense* (DRI Newsletter) 65 (November 1968). A definition of "tort" might be helpful to the nonlawyer. Unfortunately no really adequate definition of this word can be given in a sentence or two. Common definitions are "a civil wrong" and "a civil cause of action to recover for injuries not arising out of a contractual relationship." Neither is fully satisfactory. The area of law called torts covers many accident situations but is broader, including many intentional wrongs that result in injury whether or not they give rise to criminal sanctions. Fault, while often necessary for tort liability, is by no means always a prerequisite.

15. See, e.g., "DRI Board Opposes All No-Fault Plans," 9 *For the Defense* 73 (December 1968); "Basic Protection—Diminished Justice At High Cost," "Auto Compensation Plans Change—At Any Cost?" and "Alleged Savings Under Keeton Plan Disputed," 8 *For the Defense* 73 (December 1967).

16. See, e.g., "A Program for Highway Accident Prevention," 9 *For the Defense* 65, 68 (November 1968).

17. See, e.g., "Defense Memo—The Case Against the Collateral Source Rule," 8 *For the Defense,* insert between pp. 60–61 (October 1967); see also *AIA Report,* at 4. Collateral sources are payments to the victim from sources other than the injurer. Accident insurance, Social Security, Blue Cross, and employment wage maintenance plans are prime examples.

association study pointed out, making such collateral sources the primary font of accident recoveries could "lead eventually to a system or systems under which the cost of motoring would be shifted to taxpayers and groups . . . not directly related to motoring."[18] In other words, the Defense Research Institute ends up, perhaps inadvertently, with a system that is perilously close to social insurance paid for out of tax revenues and buttressed by a lot of government safety regulations. One can only assume that it is the unavailability of an adequate theoretical study of the field which has led the Institute to such an improbable result.

The Blum and Kalven Stopgap Plan

Of all the writers in the field, Blum and Kalven have been among the most aware of the frail theoretical underpinnings of most plans. Indeed, at least part of their defense of the fault system can be understood as suggesting simply that no adequate theoretical argument has been offered for any change short of either such radical and politically suspect alterations as social insurance, or even more fundamental changes such as those implied in negative income tax plans.[19] Recently, however, even they have come up with a plan they appropriately label a "stopgap."

The plan contemplates the existence of a Guaranteed Benefits system, now being tried by some insurance companies, under which all victims of automobile accidents would be offered a settlement of up to $5,000 for medical expenses, while those who would have a chance to recover under the fault system would be offered up to $7,500 in addition for all other economic losses actually suffered, provided they eschew their common law remedies. To this munificent scheme (which, incidentally, would seem to increase the current overpayment of minor injuries while hardly helping victims of major ones, and which is justified, as always, in terms of its administrative cost savings), Blum and Kalven add that

18. *AIA Report,* at 4.
19. See Blum and Kalven, *Public Law Perspectives,* at 81–85; and Blum and Kalven, "Stopgap."

> *if* it is desired to protect *all* victims one could . . . [similarly
> compensate] the victims who could not recover at common
> law . . . [by providing that any] . . . *additional cost* of [so]
> extending the compulsory Guaranteed Benefits . . . *should
> be paid for by the state out of general tax revenues.*[20]

Several things should be noticed about Blum and Kalven's plan.
First, they make precisely the opposite decision from Keeton-
O'Connell as to whether those accident costs that are placed on
driving should be placed on drivers on a first- or third-party basis,
and opt for a third-party plan. Predictably, they are fully aware
of doing this and that they have no special ground to prefer one
to the other; they justify their choice on the simple ground that it
retains the status quo.

Second, they emphasize that their plan is desirable only if we
want to compensate *all* automobile accident victims, not just those
who would recover under the fault system. Here too the absence of
a theory that would justify change, or, for that matter, the status
quo, is patent.

Finally, they reach the decision that compensation for those who
are not eligible to recover under fault should be limited to the
$12,500 of the Guaranteed Benefits plan and that the cost of this
should be assessed neither as a cost of driving nor as a cost of the
activity in which the victim was engaged, but as a general cost of
living. The $12,500 limit can be explained by their desire to stay
as close to the status quo as possible pending an adequate theory
justifying change. Placing the costs of the added protection on the
government is harder to understand, however. This allocation removes it both from the victim, where it currently lies, and from the
motorist, on whom Keeton-O'Connell would put it, and charges it
instead to the taxpayer. Again no adequate theoretical justification for this "externalization," as economists would call it, is
given. The only justification offered is the remarkable suggestion
that allocation to the government will bring into the open the

20. Blum and Kalven, "Stopgap," at 665–68 (emphasis in the original).

question of who ought in all fairness to bear accident costs that are currently left on victims.[21]

Passing over the validity of this justification, the clear fact remains that Blum and Kalven, both when they suggest changes and when they reject them for lack of justification, are asserting the need for a theory of accident law. Indeed, they seem to demand even more; they seem to demand a theory capable of calling forth and structuring empirical research from which alone would come facts that in their judgment would justify compensation plans. I suspect, however, that if we waited for such facts to be adequately proven before we made societal changes, we would rarely if ever depart from the status quo. Still, we do have the right to ask for a theoretical framework that will indicate what facts or political opinions justify what kinds of changes. Only with such a framework can we evaluate the factual premises implied in different systems and, in the absence of hard facts, make good guesses.[22]

JUDICIAL MOVES IN PRODUCTS LIABILITY LAW

The final approach I shall discuss in this introduction is not a proposal but rather the implications of judicial determinations in tort law generally, especially in the area of product liability. It is said that products liability law has become or is becoming an area of strict liability, that is, that users now often recover for defects regardless of the manufacturer's or seller's fault. But such a statement conceals more than it reveals. Does the user who is allergic to strawberries recover if the allergy occasionally kills? If not, is there a difference between such a case and 'one where, through no fault of the manufacturer, a drug that is put on the market causes dire effects in a few users? Verbal distinctions can, of course, be made, but whether these distinctions are ultimately meaningful depends on why we have product liability at all. They depend,

---

21. Id. at 668.
22. Cf. Calabresi, "Transaction Costs, Resource Allocation and Liability Rules—A Comment," 11 *J. L. & Econ.* 67, 69–70 (1968) (hereafter cited as Calabresi, "Transaction Costs").

in short, on the existence of a theory of accident law. That courts have not attempted to define such a theory is neither surprising nor troubling; it is not their job.[23] The changes they have made reflect the general attitudes of the academic world. And it is that world that must provide the theory, both for the limited changes courts can make and for the broader ones represented by some of the compensation plans I have discussed.[24]

TOWARD A THEORY OF ACCIDENT LAW

Under the circumstances, the time has come for a full reexamination of what we want a system of accident law to accomplish and for an analysis of how different approaches to accidents would accomplish our goals. To be complete, such a work would have to be mammoth. But even a work of manageable proportions can go well beyond the catchwords and try to show what goals such phrases as risk distribution, resource allocation, and even, in this context, justice, attempt to serve. In addition, such a study can consider the degree to which these goals are consistent with one another and how well the fault system accomplishes them.

The outcome of this analysis cannot be the recommendation of an all-inclusive system of accident law. That would require an

23. Cf. Learned Hand, "Have the Bench and Bar Anything to Contribute to the Teaching of Law?" 24 *Mich. L. Rev.* 466 (1926).

24. At the same conference where McKean's paper "Products Liability: Trends and Implications" was delivered, four comments by economists and lawyers on McKean's paper and on products liability theory were also presented. They are James M. Buchanan, "In Defense of *Caveat Emptor*"; Guido Calabresi and Kenneth C. Bass, III, "Right Approach, Wrong Implications: A Critique of McKean on Products Liability"; Robert Dorfman, "Comments on Roland N. McKean, 'Products Liability: Trends and Implications'"; and Grant Gilmore, "Products Liability: A Commentary." The papers and the discussion that followed deal in some detail with the theoretical and practical problems raised in this section of this book. The whole proceedings are scheduled to be published shortly. The papers are currently on file in the Yale Law Library.

For an interesting, empirically based evaluation of the changes in products liability law, see W. C. Whitford, "Strict Products Liability and the Automobile Industry: Much Ado About Nothing," 1968 *Wis. L. Rev.* 83 (1968).

evaluation of each goal in relation to each area of accidents, for the importance of each goal may well vary in the different areas in which accidents occur. Moreover, even if the goals are given the same weight in different areas, structural differences in the areas may require different systems. A system that is desirable for work accidents may not be desirable for automobile accidents, either because what we desire may be different, or because the structure of the activities involved may require different systems to accomplish the same ends. Only careful empirical research in each area can reveal the system that is best for it.[25]

The aim of this study is more limited: it is to determine what goals are best accomplished by what types of systems, what systems are best suited for dealing with combinations of goals, and what systems are most suitable in areas where one goal predominates.

I shall begin by discussing some of the common areas of confusion in previous discussions. Second, I shall state what I consider to be the two principal goals of accident law, as well as three subgoals of one of these goals, and describe the principal methods or approaches we have for achieving these subgoals. Third, I shall examine the theoretical bases of these methods, viewing the methods as means of accomplishing the subgoals, and see how they limit the methods. Fourth, I shall consider particular problems involved in the analysis of two of the methods that have been examined less adequately in the past than the others. (Incidentally, these problems exist in all of the methods, but they are most dramatic in the two I shall analyze.) Fifth, I shall evaluate the fault system as a device for accomplishing the subgoals and contrast it with other possible systems. Finally, I shall return to the other main goal, consider what we mean by it, and reexamine the fault system and other possible systems in light of it.

25. For an indication of the detail needed see W. C. Whitford, "Law and the Consumer Transaction: A Case Study of the Automobile Warranty," 1968 *Wis. L. Rev.* 1006 (1968).

Throughout, I shall try to maintain the following locutions: *goals* will mean the broadest aims of accident law (justice and cost reduction); *subgoals* will mean particular categories of the broad goals (e.g. reduction of administrative costs); *methods* or *approaches* will mean theoretical devices for achieving goals or subgoals (e.g. spreading of costs, general deterrence); *systems* of accident law will mean actual ways of allocating costs of accidents (e.g. the fault system, social insurance, or enterprise liability).

CHAPTER 2

Some Common Areas of Confusion

Some myths will make our analysis difficult if not cleared up. The first is that our society wants to avoid accidents at all costs; the second is that there is an inexorable economic law that dictates the "right" way to allocate accident losses; the third is that when critics and courts talk about distributing the risk of accidents they have a specific goal or subgoal in mind; and the fourth is that it is axiomatic that the costs of an accident be borne only by the victim or by the party who may in some sense be said to have injured him.

Avoid Accidents at All Costs

Our society is not committed to preserving life at any cost.[1] In its broadest sense, the rather unpleasant notion that we are willing to destroy lives should be obvious. Wars are fought. The University of Mississippi is integrated at the risk of losing lives. But what is more pertinent to the study of accident law, though perhaps equally obvious, is that lives are spent not only when the *quid pro quo* is some great moral principle, but also when it is a matter of convenience. Ventures are undertaken that, statistically at least, are certain to cost lives. Thus we build a tunnel under Mont Blanc because it is essential to the Common Market and cuts down the traveling time from Rome to Paris, though we know

---

1. For a more complete discussion of this point, see Calabresi, "The Decision for Accidents," at 716–21. As in that article, n. 1, the use in this book of such terms as "cost," "cheaper," "afford," and "socially more expensive," is extremely sloppy from an economist's viewpoint; I have used the terms in this unrigorous way in an attempt to make the book intelligible to noneconomists. This effort may be misguided, but I think it is essential. It would not be too difficult to translate these terms into their relatively precise economic meanings. I have not done this consistently, however, because it would make the book less readable. Some appropriate definitions may be found in Calabresi, "Risk Distribution," at 503–04, nn. 15, 18.

that about one man per kilometer of tunnel will die. We take planes and cars rather than safer, slower means of travel. And perhaps most telling, we use relatively safe equipment rather than the safest imaginable because—and it is not a bad reason—the safest costs too much. It should be apparent that while some of these accident-causing activities also result in diminution of accidents— the Mont Blanc tunnel may well save more lives by diminishing traffic fatalities than it took to build it—this explanation does not come close to justifying most accident-causing activities. Railroad grade crossings are used because they are cheap, not because they save more lives than they take.

ECONOMIC LAWS GIVE ABSOLUTE ANSWERS

Since we are not committed to preserving life at any cost, the question is the more complex one of how far we want to go to save lives and reduce accident costs. This leads us to the second myth: that economic theory can answer the question. Just as economic theory cannot decide for us whether we want to save the life of a trapped miner, so it cannot tell us how far we want to go to save lives and reduce accident costs. Economic theory can suggest one approach—the market—for making the decision. But decisions balancing lives against money or convenience cannot be purely monetary ones, so the market method is never the only one used. The decision to build the Mont Blanc tunnel is not based solely on whether the revenue received from tolls will pay for the construction costs, including compensation of the killed and maimed. Neither is the decision to permit prostitution based solely on whether it can pay its way. Such pure free enterprise decisions have never been acceptable and have been, in fact, rejected by even the most orthodox of classical economists, who did, however, feel it necessary to explain the rejection through the use of such terms as external social costs and benefits, concepts which are not self-defining and are in fact as narrow or as broad as any society cares to make them.[2]

2. See, e.g., A. C. Pigou, *The Economics of Welfare* (4th ed. London, Macmillan, 1932).

The issue, whether or not expressed in terms of hidden social costs or hidden social savings theories, is how often a decision for or against an activity should be made outside the market. Such decisions operate on the one hand to create subsidies for some activities that could not survive in the marketplace, and on the other to bar some activities that could more than pay their way. The frequency with which decisions to ignore the market are made tells something about the nature of a society—welfare, laissez faire, or mixed. It is clear, however, that in virtually all societies such decisions to overrule the market are made, but are made only sometimes.

In accident law too, the decision to take lives in exchange for money or convenience is sometimes made politically or collectively without a balancing of the money value of the lives taken against the money price of the convenience, and sometimes made through the market on the basis of such a value. The reasons for choosing one way rather than the other are not entirely reasons of principle. Great moral issues lend themselves to political determination and must be decided in whatever political way a society chooses. But whether to use rotary mowers instead of reel mowers and what method to use for making steel are questions not easily answered collectively. For one thing, they occur too frequently. Every choice of product and use involves, tacitly or otherwise, a decision regarding safety and expense. The dramatic cases can be resolved politically. We ban the general sale of fireworks regardless of the ability or willingness of the manufacturer to pay for all of the injuries resulting from their use. But we cannot deal with every issue involved in every activity through the political process. In most cases, the marketplace serves as the rough testing ground. A manufacturer is usually free to employ a process that occasionally kills or maims if he is able to show that consumers want his product badly enough to enable him to compensate the injured. Economists would say that, except in some areas where collective decisions are needed, this is the best method for deciding whether the activity is worth having. But the tautologous nature of this statement makes it clear that ultimately, we collectively, and not economics, are the boss.

In other words, although the market can help us to decide how far we wish to go to avoid accidents, it cannot solve the whole problem for us. And when we overrule the market and ban an accident-causing activity that can pay its way or subsidize an activity that cannot, we are not violating absolute laws. We are making the same type of choice between accidents and accident-causing activities that the market makes, but we are choosing, for perfectly valid reasons, to make it in a different way. We are preferring a collective approach or method (e.g. because it enables consideration of nonmoney costs which the market cannot deal with, or because in the particular instance it is cheaper) to a market approach, even though the market might allow for individual differences in tastes and desires that the collective decision might tend to ignore.[3]

RISK DISTRIBUTION IS SELF-EXPLANATORY

The third myth involves the meaning of risk distribution. It has often been suggested that distributing the risk of accidents requires

3. Although economic theory does not give absolute answers to the problems of accident law, it remains a fundamental tool for analyzing the problems. See, e.g., Kenneth J. Arrow, *Social Choice and Individual Values* (2nd ed. New York, John Wiley & Sons, 1963). For some of the more recent significant articles by economists dealing with the problem of accidents, omitting those cited elsewhere in this book, see Gary Fromm, "Aviation Safety," 33 *L. & Cont. Probs.* 590 (1968); Simon Rottenberg, "On the Social Utility of Accidental Damage to Human Resources," in *Federal Programs for the Development of Human Resources* (papers submitted to the Subcommittee on Economic Progress of the Joint Economic Committee of the Congress of the United States, 90th Congress, 2nd Session) (Washington, Gov. Printing Office, 1968), 2, 491; T. C. Schelling, "The Life You Save May Be Your Own," in S. B. Chase, Jr., ed., *Problems in Public Expenditure Analysis* (Washington, The Brookings Institution, 1968), at 127; Joseph J. Spengler, "The Economics of Safety," 33 *L. & Cont. Probs.* 619 (1968); William Vickrey, "Automobile Accidents, Tort Law, Externalities, and Insurance: An Economist's Critique," 33 *L. & Cont. Probs.* 464 (1968); Oliver E. Williamson, Douglas G. Olson, and August Ralston, "Externalities, Insurance, and Disability Analysis," 34 *Economica* 235 (1967).

drivers rather than pedestrians to pay for automobile accidents, employers rather than employees to pay for work accidents, and so forth. Yet advocates of such systems of loss allocation often fail to explain or justify this and assume that the term risk distribution is self-explanatory. Actually, they may be using the term to mean three quite different things. The first possible meaning is the accomplishment of the broadest possible spreading of losses, both over people and over time. The second is the placing of losses on those classes of people or activities that are best able to pay, usually the "wealthiest," regardless of whether this involves spreading. The third is the placing of losses on those activities that, in some undefined sense, engender them.

Unfortunately, these meanings, while they represent valid methods for achieving valid aims, are not always consistent with one another. They are, moreover, supported by quite different ethical and economic postulates—postulates that are probably not accepted equally by anyone, and certainly not equally accepted by everyone. The first and second meanings of risk distribution represent two different methods for achieving a common subgoal which may loosely be called compensation. (I shall sometimes use this term, but more often will call the aim "secondary accident cost avoidance".) The first meaning of risk distribution I shall call the "risk spreading" method; the second I shall call the "deep pocket" method. The third meaning of risk distribution has very little in common with the first two except that it has been confused with them. It represents one method for achieving a different subgoal of accident law: the reduction of the immediate costs of accidents. In my locution, it represents a particular approach to achieving "primary accident cost avoidance." I call it the general deterrence or market approach.[4]

---

4. Roger C. Cramton, drawing on the term "general prevention" used by Andenaes in connection with the preventive effects of punishment, has used the terms "general deterrence" and "special deterrence" to mean, respectively, the influence of a threatened consequence upon the general population to which the legal command is addressed, and the effect of punishment

A NECESSARY FINANCIAL LINK EXISTS BETWEEN
INJURERS AND VICTIMS

The fourth myth is that there is any necessary financial link between injurers and victims or, more broadly, that we are limited, in choosing who should bear the burden of accident costs, to these two groups. There is no such necessary link, just as there is no inexorable requirement that victims bear their own accident costs.[5] The question of who should bear the costs of a particular accident, or of all accidents, is to be decided on the basis of the goals we wish accident law to accomplish. Thus it is a policy question whether accident costs should be (1) borne by particular victims; (2) paid on a one-to-one basis by those who injure a particular victim; (3) borne by those broad categories of people who are likely to be victims; (4) paid by those broad categories of people who are likely to be injurers; (5) paid by those who in some sense violate our moral codes (in some sense are at fault) according to the degree of their wrongdoing, whether or not they are involved in accidents; (6) paid by those who in some actuarial sense are most likely to violate our moral codes; (7) paid from the general coffers of the state or by particular industry groups in accordance with criteria (such as wealth) that may be totally unrelated to accident involvement; or (8) paid by some combination of these methods.

---

on the person who experiences it. See Cramton, "Driver Behavior and Legal Sanctions," in *Driver Behavior—Cause and Effect* (Proceedings of the Second Annual Traffic Safety Research Symposium of the Automobile Insurance Industry, 1968), 181, 183–189. See generally, Johannes Andenaes, "The General Preventive Effects of Punishment," 114 *U. Pa. L. Rev.* 949, 949–54 (1966); Andenaes, "General Prevention—Illusion or Reality?" 43 *J. Crim. L., C., & P.S.* 176, 179–81 (1952). In my locution, Cramton's "general deterrence" would be described as one type of specific deterrence. See infra pp. 95–96.

5. We are, however, limited in our allocation to the extent that potential accident victims fear pain and suffering regardless of compensation, so that they will be unaffected in their choices among acts and activities by our decision whether or not to compensate them for pain and suffering. See infra pp. 217–25.

It should be clear even from this partial list of possibilities that there is also no necessary relationship between the criteria for allocating compensation and those for assigning the costs of compensation. All these alternatives are real possibilities depending on the policies we wish to pursue and the goals we wish accident law to accomplish. This is not to say, of course, that such broad choices are or should be open to the *courts*. That is an altogether different issue, with which this book is not especially concerned. Rather, it means that, in considering the bases of accident law, there are virtually no limits on how we can allocate or divide the costs of accidents. What we choose, whether intentionally or by default, will reflect the economic and moral goals of our society. Accordingly, one aim of this book will be to suggest which goals and subgoals are implied in different possible systems of accident law and what importance different possible allocations must in fact give to each of the different goals and subgoals. And as we do not want to accomplish any one of these aims totally at the expense of the others, another aim of this study will be to show how our goals and methods conflict with one another at times and preclude the complete achievement of any particular one. This study will also show, however, that if perfection is not demanded, a fair degree of accommodation of conflicting aims and methods is possible.

One final introductory word of caution may be useful. When we deal with accidents we are dealing with costs, for that is what accidents involve. We are, to be sure, also dealing with emotional and moral attitudes, but we are always dealing with these in relation to costs. If we were not, we would wish to avoid accidents "at all costs." It follows that in examining any approach to accidents we must always keep in mind the cost of establishing and effectuating the approach, as well as the benefits the approach is expected to bring about. These costs and benefits, moreover, must be compared with the costs and benefits of alternative approaches. We must, in short, always ask whether the game is worth the candle, not only in terms of the cost of the candle but also in terms of other games we might be playing.

CHAPTER 3

Goals and Subgoals of Accident Law

What, then, are the principal goals of any system of accident law? First, it must be just or fair; second, it must reduce the costs of accidents.

JUSTICE

Justice, though often talked about, is by far the harder of the two goals to analyze.[1] It is often said that a particular system of accident law, be it fault, social insurance, or enterprise liability, is supported by one's sense of fairness or justice. But such statements are rarely backed up by any clear definition of what such support means, let alone by any empirical research into what is considered fair.

In fact, it is doubtful that such empirical research would tell us very much anyway. As one scholar has observed, it is much easier to describe instances of *injustice* than examples of justice.[2] We are much surer that particular processes or results are unfair than that particular arrangements are just in some positive sense. We can readily document specific injustices that occur in existing systems, such as the fault system or workmen's compensation. But the requirements of fairness that those systems may meet are diffi-

1. Though I list justice or fairness as a goal, it will soon be apparent that in this book I do not treat it as a goal of the same type as cost reduction but as a veto or constraint on what can be done to achieve cost reduction. Viewed this way fairness becomes a final test which any system of accident law must pass. It is a test that requires that our many goals not specifically dealt with under cost reduction be adequately handled by the proposed system. For this reason I treat certain goals such as avoidance of undesirable changes in income distribution, which economists would lump under justice, as part of cost reduction. See infra notes 4, 6. Compare McKean, "Products Liability: Trends and Implications."

2. See Edmond N. Cahn, *The Sense of Injustice* (Bloomington, Indiana University Press, 1964).

cult to define and therefore are usually stated in generalities, in hope of striking a responsive chord. This responsive chord, however, may be an inadequate guide to what our reaction would be if the system were changed. Conversely, while it is fairly easy to argue that particular untried systems will cure current injustices, it is much harder to foresee the injustices they may create.

More important, claims that particular systems are just, like those that justice is in some sense a goal concurrent with accident cost reduction, fail to ring true. They seem to suggest that a "rather unjust" system may be worthwhile because it diminishes accident costs effectively; or, conversely, that there is one system that can be termed just to the exclusion of all others, i.e. that is supported by justice in the same sense that economic efficiency may prefer one system to all others. But the words just and unjust do not sound right to me in either of the statements. They ring true in rather different contexts, as when we say that we reject a particular system or parts of it as unjust, or that a system taken as a whole does not violate our sense of justice. This suggests that justice is a totally different order of goal from accident cost reduction. Indeed, it suggests that it is not a goal but rather a constraint that can impose a veto on systems or on the use of particular devices or structures within a given system (e.g. administrative tribunals under the fault system) even though those same structures might not be unjust in another system (e.g. administrative tribunals under workmen's compensation).

All this discussion may make the concept of justice seem both negative and elusive. But it affords no excuse for ignoring justice in discussing accident law. Our reaction to accidents is not a strict dollars-and-cents one. If it were, I doubt that we would accept railroad crossing accidents because it costs too much to eliminate grade crossings and yet spend "whatever it takes" to save a known individual trapped in a coal mine.[3] An economically optimal system of reducing accident costs—whether decisions are made col-

3. For some thoughts on this apparent paradox, see Calabresi, "Reflections on Medical Experimentation in Humans," *Daedalus* (J. Am. Ac. Arts & Sci.) Spring 1969), 387.

lectively, through the market, or through a combination of both
—might be totally or partially unacceptable because it strikes us
as unfair, and no amount of discussion of the efficiency of the system would do much to save it. Justice must ultimately have its due.

But if the elusiveness of justice cannot justify ignoring the concept, it at least justifies delaying discussion of it. The fact that what
is unfair is easier to define than what is fair, like the fact that what
is fair in one system may be unfair in another, indicates that it
would be better to examine the requirements of accident cost
reduction first and then to see how various untried methods and
systems suggested by that goal compare in terms of fairness with
the systems we use today—how, in other words, they comply with
our general sense of fairness and whether they are more or less
likely to create specific instances of injustice than the current systems. Such an approach may not lead us to the fairest systems possible but it may well indicate whether change is desirable.

REDUCTION OF ACCIDENT COSTS

Apart from the requirements of justice, I take it as axiomatic
that the principal function of accident law is to reduce the sum of
the costs of accidents and the costs of avoiding accidents. (Such
incidental benefits as providing a respectable livelihood for a
large number of judges, lawyers, and insurance agents are at best
beneficent side effects.) This cost, or loss, reduction goal can be
divided into three subgoals.

The first is reduction of the number and severity of accidents.
This "primary" reduction of accident costs can be attempted in
two basic ways. We can seek to forbid specific acts or activities
thought to cause accidents, or we can make activities more expensive and thereby less attractive to the extent of the accident
costs they cause. These two methods of primary reduction of accident costs are not clearly separable; a number of difficulties of
definition will become apparent as we consider them in detail.
But the distinction between them is useful because from it flows

two very different approaches toward primary reduction of accident costs, the "general deterrence" or market method and the "specific deterrence" or collective method.[4]

The second cost reduction subgoal is concerned with reducing neither the number of accidents nor their degree of severity. It concentrates instead on reducing the societal costs resulting from accidents. I shall attempt to show that the notion that one of the principal functions of accident law is the compensation of victims is really a rather misleading, though occasionally useful, way of stating this "secondary" accident cost reduction goal. The fact that I have termed this compensation notion secondary should in no way be taken as belittling its importance. There is no doubt that the way we provide for accident victims *after* the accident is crucially important and that the real societal costs of accidents can be reduced as significantly here as by taking measures to avoid accidents in the first place.[5] This cost reduction subgoal is sec-

4. See supra note 4, Chapter 2. Many economists would not view the introduction of collective desires into the primary cost avoidance decision as a part of cost reduction since consideration of collective desires almost inevitably involves interpersonal comparisons of utility. This makes traditional economic analysis difficult. Accordingly they tend to deal with such desires under justice. See McKean, "Products Liability: Trends and Implications." I prefer to deal with it under cost reduction for purely practical reasons. The choices required by the introduction of collective valuations are analytically similar to those made by individuals in the market. They are very different from the much more general constraint imposed by the requirement that any proposed system of accident law be just or fair. See supra note 1, infra note 6. See also Calabresi and Bass, "Right Approach, Wrong Implications: A Critique of McKean on Products Liability."

5. See in this connection *AACP,* at 124 ff.; Conard, "Automobile Injuries," at 294–95; Clarence Morris and James C. N. Paul, "The Financial Impact of Automobile Accidents," 110 *U. Pa. L. Rev.* 913, 918 (1962) (cited hereafter as Morris and Paul, "Financial Impact"). Conard divides postaccident costs into rehabilitative, subsistence, and maintenance. The first indicates proper medical treatment, including psychological readjustment and occupational retraining; the second indicates simply the providing of the necessities of life for those whom accidents have rendered incapable of providing for themselves; and the third indicates the maintenance of a basic income level for such individuals above the purely subsistence level. Clearly, these costs are substantial.

ondary only in the sense that it does not come into play until after earlier primary measures to reduce accident costs have failed.

The secondary cost reduction goal can be accomplished through the two methods outlined in Chapter 2, both of which usually involve a shifting of accident losses: the risk (or loss) spreading method and the deep pocket method.[6]

The third subgoal of accident cost reduction is rather Pickwickian but very important nonetheless. It involves reducing the costs of administering our treatment of accidents. It may be termed "tertiary" because its aim is to reduce the costs of achieving primary and secondary cost reduction. But in a very real sense this "efficiency" goal comes first. It tells us to question constantly whether an attempt to reduce accident costs, either by reducing accidents themselves or by reducing their secondary effects, costs more than it saves. By forcing us to ask this, it serves as a kind of general balance wheel to the cost reduction goal.

These, then, are the principal subgoals into which the goal of accident cost reduction can be divided—primary accident cost reduction, which includes the general deterrence or market method and the specific deterrence or collective method; secondary accident cost reduction, which includes the risk spreading and the deep pocket methods; and the tertiary or efficiency cost re-

---

6. Economists, unlike lawyers, tend to treat secondary cost reduction under the rubric of justice. See McKean, "Products Liability: Trends and Implications." The reason, the same given for treating collective desires under justice, is that reduction of secondary costs usually entails interpersonal comparisons of utility and hence is not amenable to traditional economic efficiency analysis. I treat it under cost reduction because what can be said about reducing secondary costs is much more concrete than what can be said about the catchall of goals we deal with under justice. As a result we are willing to have trade-offs between spreading and economic efficiency, while we would not tolerate trade-offs between justice and economic efficiency. See Calabresi and Bass, "Right Approach, Wrong Implications: A Critique of McKean on Products Liability." My treatment of secondary costs follows from my decision to treat justice as a veto or constraint involving a catchall of goals rather than as a concurrent goal with cost reduction, since that decision requires me to give separate treatment to any significant goals among which we might have trade off. See supra notes 1, 4.

duction. Each of these subgoals and the relationships among them will be examined in this study. Primary and secondary accident cost reduction will be discussed separately. Tertiary cost reduction, because it requires us to ask whether particular methods of achieving the other subgoals are worth their administrative costs, will be discussed primarily in conjunction with the other two subgoals.

It should be noted in advance that these subgoals are not fully consistent with each other. For instance, a perfect system of secondary cost reduction is, as we shall see, inconsistent with the goals of reducing primary accident costs. We cannot have more than a certain amount of reduction in one category without forgoing some of the reduction in the other, just as we cannot reduce all accident costs beyond a certain point without incurring costs in *achieving* the reduction that are greater than the reduction is worth. Our aim must be to find the best combination of primary, secondary, and tertiary cost reduction taking into account what must be given up in order to achieve that reduction.

In this sense, it may seem unwise to divide accident cost reduction into three subgoals at all. It might seem better to lump all accident costs together and concentrate on finding that point at which further accident cost reduction is not worth its costs, especially since the division of accident cost reduction into subgoals is ultimately an arbitrary one. The differences between primary and secondary accident costs are not fixed nor are they always clear. Is failure to get medical care and therefore to mitigate damages a primary or secondary cost of an accident? Would the dislocation and unemployment that might result from banning motorcycles be a primary accident avoidance cost (because it is a cost in forgone pleasure or profit borne in order to avoid accidents) or would it be a secondary accident avoidance cost (because it is an economic and social dislocation cost resulting from primary accident costs or their avoidance)? The same is true with respect to tertiary accident costs. When we say that the administrative costs of instituting a system to reduce accident costs would be too great in comparison with the savings the system would bring (a typical tertiary cost statement), it is not very different from the statement that further reduction of speed limits would cost more than the accident costs it would prevent (a clear primary cost avoidance statement).

Nevertheless, the division of accident costs into three rough categories (and of the accident cost reduction goal into three subgoals) is useful for analytical purposes. Although each category of costs cannot be clearly defined, especially in the fringe areas, the methods available for reducing costs, which in a loose sense fit each of the categories, are very different from one another. As a result, the division is extremely practical, if only to enable a rational discussion of methods. This is especially so because different writers assign vastly different magnitudes and importance to the costs and cost reduction potential available in these three categories. Some emphasize the need to diminish the burdens of unspread accident costs, others center on the massive administrative costs entailed by existing systems, and still others argue that the best way to reduce accident costs is to reduce the number of accidents and their immediate costs by inducing people to act safely and use safer equipment.[7] Since there is no adequate empirical data available from which to determine who is correct, and since the costs that are important in one type of accident may not be as important in another, there is an advantage in considering separately what methods accomplish each type of cost reduction best and what methods accomplish cost reduction well in all three areas. This kind of analysis enables decisions to be made in specific areas of accidents, based on the empirical data available and the political judgments applicable to each particular area.

In addition, the division into rough subgoals is useful because the types of costs in each category are not always completely fungible. Reduction of primary accident costs may be given greater significance in some situations than the monetary weight we are

7. Compare, e.g., Morris and Paul, "Financial Impact," at 913; *AACP;* and Jeffrey O'Connell, "Taming the Automobile," 58 *Nw. U.L. Rev.* 299 (1963).

willing to give to these costs would seem to justify. Accordingly, systems of primary accident cost avoidance that are inefficient in strictly monetary terms may find favor nonetheless. One could, of course, attempt to give a "cost" value to this extra desire to avoid the accident. But that would involve stretching the term costs to the point of rendering it useless. Indeed, it would involve much the same kind of misuse of terms that would occur if one tried to subsume the goal of justice into cost saving by giving money values to feelings of fairness and unfairness. This could be done verbally, but it would not help analysis of the nonmonetary factors and would render such terms as costs so vague that they would no longer be useful for the monetary factors either. Separate analysis of different categories of accident costs enables us to consider how best to deal with each and helps us to isolate and consider the non-cost factors involved when we try to combine the different categories and reduce their total. We must remember, however, that the divisions we have made are only analytical ones and that the main goal is the maximum reduction of the sum of accident costs and the costs of avoiding accidents that can be accomplished in a just way.[8]

Other Goals outside Accident Law

One could, of course, consider the goals of accident law more broadly and ask what accident law may do to cure evils in our society that are not a result of accidents. The list of possibilities would be endless, and any analysis of accident law would be virtually impossible. Nevertheless, we should be aware that accident law, like any other branch of law, can be used to accomplish an enormous variety of goals.[9] Thus systems of accident law seem to have found support in the past because they gave hidden subsidies

8. Compare, supra notes 1, 4, and 6.
9. The tax laws have long been used as an adjunct to criminal law enforcement, as Al Capone could have testified. Although the acceptability of some such devices that are commonly used as criminal law enforcement measures rather than as means of raising revenues is now being questioned, their efficaciousness has long been apparent.

to developing industries at a time when subsidies to such industries were probably desirable.[10] In other instances, people have sought to use accident law as a means of reducing inequalities in income distribution, or of attacking problems of depression and unemployment. One author has even suggested that some systems of accident law could act as a tax on monopoly and perhaps help meet some of our goals in that area.[11]

Regarding these and similar goals, the fact is that we usually would do far better to attack the particular problem directly rather than through accident law. If subsidies to developing industries seem sensible, it is best to give them openly, with visible decisions as to who should pay, rather than through a system which removes some or all of the costs of accidents from the activities causing them and hides this subsidization by placing these costs on undefined or unrepresented groups.[12]

I do not mean to say that such "outside" goals can be totally ignored. In a negative sense they may be quite significant. We do not want our treatment of accidents to be too inconsistent with our goals in other areas. A system of accident law that exacerbates unequal distribution of income or favors monopolies will violate our moral framework, therefore seeming unjust. To this extent these outside goals remain relevant and will tend to prevent some systems from gaining acceptance. Whether this is a good result in any given case will depend not only on whether there are outside means for redressing the undesirable outside effects of the proposed system of accident law, but also on whether the un-

10. For further discussion, see Calabresi, "Risk Distribution," at 516, and works there cited.

11. Id. at 507–14, 524–28.

12. But see discussions of the Warsaw Convention explaining its origin from the idea that the fledgling airlines should not be liable to crash victims beyond a low maximum amount in order to protect and strengthen the industry. *New York Times,* Oct. 24, 1965, § 4, at 7, col. 2. The argument is still made that some airlines in developing countries and elsewhere would not be able to withstand a series of expensive liability judgments and that therefore the hidden subsidy should be continued in order to preserve the benefits of air service.

desirable effects will *in fact* be redressed if the system of accident law is adopted.[13] If there are no readily available outside means for redressing the undesirable effects, or if attempts to redress them adversely affect other accident cost reduction goals, then it is proper to view these outside effects as costs of accidents and consider them in our analysis of such costs. Indeed, secondary accident costs which are essentially costs of rapid changes in income distribution are included for just this reason.

All in all, however, there is little point in discussing outside goals in the abstract. Where they seem to be especially pertinent to particular systems of accident law they will, of course, be mentioned. More often they will blend into the general background of what makes a system of accident law fair.

13. Cf. Paul A. Samuelson, *Foundations of Economic Analysis* (Cambridge, Harvard University Press, 1953), Chapter 8, esp. at 214.

PART II

Subgoals of Accident Cost Reduction and Methods for Achieving Them

In discussing each of the above mentioned subgoals of accident law, their theoretical and practical justifications, and the principal methods for achieving them, we must be especially aware of one danger. In concentrating on any one goal, we may lose sight of the fact that no system of accident law should be designed with only one goal in mind. The significance of some goals may depend on the existence of others. If primary accident cost avoidance were not a goal, for example, the compensation aim could very easily be discussed in terms of its ideal solution—a system of general social insurance—and this may be precisely what is at the root of some of the approaches I have categorized as social insurance and welfare legislation plans. But given the goal of primary accident cost avoidance, general social insurance may not always be the best solution. Conversely, primary accident cost avoidance may not, standing alone, suggest any particular system. It may leave us indifferent—let us assume for the moment—between fault and enterprise liability, or between first-party insurance plans like Keeton-O'Connell and third-party insurance plans, and as such may seem to be too vague a goal to bother with. But if one of these systems conflicts with another goal, such as secondary accident cost avoidance, while the other does not, and if in addition other systems that do *not* conflict with our compensation aims violate even the vague requirements of primary accident cost avoidance, then deterrence of primary accident costs must be considered in choosing among these systems.[1] The Blum and Kalven stopgap plan, for example, in removing part of automobile accident costs from both victims and injurers and placing them on the general

---

1. A major fault of some recent analysis has been this tendency to reject any given plan because it fails to do some one thing perfectly, even though it may accomplish the overall mixture rather well, and better than the existing system. See Calabresi, "Fault, Accidents and the Wonderful World of Blum and Kalven," 75 *Yale L.J.* 216, 221 (1965) (cited hereafter as Calabresi, "The Wonderful World").

public, seems particularly oblivious to the importance of this last consideration. As a result of these relationships among our various subgoals, I will occasionally be forced to anticipate discussions of other subgoals in order to complete the analysis of the one under discussion.

CHAPTER 4

Secondary Accident Cost Avoidance:
The Loss Spreading and Deep Pocket Methods

THEORETICAL BASES

The justification found most often among legal writers today for allocation of accident losses on a nonfault basis is that accident losses will be least burdensome if they are spread broadly among people and over time.

Analogues to these views can be found in economic theory. The advantages of interpersonal loss spreading would probably be stated as a pair of propositions: (1) taking a large sum of money from one person is more likely to result in economic dislocation, and therefore in secondary or avoidable losses, than taking a series of small sums from many people;[1] (2) even if the total economic dislocation were the same, many small losses would be preferable to one large one simply because people feel less pain if 10,000 of them lose one dollar apiece than if one person loses $10,000.

While the first of these propositions is an empirical generalization not too difficult to accept, the second is a variant of the empirical generalization known as the diminishing marginal utility of money theory. This theory has been in substantial disfavor among modern economists because as an empirical generalization it cannot be proven to be universally true, and because it has been shown to be invalid in certain situations. Studies have indicated, for example, that a loss of a relatively small amount of money, if it results in a drop in social status, may be nearly as significant to an individual as a much larger loss causing no substantial change in

1. This statement of the proposition is not, of course, original. See, e.g., W. Feezer, "Capacity to Bear Loss as a Factor in the Decision of Certain Types of Tort Cases," 78 *U. Pa. L. Rev.* 805, 809–10 (1930).

his social position. On the other hand, a relatively small loss, if it can be borne without giving up certain symbols of social status—be they a house on the right street or a television set—feels infinitely smaller to people than an only slightly larger loss that does involve a loss in status.[2]

Despite the weaknesses of the strictly utilitarian plain-pleasure analysis underlying the marginal utility of money theory, with its implication that a five-dollar loss divided among five people *necessarily* hurts less than the same loss placed on one person, the basic justification for loss spreading remains strong. We need merely recognize that social dislocations, like economic ones, will occur more frequently if one person bears a heavy loss than if many people bear light ones to find an adequate support for the spreading of losses.[3]

A variant of the notion that secondary losses of accidents can be reduced by spreading them broadly is the deep pocket notion. This holds that secondary losses can be reduced most by placing them on the categories of people least likely to suffer substantial social or economic dislocations as a result of bearing them, usually thought to be the wealthy. One can conceive of societies or situations, however, where social and economic dislocations would be minimized by placing accident losses on other groups, perhaps even on the poor (highly regressive taxes are certainly not unknown). The principal difference between this method and loss spreading is that this method implies that partial spreading can

2. See generally Milton Friedman and L. J. Savage, "The Utility Analysis of Choices Involving Risk," 56 *J. Pol. Econ.* 279 (1948). Even before the Friedman-Savage approach, the notion of diminishing marginal utility of money had fallen into substantial disfavor with economists. See ibid., and Blum and Kalven, "The Uneasy Case for Progressive Taxation," 19 *U. Chi. L. Rev.* 417 455–79 (1952).

3. The idea that secondary social effects are more likely when losses are concentrated may also derive support from the notion that people's wants are significantly dependent on the wants of their neighbors. Thus C. J. Taney may feel his losses less if C. J. Marshall and C. J. Chase, his neighbors, suffer similar losses. See generally James S. Duesenberry, *Income, Saving and the Theory of Consumer Behavior* (Cambridge, Harvard University Press, 1959).

reduce secondary costs better than total spreading if the right people are made to pay.

The bases for this notion are not hard to find in either economics or politics. The theory of the diminishing marginal utility of money implies that a dollar taken from a rich man causes less pain than one taken from a poor man, and that therefore shifting losses from the poor to the rich is a good thing in itself. As noted, this theory is currently out of favor. But even if we cannot say that it has universal validity, we are accustomed to operating under this assumption as voters. Even if the economist refuses to say that the last $10,000 of a millionaire's income is worth less to him than the last $1,000 of a poor man's income is worth to the poor man, the Internal Revenue Service, on instructions from the people, says just that. An argument can be made for letting our system of accident loss allocations work the same way as our tax code does and take from the rich, by and large, to give to the poor, more or less. Needless to say, in order to find the argument at all attractive one must first agree with the voters' choice in favor of highly graduated taxes. If one does, one may well favor systems that, while spreading, differentiate according to ability to pay, rather than systems that merely spread losses evenly among the rich and poor.[4]

Conversely, there are systems of compensation in which the rich accident victim recovers more than the poor.[5] A man who once earned $10,000 and is incapacitated might recover $6,000, while one who once earned $4,000 and is equally incapacitated might recover $4,000. One is more likely to favor such a program of income maintenance if one disapproves of the pure theory of the diminishing utility of money, since one would then believe that the loss of social status suffered by a victim is a more important object for social action (once a decent minimum income is achieved) than the

4. See, e.g., Blum and Kalven, *Public Law Perspectives*, at 55–56.
5. For an interesting discussion of the role to be played by economic reparations in a system of accident law, see Conard, "Automobile Injuries," at 279, 294 ff., esp. 301, 304–05, and n. 94. See also supra note 5, Chapter 3, and materials there cited.

restoration of all victims to a particular income above that minimum. A compromise approach would be a loss spreading system
that collected on a deep pocket basis and then distributed in a way
that provided some measure of income maintenance, thus "re-
imbursing" some of the rich. Such a system would tax the uninjured
rich to maintain the income and social status of the injured rich,
as well as of the poor. As such, it is still a deep pocket approach to
loss spreading, for less than total spreading is deemed to do a
better job of reducing secondary accident costs than full spreading.

To many accident victims, interpersonal loss spreading may be
less important than loss spreading over time. As many writers
have suggested, the immediate rehabilitation of the victim whenever possible is the best way of minimizing secondary costs once an
accident has occurred.[6] When the cost of rehabilitation must be
paid unexpectedly and immediately by the victim and his family,
the disruptive effect may be disastrous. Rehabilitation may therefore be forgone or it may be incomplete. Even if we adopt no devices for interpersonal loss spreading, the threat of disruption is diminished if such pressing costs as that of rehabilitation can be
spread over the victim's past and future earnings.

Some intertemporal spreading is achieved through insurance,
although insurance is often thought of chiefly as a device for accomplishing interpersonal spreading. Intertemporal spreading
could also be accomplished by borrowing after the accident. But
borrowing is unlikely to give adequate intertemporal spreading
since low-income families, who have the greatest need to borrow
in order to achieve intertemporal spreading, may not be able to
borrow against meager future earnings. Nor can they borrow
against future compensation unless that compensation is relatively
guaranteed.[7] Indeed, one of the major charges being leveled

6. See Morris and Paul, "Financial Impact," at 913, 918–26, for a stud
showing the extent to which the present system of accident law leaves vic
tims inadequately compensated in a narrowly defined economic sense. C
Conard, "Automobile Injuries," at 294 ff., and *AACP,* at 124.

7. The present system does provide for a limited form of borrowin
through the contingent fee system. This system enables many victims to ob

against the fault system today is that it combines delay with un-certainty of compensation, thus increasing the need for inter-temporal spreading while making it difficult for those who need it most. This hampers rehabilitation and increases secondary losses substantially.[8]

Where delay in compensation is not caused by uncertainty, the problem is greatly reduced. The only remaining obstacle to inter-temporal spreading is the cost of borrowing (even a low-income family should be able to borrow against certain compensation). And this obstacle may be just another expression of the fact that spreading, whether intertemporal or interpersonal, costs money and may not be worth the cost.

The need for interpersonal and intertemporal loss spreading to diminish secondary costs is certainly great. But secondary accident cost avoidance cannot be the only aim of a system of accident law. This should be clear from the fact that loss spreading and deep pocket do nothing to reduce the *primary* costs of accidents, whereas most people seem to want at least some primary accident cost reduction.

If secondary cost avoidance were our sole aim, there would be no justification for limiting compensation to accidents and not giving equal compensation for illness, old age, and all the other troubles of this planet. Of course, we do compensate to some ex-tent in fields other than accidents. But it is the fact that we only do it to some extent that is crucial. Why is compensation for ill-ness, even in highly welfaristic countries, much less complete than compensation for accident victims? Surely if the type of cost re-duction with which we are concerned is solely or principally that accomplished by diminishing secondary costs—social and eco-

---

ain legal services without any cash outlay at a time when they could not other-wise afford them. But what can be borrowed is not what is most urgent in the majority of cases (medical treatment and subsistence would seem to rank head of these expenses). Cf. infra note 23, Chapter 9.

8. See, e.g., Conard, "Automobile Injuries," at 295–98.

nomic dislocations—then a generalized system of social insurance covering all types of severe injuries would be the only practical answer. Payments into the social insurance fund could be spread as widely as possible or allocated to those especially able to pay, depending on whether we preferred the spreading or the deep pocket approach. But either way, secondary cost avoidance could be achieved in an extremely efficient fashion.[9] The answer is, of course, that accidents, unlike most diseases,[10] can easily be reduced in number and severity, and that such primary cost reduction can —indeed must—be an important aim of whatever system of law governs the field. Accordingly, perfect systems of secondary cost avoidance, if they give poor primary cost avoidance, may be totally unacceptable.

Nevertheless, compensation remains a fundamental aim of accident law. If its theoretical basis lies in certain notions about social and economic costs caused by concentrated losses, its practical bases lie in the fact that accidents are a source of some of the most dramatic concentrations of costs in our society. Some writers have attempted to equate the need for compensation of accident losses with the problem of poverty, thus making it essentially an adjunct of the more general problem of improper distribution of income.[11] It is certainly true that some of the direst examples of

9. There might be perfectly respectable political objections to such a social insurance system, despite agreement that compensation is the over-riding goal and despite the fact that social insurance is the cheapest way of accomplishing it.

10. I say "most" diseases because there are some diseases, often described as "occupational," "work-related," or "product-related," which can be treated in the same way that accidents are treated, as it has been shown that their incidence can be reduced in the same way that accidents costs can be reduced Such relationships as that between coal dust and miners' lung diseases, o cigarettes and cancer, come to mind immediately. Even in other diseases, pri mary cost reduction may play a part. One could build a whole theory of pri mary cost avoidance in terms of incentives to discover cures, for example Usually, however, we apparently do not believe that a different allocation o most disease costs would do much to spur reduction of their number o severity.

11. See Blum and Kalven, *Public Law Perspectives,* at 83; and Blum and Kalven, "The Empty Cabinet, at 271–72.

poverty stem from accident situations. But I suspect that even if poverty were eliminated by a guaranteed minimum income, we would still find too severe those social and economic dislocations resulting from the fact that some unspread accidents costs reduce people from a good to a minimum standard of living. In other words, since the economic and social costs of unspread accident losses result as much from the *change* in social and economic status caused by the accident as from the actual economic condition in which the accident may leave people, no discussion defining the problem in terms of poverty alone is sufficient.[12] In this sense, compensation plans like the Blum and Kalven stopgap plan and the minimum nonpoverty level social insurance plans must be interpreted either as ignoring the change-in-status aspect of secondary accident costs or as having decided for unspecified reasons that this aspect is unimportant.

The previous discussion presupposes that people either cannot or for some reason do not provide on their own for sufficient spreading of the risks of accident costs. The reasons for this are many and worth examining, for they will be of great significance in helping us to evaluate different systems for avoiding secondary accident costs.[13] But before we examine them, we must discuss the principal systems by which accident loss distribution can take place in our society: social insurance, private risk pooling (insurance), and enterprise liability (a term that actually signifies two quite different systems).

12. That we do feel this way is shown by the fact that we give greater compensation to the rich than to the poor under our current system (see supra note 5, Chapter 4, and accompanying text). We feel that there is an overall loss minimization in this procedure, in that the disruption to society is decreased as the change in economic status is minimized. Blum and Kalven discuss the poverty aspect of compensation in *Public Law Perspectives,* at 38; see also Morris and Paul, "Financial Impact."

13. Conard, "Automobile Injuries," at 302, mentions a couple of problems with reliance on individual initiative in this respect. To the extent that sufficient spreading of accident costs involves some permanent redistribution of income, the problem is an obvious one, for to that extent we will always require compulsion to accomplish our goal.

SYSTEMS OF ACCIDENT LOSS DISTRIBUTION

Social Insurance

Social insurance is the easiest system of distributing losses to define and may at first glance seem the most attractive. Its attractiveness lies in the fact that it allows for just the degree of risk spreading or deep pocket we want and permits us to achieve it in a remarkably inexpensive way.[14] Indeed, if secondary cost avoidance were the only aim of accident law, there would be little reason for stopping short of general social insurance paid out of taxes and covering all accidents.

Who would pay what taxes to establish the compensation fund would depend on whether we wanted complete spreading of losses or some element of deep pocket in our loss spreading. If we were serious about *total* loss spreading, everyone would pay an equal amount. If instead, as seems likely, we wished to mix our loss spreading with some income redistribution, then the tax feeding the fund could be geared to whatever progressive or regressive income redistribution we wanted to accomplish. This might be described as optimal, as against total, loss spreading.

A very different approach would be implicit in an attempt to tax people on the basis of their tendency to "cause" accident costs, i.e. their accident-proneness.[15] Such an attempt would immediately suggest that the objective was primary accident cost deterrence rather than spreading. Indeed, the very fact that some would bear a greater loss burden than others and would do so in relation to factors other than the desired income redistribution would mean than full or optimal spreading was not the sole motivating force. Such a way of handling social insurance would involve not only some concentration of accident losses, but greater tertiary or ad-

14. *AACP* at 52–55 presents the loss-shifting expenses of major reparation systems in 1960. It should be noted that the authors were unable to estimate collection expenses for private loss insurance, social insurance, or public welfare programs, but stated that about 25% of the *total* payments to automobile injury victims was consumed by collection expenses, chiefly attorneys' fees.

15. See supra note 8, Chapter 1, on my use of the term "cause."

ministrative costs as well, for people would have to be placed in appropriate risk categories for taxation purposes. In all events, since such a way of raising money for a compensation fund would be based on the primary rather than the secondary cost avoidance aim, its analysis and desirability compared with other methods of primary cost avoidance are best discussed later.[16]

Private Insurance or Voluntary Risk Pooling

The most common system of distributing losses is, of course, private or voluntary insurance. If it happened to bring about in an efficient way the degree of risk spreading and deep pocket allocation we collectively desired, we would all be delighted because it appeals to us politically as the "freest" way. The reasons why it probably does not suffice will be discussed later.

At this stage, there are three interesting things to note about private insurance. First, it generally involves a combination of intertemporal spreading, limited interpersonal spreading or pooling, and a limited degree of concentration of losses according to involvement or accident-proneness. Second, the degree of pooling that occurs is a function more of what it costs insurance companies to differentiate among categories of insured than of any clearly defined collective choice of what degree of spreading is most desirable from a societal point of view.[17] Third, unless the pools are subsidized or government controlled, private insurance will not reflect the aims of the deep pocket approach in allocating accident costs.

Most private insurance involves a substantial element of intertemporal loss spreading. In this sense it is just a form of saving. If all people had equal accident costs and had them at the same age, insurance would be no more than the putting aside of money to meet the accidents when they come. Despite the fact that accident

16. See Franklin, "Replacing the Negligence Lottery: Compensation and Selective Reimbursement."

17. See infra pp. 60–63. This differentiation might result in an overall reduction of accident costs. See infra p. 63.

costs do not occur with such certainty, a part of insuring is likely to be no more than a prepaying of those accident costs each of us is likely to have. As such, it is no more than a rather complicated way to save.

But private insurance is more than saving. It protects the insured against two types of risk, that of having above average accident costs and that of having accident costs sooner than the average. Protecting against each of these risks involves interpersonal loss spreading. The man who has his accidents "early" spreads to the man who has his accidents "late." And the man who has above average accident costs spreads a portion of them to the man who has fewer than the average. This is fine if loss spreading is what the insureds had in mind in the first place. Indeed, from the standpoint of total loss spreading, the ideal would be for all insureds to be in one great pool so that the burden of all accidents would be evenly distributed among all people.

In fact, however, as private insurance becomes more refined, the large pool becomes less common. Groups are divided into risk categories. Premiums differ according to the presumed accident-proneness of each category, i.e. according to predicted accident costs and according to whether the accident costs are likely to occur early or late.[18] People are generally invited to spread their losses only among those who are thought to be roughly as accident prone as they. As a result, private insurance charges some groups much more than others. This may not be bad, but to the extent that this categorization takes place, something other than loss spreading is occurring and some goals other than loss spreading are being served.

The interesting thing about this differentiation into risk categories is that if it were possible to know exactly how "risky" each person is, each person would form his own category. The result would be that insurance would no longer spread losses interper-

18. The best example of insurance subcategorization according to an "early-late" factor is life insurance, where the only question from the insurer's point of view is whether an individual's death will occur early or late.

sonally at all. It would become just the type of intertemporal loss spreader I described previously, when I assumed that all insureds had *equal* risk potential. Under this kind of perfect individualization, there would be a high degree of concentration of losses on those who are accident prone, and our collective desire for loss spreading would not be met. We would have something very close to one approach to primary accident cost avoidance—perfect general deterrence, a concept I will discuss later. It will become clear then that with the perfect knowledge necessary for such perfect individualization, we really would not have "accidents" at all, though we might have severe concentrations of losses nonetheless.

In effect, then, private insurance, like social insurance, can range from a single risk pool that achieves close to total loss spreading, to a substantial differentiation according to accident-proneness that abandons total spreading for the advantages of achieving a closer relationship between what one must pay and the accidents one "causes". I say it is like social insurance because, as we have seen, a social insurance fund can be collected from all people equally (resulting in total loss spreading) or from people or activities in accordance with their accident-proneness (resulting in some concentration of losses and some primary accident cost deterrence).

One could go further and describe how certain types of assigned risk pools within an essentially private system could be made quite analogous to a deep pocket method of raising a social insurance fund, but such an analogy would be incomplete. A better one would exist if a subsidy based on income were given to people on condition that they get insurance, such a subsidy to be raised through taxes according to ability to pay. But this, like all deep pocket notions, would involve some compulsion and hence would be a move away from the pure world of private insurance.[19]

This discussion may seem rather simple and unnecessary. But

19. A system of general subsidies, unrelated to insurance or accidents, from which payments could be used for insurance if the recipients wished, would be another matter. The above discussion assumes a system of subsidies triggered essentially by placement of loss on a party, or at least by the statistical probability of such placement.

unfortunately, it is far from either. All too often writers dealing with loss spreading seem to proceed on the assumption that wide loss spreading is the goal, while at the same time bemoaning the fact that there is not greater differentiation into risk categories. The fact is that here, as in a social insurance context, there is a basic conflict between the spreading we want and the allocation of accident costs according to accident-proneness (primary cost deterrence) we seem to need.

The interesting thing about the balance struck between loss spreading and general deterrence in private insurance is that the degree of differentiation into categories and the concomitant concentration of costs on certain accident-prone groups are not the result of a reasoned collective decision (as they would be, for better or for worse, under social insurance), but depend instead on the degree to which insurance companies view further differentiation as an economically advantageous step. While in theory this might reflect free market decisions based on the cost of further differentiation and the desire of people for categorization by accident-proneness rather than for more complete loss spreading, it is unlikely that the decision in practice reflects these rather complex and somewhat contradictory forces. Ultimately, my skepticism here reflects in part my belief, explained later, that people individually do not or cannot voluntarily insure against accident risks to the degree they collectively deem desirable.[20]

Enterprise Liability

The third and fourth ways of achieving wide spreading of accident losses are usually both referred to as enterprise liability, although they are quite dissimilar. The first of these, which really has little to do with enterprises, places losses on those categories of people who are most likely to insure or, to the extent that they do not insure, are able to self-insure adequately (i.e. bear any likely accident loss without causing secondary losses, and ultimately cover this loss by internal intertemporal spreading—in other words, saving).

20. See generally infra pp. 55–64.

The second system involves placing losses on those who are in a position to pass part of the loss on to purchasers of their products or to factors employed in the production of their products (including labor and capital), in this way bringing about a fairly wide spreading of accident losses. These two meanings of enterprise liability are related only in the sense that it is commonly believed that those who are most able to pass accident costs on to purchasers or to factors of production are also the most likely to insure or self-insure adequately.

Since, as has frequently been pointed out, social insurance can make all parties equally likely insurers and equally effective loss spreaders,[21] the first of these systems of allocating losses presupposes, in effect, a decision not to have social insurance. It probably also presupposes some dissatisfaction with private insurance as a means of loss spreading. The very fact that liability would be determined on the basis of who is most likely to insure assumes either a difference in the cost of private insurance to different parties for the same risk (depending on who insures) or a belief that decisions not to insure but to bear unspread losses instead would bring about secondary costs that society wishes to avoid. In other words, this system of allocating losses implies that even within a basically noncompulsory system, we prefer a legal framework that tends to cause more losses to be pooled to a framework that would result in less loss spreading. This is not to suggest that the real reasons for the popularity of enterprise liability as a system of loss allocation may not lie *outside* the realm of loss spreading. I only want to point out that compared with the voluntary loss spreading brought about by private insurance and the compulsory loss spreading involved in social insurance, enterprise liability in this first meaning can be viewed as a system of semicompulsory loss spreading.

How this semicompulsion works is worth examining. The law cannot avoid placing accident costs on someone. It can for example

21. See Blum and Kalven, *Public Law Perspectives*, at 56–57. Their analysis raises problems regarding the externalization of costs, however. See Calabresi, "The Wonderful World," at 234–35; and infra pp. 144–50.

decide (1) to leave them on the injured party, (2) to shift them to another party to the accident, (3) to divide them among the parties involved, or (4) to remove them from the involved parties and place them on the taxpayers. The last involves compulsory spreading, but none of the others do so long as the parties involved are free to decide by contract with each other who will bear the loss. If such indemnificatory or exculpatory agreements are allowed, placing the losses on the party thought to be the best avoider of secondary costs does not compel spreading because in theory he was free to reach an agreement with other poorer avoiders of secondary costs who might be involved in the accident that they rather than he would bear any loss that might occur. Conversely, placing the losses on the inadequate spreaders does not compel secondary losses because in theory they were free to contract with the better spreader to bear the loss. Actual compulsion only enters the picture if such preaccident agreements are barred. The fact that exculpatory and indemnificatory agreements are often barred, especially in situations where the initial loss bearer is a good spreader, indicates that we often deem compulsion to be justified and that *one* of the reasons we use to justify compulsion is the need to minimize secondary losses. (Another reason we use to justify compulsion is the notion that, because of the ignorance or incapacity of one of the parties, compulsion of that party is inherent in allowing exculpatory agreements.) It does not suggest, however, that where such agreements are allowed compulsion is used.

Since indemnification agreements between potential injurers and victims are often unfeasible, loss spreading can often be maximized without the need to bar such agreements. One cannot conceive of a driver seeking indemnification agreements from every pedestrian he may hit, or, for that matter, a pedestrian seeking an agreement to bear accident losses from every driver who may hit him. In such situations, the law cannot avoid determining how the losses will be divided among the parties to an accident. A decision of who shall bear the loss on the basis of who is likely to farm out the risk or self-insure adequately will therefore maximize loss spreading in such situations without increasing the degree of compulsion beyond that which is inherent in the fact that indemnification agreements are not feasible. (Similarly, no increase in compulsion would be entailed in a decision to bar exculpatory agreements if one genuinely believed that because of the ignorance of one of the parties an agreement free from compulsion was impossible.)

Such decisions reflect a societal belief in favor of broad loss spreading, though they do not necessarily imply that we are willing to increase compulsion to achieve it. They are, in short, prime examples of enterprise liability in its first meaning operating as a system of semicompulsory spreading.[22] (In this sense we can readily understand judicial decisions which bar exculpatory or indemnificatory clauses in some product liability situations and allocate responsibility to categories of defendants who are good spreaders in other tort situations where agreements are not feasible.) It should again be emphasized, however, that the consequences, and hence perhaps the popularity of enterprise liability go far beyond the establishment of semicompulsory spreading.

The second meaning of enterprise liability as a system of allocating losses involves choosing a risk bearer not because he is the most likely insurer, but because he is most likely to be able to pass on part of the loss burden to buyers of the products he makes or to factors of production employed in making his products, thus distributing the loss broadly. The determination of the degree to which enterprises are in fact able to spread losses forward to consumers and backward to production factors is a very complicated matter involving, among other things, whether the enterprise operates in a competitive or a monopolistic industry. This is an issue with which I have already dealt at great length elsewhere and which does not need substantial further discussion here.[23]

For the scope of this book it is sufficient to say that, at least after an initial period of taking hold, a system that places liability on

22. See Infra pp. 161–73.
23. See generally Calabresi, "Risk Distribution," esp. at 519–27.

enterprises probably does accomplish a fair degree of loss spreading. The people who ultimately pay the spread burden of losses are, however, very different from those who pay the spread burden under social insurance. In social insurance the payers would probably be chosen either to achieve the broadest possible spreading or to achieve broad deep pocket spreading. The payers under enterprise liability are much more akin to those who would be chosen to pay if the social insurance fund were financed with primary cost avoidance notions in mind. Indeed, the very use of enterprise liability, which is more expensive to administer than simple social insurance, would indicate that spreading was not the only goal, suggesting some desire to place costs on those activities that are thought to engender them, that is, to accomplish some primary accident cost deterrence. Accordingly, I prefer to postpone until after my discussion of primary cost avoidance the question of how much spreading enterprise liability in this second sense accomplishes.

Like the first system of "enterprise liability", however, the second implies a certain amount of favoritism toward loss spreading and occasionally even a certain amount of compulsory spreading. Here, just as in the case where a party is chosen to bear the loss because he is the most likely insurer, the law uses the practical difficulties of striking bargains of indemnification to assure broad loss spreading. And to the extent that it forbids agreements exculpating enterprises from liability, it compels losses to be borne in a way that is expected to produce broad spreading.

The fact that systems such as social insurance and enterprise liability, which involve more than voluntary spreading, find substantial favor suggests a belief that people do not individually insure voluntarily to the degree necessary to provide for the spreading of losses that collectively they consider best for society. To put it another way, there seems to be a feeling in our society that we need more loss spreading than people are individually willing to buy.

Why Private Insurance May Give Inadequate Loss Spreading

The preceding discussion raises the question of why free individual decisions about insurance are not likely to bring about the amount and type of loss spreading we collectively want. To the extent that we are concerned with deep pocket—that is, with type rather than amount of spreading—no further discussion is needed, for private insurance without compulsion or control cannot make the choice of who pays depend on who is most able, from a collective point of view, to bear the burden. Accordingly, the following discussion will be concerned only with the amount of spreading that voluntary insurance affords. I believe that there are five principal reasons, whose significance and acceptance vary, why many critics feel that private insurance gives inadequate risk spreading.

Paternalism

The first and most controversial reason is simply the old paternalistic one—that people do not know what is best for themselves. In its most extreme form, it calls into question the very notion of a free market. Stated blatantly, it is a belief that people are likely to be happier if a central authority makes decisions for them than if they make decisions for themselves. I shall have more to say about this notion later, when I discuss the economic and ethical postulates of the general deterrence approach to primary accident cost avoidance. Here it is enough to say that while this notion has always had some adherents, and has perhaps gained more in recent years, in its extreme form it still does not command much assent in our society.

Inability to Value the Risk Properly

A more measured, more acceptable version of the paternalistic notion is at the root of the second reason. This approach does not question the general proposition that people know what is best for themselves by and large but is based instead on the view that in the area of accidents they often do not. This notion is three-sided.

First, individuals choosing between insurance and taking their chances often do not have the data necessary to determine how great the risk is, how large the losses are apt to be if they occur, and how serious the secondary results of such losses would be. If they had that data, their decision whether to buy insurance might be different. A concomitant of this view is that there are others more aware of the financial implications of the risk and therefore better able to make the choice whether to insure. Thus, some individuals who buy particular products will not know how risky they are, while the manufacturer, because he can view the risk as a statistic, can evaluate it clearly.[24]

Second, even if individuals had adequate data for evaluating the risk, they would be psychologically unable to do so. The contention is that people cannot estimate rationally their chances of suffering death or catastrophic injury. Such things always happen to "the other guy," and no amount of statistical information can convince an individual that they could happen to him. Whether people know what is best for themselves in other areas is, therefore, irrelevant to the conclusion that they do not know what is best in deciding between insuring themselves and bearing the risk of an unspread accident cost. Some adduce evidence of this psychological truth from the fact that people are much more likely to carry liability insurance (for injuries "the other guy" may receive) than personal accident insurance (for injuries they may receive).[25] Others just say it is a self-evident fact.[26] Either way, this notion

24. In strictly economic terms, we might express the individual's lack of awareness of the risk as a high information cost.

25. This point is made in *AACP* at 128: "the threat of having all one's wealth taken by the arm of the law seems somehow more persuasive than the threat of losing it all in an uncompensated accidental injury."

26. Occasionally, this psychological inability to view rationally the chances of one's own death or catastrophic accident operates to overemphasize the risk. There seems to be little doubt that people think airplanes more dangerous than they in fact are. But the people who fear flying so much are not usually those

implies that someone other than the individual, someone who *can* make a rational evaluation of the risk involved, is better suited to decide the optimal degree of loss spreading. This someone can be thought of as "society," which represents our collective judgment when we view accidents as a whole and therefore are not confused by the individual's inability to conceive of serious accidents happening to himself.

The third aspect of this semipaternalistic approach is somewhat harder to define. It is not based solely on the psychological inability to conceive of oneself as gravely injured, nor solely on the lack of data on accident risks. Instead, it is a more generally paternalistic view. We do not need to deny that there are many areas where people do know best for themselves in order to affirm that there are some where they do not. In general, the areas where individuals do not know best for themselves are those where the choice is between immediate cost and long-range cost. In such cases, people tend to choose the immediate "good life" and regret it later. This may be termed the "Faust attitude." A correlate of this view is that people as a group, or people when they set up general or collective norms, are less likely to view only the short run than are people deciding individually. They are less likely to yield to temptation collectively. Thus, it is argued, people do not save up for doctors' bills, do not provide for their retirement, do not insure adequately, and yet are basically happy if they are forced to do so.[27] It is easy to see that this attitude implies that a fair degree of "collectively self-imposed" compulsion is needed to achieve optimal loss spreading.

---

for whom not flying involves any real cost. Those who must fly, for whom not flying would be a real burden, probably view their chances of having an accident in the same underestimated manner in which most of us view the risk of car accidents.

27. Other examples of self-imposed restrictions which force us to forgo short-run temptations for long-run benefits come readily to mind. Perhaps the most dramatic is the Bill of Rights, which reflects a societal decision not to yield to certain temptations of the moment, even if backed by a majority, because of their long-run undesirability.

All three of these facets of the semipaternalistic thesis share the notion that someone other than the individual can best determine the present value of his accident loss risks and, therefore, the amount of insurance that is best for him. In theory, they may differ as to who is best suited to make this choice. In practice, however, the three coalesce into one and, combined with other reasons for thinking that individuals cannot, without outside help, choose best for themselves, create dissatisfaction with purely private insurance as a system of loss spreading. This dissatisfaction usually results in support for systems that involve some collectively decided compulsion and some placing of the choice on more likely insurers and on groups who have better access to risk data, with some individual choice at the edges.

The Individual May Not Bear the Costs
of Failing to Insure

A third general reason why we may feel that individual choices concerning insurance do not give us the degree of loss spreading we desire lies in the fact that often the individual does not have to bear all the costs that result if he chooses to leave losses unspread. The most obvious example of this is the case of the judgment-proof driver.[28] If he buys liability insurance, he pays approximately the costs of accidents that, statistically speaking, he will "cause". If he does not buy insurance he will not pay for the accident costs he causes, since blood cannot be gotten from a stone. His choice between insuring and not insuring does not take into account the costs his choice may entail for others and therefore would not, even under the least paternalistic outlook, result in the degree of loss spreading society wants.[29] In order to achieve the

28. The judgment-proof driver is the individual who has no money to pay for damages he causes or whose assets would be unavailable to satisfy a judgment against him because of bankruptcy laws.

29. There remains the possibility that those who end up paying could bargain with the judgment-proof driver to insure. However, this would still result in a less than optimal degree of loss spreading, as it would entail needless

desired loss spreading the individual must be made either to bear costs equivalent to those he causes (a rather difficult thing to do without offending other justice type goals), or to insure. It is not hard to see why society, which bears the costs of his noninsurance, frequently compels insurance.[30]

There are more complex examples of the same situation. An individual may fail to insure against injury to himself because he expects society to pick up at least part of the tab if he is left destitute. A choice between insuring and not insuring predicated on such expectations would not take into account all the costs involved. In effect, the man is a Faust who chooses the good life now, *knowing* that Marguerite's hard work will save him in the end. Society can react to such an attitude in two ways. It can either refuse to pick up the tab at the end or compel insurance in the first place. The first is out of style, in part because things are not always as neat as our analysis would make them; it is often difficult to separate cases where—failing society's intervention—the unspread loss would fall on Faust alone, from cases where it would fall in part on innocent parties, such as his family. It is also out of style because notions of justice make us feel sorry for Faust (the legend would not have the appeal it does if this were not so). The result is that Faust can be pretty sure that he will be saved in the end, and that society, to protect itself, must exact the cost of that salvation from him early in the game. In other words, some degree of compulsion in determining the degree of loss spreading is again necessary.

---

transaction costs. See Calabresi, "Transaction Costs." And wherever the costs of compelling the judgment-proof driver to insure are less than the transaction costs of such bargains, we are likely to opt for compulsion.

30. Analogously, part of the explanation for public housing programs lies in society's unwillingness to bear the secondary costs of inadequate housing. Unlike compulsory insurance, however, the cost of public housing is borne out of general taxes, so that an income redistribution effect is added to the secondary cost avoidance effect. Any primary cost avoidance lost is presumably not worth the redistribution effect gained.

The Costs of Loss Spreading May Differ Depending on Who Chooses Whether to Insure

A fourth reason why a purely free market determination of the degree of loss spreading may not suffice lies in the fact that the cost of spreading may differ depending on who decides whether or not to spread. In other words, buying insurance against the same risk may be cheaper for one party than for another. Under these circumstances, one potential party to an accident may decide that it is better to bear the risk than to pay for insurance, while a party for whom insurance is cheaper may for that very reason decide the opposite.

It may be argued that since the party for whom insurance is more expensive can always, in a free market, pay the other to bear the risk, thus taking advantage of the other's ability to insure cheaply, the fact that costs of insurance may differ is unimportant. In an economist's perfect world, this would be true. But as we have already seen, such an indemnity contract might not be feasible (how can one collect all potential parties to accidents?), and even if it were, would not be without cost. As a result, it remains true that placing the initial burden on the party who can insure most cheaply would bring about the best comparison between the cost of spreading the loss and the cost of bearing the risk of an unspread loss.

This fourth reason does not by itself justify compulsory loss spreading; it does, however, justify semicompulsion. It is likely to cause us to enact laws that place the initial accident loss burdens on those parties that, because spreading is cheapest for them, are most likely to spread the loss broadly and thus increase the degree of loss spreading beyond that which would normally occur.

How Insurance Operates

The fifth reason why private insurance may not achieve the degree of spreading we want is somewhat different from the others. The others depend essentially on the attitudes of individuals toward the choice between insuring and bearing the risk of unspread losses. The final factor depends instead on how risk categories are arrived at by insurance companies.

I have discussed earlier how private insurance tends not to put all would-be insureds into a single pool, but to distinguish them somewhat according to accident-proneness. I have also noted that this tendency, though perhaps desirable for primary accident cost deterrence, prevents "total" loss spreading through private means. The question here is whether or not the degree of differentiation and concomitant concentration of losses resulting from private insurance is likely to reflect an aggregate of individual choices regarding how much differentiation and pooling is wanted in relation to the costs involved in differentiating.

No simple answer to this question seems possible to me. An insurance company will only undertake the cost of differentiation if it can gain a competitive advantage by so doing. A company would hope that by differentiating it could separate out a group involving substantially lower risks and offer insurance to this group at rates that would cover the cost of the differentiation and still be sufficiently lower than previous rates to attract a large number of people who fell into that lower risk category. Enough such people would have to be drawn away from other companies to make up for the loss of the higher risk people hitherto in the single pool. They would presumably switch to insurance companies that did not differentiate and could, therefore, charge them lower premiums.

If, however, the differentiation proved initially worthwhile, and if insurance is, in this respect, a relatively competitive business, sooner or later all the companies would have to accept the same or a similar differentiation. The company that did not differentiate at first would find that it was losing all the lower risk members of its pool to the company that did. It would therefore be forced to raise its premiums to those who remained. Over time, these premiums would have to rise to the same level as those the differentiating company charged to the higher risk group. The nondifferentiating company would then have no competitive advantage in this higher risk group and would do well to compete for the lower risk group by offering them the same lower rates offered by the differentiating company—in other words, to start differentiating.

This analysis indicates that the degree to which insurance companies differentiate is not the product of the degree of loss spreading people a priori want. It depends instead on the variance in accident-proneness among those in any given risk pool and on the cost of further differentiation. These two factors will determine whether an insurance company can, as a result of differentiation, offer premiums low enough to attract a group large enough to make the change worthwhile.

Once the differentiation is made, no member of the lower risk group is likely to pool himself voluntarily with a higher risk category. The result of the differentiation, then, is to identify groups that either cannot insure or can only insure at rates that prevent them from undertaking the activity involved. In other words, high risk groups may face the choice of paying a very high insurance burden, taking the risk of engaging in the activity without insurance, or, what may often be the greatest burden of all, giving up the activity. At this point, society often intervenes with subsidies or compulsory assigned risk pools because it is considered unfair to exclude certain groups from certain activities as a result of their identifiable accident-proneness. The treatment of physically handicapped workers is a prime example of this.

I should like to emphasize that I am not necessarily criticizing differentiation, even if it does impose a greater burden on accident-prone groups. In terms of the general deterrence approach to primary accident cost avoidance, such differentiation may be essential. I am, however, pointing out that the extent to which private insurance leads us away from fairly complete loss spreading depends on considerations other than the amount of spreading desired. To put it another way, if people asked themselves whether they preferred to be in one pool with broad spreading or have the pool broken into two categories, one of which would pay small premiums and the other very high ones, they might very well prefer, before knowing their own category, to stay where they were, but be unwilling to go back to the large pool once they knew they were in the lower category. Since the determination of an individual's category may occur for reasons unrelated to whether there was satisfaction with the original single pool arrangement, the resulting categorization may not represent the degree of loss spreading desired.

I have expressed all this in conditional terms because the problem is actually more complicated. In the first place, my whole analysis has presupposed a degree of competition in the insurance industry that may not exist. In the second place, the very differentiation we have discussed should in theory sufficiently reduce accidents through the primary accident cost avoidance it would bring about, so that all parties—both high and low risk—could be made better off than they were before.[31] But in practice it is doubtful whether differentiation would give rise to savings sufficient to enable the low risk categories not only to compensate the high risk ones for having to forgo the activity or pay higher premiums, but also to pay the administrative costs of effectuating such compensation. Compensation, moreover, would not occur in the absence of compulsion. Without compulsion, why should the low risk categories compensate the high risk ones? Once again, therefore, we return to the fact that private insurance alone may not lead to the degree of spreading society desires. If the theoretical compensation of high risk categories just described is in reality economically feasible, it may be that private insurance supplemented by compulsory payments to high risk groups gives us the best approach to spreading. But it is equally possible that direct collective decisions on how broadly to spread losses, coupled with other devices to achieve primary cost avoidance, would give us the best all around result.

31. This is, of course, no more than what I call general deterrence in operation. See infra pp. 68–75.

I have suggested that there are various reasons for believing that the amount and type of loss spreading that would occur spontaneously or "naturally" in our society, i.e. without government intervention, would not be sufficient and that therefore it is not surprising that we have government intervention and even compulsion in favor of spreading. In this section, I have attempted to state some of the most significant or more frequently mentioned reasons for this belief. They are of very different types. They probably will not all appeal to any one reader; they certainly do not all convince me. This is especially true since some of the imperfections in natural loss spreading result from the existence of goals other than secondary cost avoidance, which some readers may not accept. Still, it is unlikely that very many will reject *all* of these reasons. And ultimately, that is all this stage of the analysis requires. Its aim is simply to point out that we cannot a priori assume that compulsory insurance or loss spreading is bad and that the ideal amount of secondary cost avoidance can be attained if we just let people buy the amount of insurance they want. The result is that we cannot ignore secondary cost avoidance as a goal in evaluating alternative systems of accident law.

THE WORLD OF TOTAL RISK SPREADING

Thus far in this chapter I have been concerned with analyzing secondary cost avoidance, both in its pure spreading version and in its deep pocket version, as a subgoal of accident law. I pointed out that various systems for accomplishing loss spreading give less than total spreading and suggested that the absolute minimization of secondary costs of accidents cannot be the only goal of accident law. A system that compensates for accidents perfectly once they have occurred but does nothing to prevent them in the first place is obviously not desirable. By way of emphasizing some of the scarcely less obvious implications of this obvious statement, it may be well to examine briefly exactly what the concept of a world of total spreading of accident losses implies.

In a world where accident costs were totally spread, there would be no financial incentives to avoid accidents other than fear for one's own safety. Even that incentive would be reduced to the extent that the injuries one might suffer could be adequately compensated for financially.[32] Total spreading would mean that all accident losses would be paid for—as well as one can ever compensate for accidents with money—and the cost spread either in as broad a way as possible or among those "best able" to pay, depending on whether our hypothetical world were of total or deep pocket spreading. A vague kind of moral sense might cause us occasionally to be safety-conscious, but where the less safe acts or activities had any substantial attraction and where the harm to others was not obvious, it would not be a very effective incentive for the mass of people.

The knowledge that the tab will have to be paid somehow could also have some indirect effects. People might worry about the fact that the tax to support the spreading fund would rise if there were increased accident costs. But this would no more cause a *substantial* incentive toward safety for any individual than the knowledge that all producers in a highly competitive industry would be better off if prices were kept high keeps individual producers from cutting prices. And the reasons are the same. Each individual is better off doing what he wants, taking the risky way if it holds some attraction, because this gives him direct and immediate benefits. Taking the safer and less immediately attractive way will pay off only if all other individuals do likewise. And the others, since there are too many of them, cannot be trusted—without compulsion—to take the safer way. Without compulsion, everyone knows that the others will take the most attractive way even if it results, in the long run, in a higher tax. And so everyone decides since the higher tax is inevitable not to be a sucker and choose the

32. We usually think of permanent disabilities and pain and suffering as not being compensable in money. It is hard to imagine significant changes in our ideas in this area. See infra pp. 215–25, on pain and suffering generally. But if medicine ever perfects the art of transplanting human limbs and organs so that organs become totally fungible, then we might be in a world where all costs except those of pain and suffering could be spread.

safer, less attractive way and then have to pay the higher tax anyway.

The key phrase in all this is, of course, "without compulsion." Compulsion forces people to take the safer way and be better off despite themselves. And it is inevitable that the more a society moves toward total loss spreading, the more it becomes subject to pressures for compulsion in the control of accidents. In such a society the specific deterrence or collective approach to primary accident cost avoidance (the prohibition, often with criminal penalties, of accident-causing behavior) becomes essential. Even a cursory examination of the proposals of those who, consciously or unconsciously (like the Defense Research Institute), are moving us toward social insurance of automobile accidents makes this evident. But the use of specific deterrence is itself inconsistent with total loss spreading, since criminal penalties or fines providing sufficient deterrence can be very severe unspread burdens.

Indeed, in terms of secondary costs, it may well be that the burdens that would be suffered as a result of collective control of certain activities and prohibitions of others would be greater than those that would be suffered if we left some part of accident losses unspread in the first place. Even if that were not so, one might question whether we could, in terms of fairness, tolerate the kind of wholesale prohibition of activities that the total spreading of the economic costs of accidents requires.[33] And one might also question whether such detailed specific control could keep up with changes in the causes of accident costs, or if we could reasonably judge when a risky activity was desirable despite its riskiness. Finally, one may well ask whether the *cost* of achieving sufficient primary cost reduction by such direct means would not be prohibitive, since such collective rules would require collective consideration and policing of the most minute details of countless activities.

In sum, the world of total accident loss spreading does not seem acceptable because it would encourage more accidents than most

33. See infra pp. 111–13.

of us would deem desirable. And total loss spreading combined with direct prohibitions against accident-causing activities is unlikely to be acceptable for a wide variety of reasons, only some of which have been mentioned here and all of which will be examined in detail when consideration is given to the specific deterrence method of primary accident cost avoidance.[34] It follows that despite our perfectly valid desire for loss spreading, there are great advantages in leaving accident costs unspread *to some extent.* But a determination of the degree to which we want accident losses concentrated depends substantially on an analysis of primary accident cost avoidance as a goal.

34. See infra pp. 107–13.

CHAPTER 5

Primary Accident Cost Avoidance:
The General Deterrence Approach

As suggested earlier, the primary way in which a society may
seek to reduce accident costs is to discourage activities that are
"accident prone" and substitute safer activities as well as safer
ways of engaging in the same activities.[1] But such a statement
suggests neither the degree to which we wish to discourage such
activities nor the means for doing so. As we have seen, we certainly do not wish to avoid accident costs at all costs by forbidding
all accident-prone activities. Most activities can be carried out
safely enough or be sufficiently reduced in frequency so that there is
a point at which their worth outweighs the costs of the accidents
they cause. Specific prohibition or deterrence of most activities
would cost society more than it would save in accident costs prevented. We want the fact that activities cause accidents to influence our choices among activities and among ways of doing them.
But we want to limit this influence to a degree that is justified by
the cost of these accidents. The obvious question is, how do we do
this?

There are two basic approaches to making these difficult "decisions for accidents," and our society has always used both,
though not always to the same degree. The first, which I have
termed the specific deterrence or collective approach, will be discussed later. At present it suffices to say that it involves deciding
collectively the degree to which we want any given activity, who
should participate in it, and how we want it done. These decisions may or may not be made solely on the basis of the acci-

1. We could call a safer way of engaging in an activity "a safer activity."
However, I believe a rough distinction between the two terms to be useful,
and I will try to maintain it. For elaboration, see infra pp. 73–74.

dent costs the activity causes. The collective decisions are enforced by penalties on those who violate them.

The other approach, and the one I wish to discuss first, involves attempting instead to decide what the accident costs of activities are and letting the *market* determine the degree to which, and the ways in which, activities are desired given such costs. Similarly, it involves giving people freedom to choose whether they would rather engage in the activity and pay the costs of doing so, including accident costs, or, given the accident costs, engage in safer activities that might otherwise have seemed less desirable. I call this approach general, or market, deterrence.

The crucial thing about the general deterrence approach to accidents is that it does not involve an a priori collective decision as to the correct number of accidents. General deterrence implies that accident costs would be treated as one of the many costs we face whenever we do anything. Since we cannot have everything we want, individually or as a society, whenever we choose one thing we give up others. General deterrence attempts to force individuals to consider accident costs in choosing among activities. The problem is getting the best combination of choices available. The general deterrence approach would let the free market or price system tally the choices.

THEORETICAL BASIS

The theoretical basis of general deterrence is not hard to find. The problem posed is simply the old one of allocation of resources which for years has been studied in the branch of economics called welfare economics; the free market solution is the one traditionally given by welfare economics. This solution presupposes certain postulates. The most important of these, and the only one we need consider now, is the notion that no one knows what is best for individuals better than they themselves do. If people want television sets, society should produce television sets; if they want licorice drops, then licorice drops should be made. The proportion of television sets to licorice drops, as well as the way in which each is made, should also be left up to individual choices because, according to the postulate, as long as individuals are adequately informed about the alternatives and as long as the cost to society of giving them what they want is reflected in the cost to the individual, the individual can decide better than anyone else what he wants. Thus the function of the prices of various goods must be to reflect the relative costs to society of producing them, and if prices perform this function properly, the buyer will cast an informed vote in making his purchases; thus the best combination of choices available will be achieved.

The general deterrence approach treats accident costs as it does any other costs of goods and activities—such as the metal, or the time it takes, to make cars. If all activities reflect the accident costs they "cause," each individual will be able to choose for himself whether an activity is worth the accident costs it "causes." The sum of these choices is, *ex hypothesis,* the best combination available and will determine the degree to which accident-prone activities are engaged in (if at all), how they are engaged in, and who will engage in them.[2] Failure to include accident costs in the prices of activities will, according to the theory, cause people to choose more accident-prone activities than they would if the prices of these activities made them pay for these accident costs, resulting in more accident costs than we want. Forbidding accident-prone activities *despite* the fact that they can "pay" their costs would, in theory, bring about an equally bad result from the resource allocation point of view. Either way, the postulate that individuals know best for themselves would be violated.

A hypothetical example may help clarify this. In Athens, accident costs are in some way or other charged to the activity that

2. The sum of individual choices will not necessarily be the best combination available, however, if the activities' other costs are not reflected in their prices. Thus if the petroleum industry were subsidized, we might have too much driving as against walking, even though both driving and walking bore their proper share of the costs of accidents. And some economists would contend that once one cost is not reflected properly, the reflection of other costs may even worsen the overall result in terms of proper resource allocation. See infra pp. 86–88.

engenders them. Sparta is a society in which all accident costs are borne by the state and come out of general taxes. C. J. Taney, a businessman in Athens, has one car and is considering buying a used car in addition. The cost of owning the second car would come to about $200 a year, plus an addition to his insurance bill of another $200. Alternatively, the cost of train fares, the taxis he would occasionally need to take, and the other expenses incurred to make up for not having a second car come to about $250. Contrasting the $400 expense of owning a second car with the $250 expense of riding in trains and taxis, he decides to forgo the car.

If Taney lived in Sparta, on the other hand, he would have to pay a certain sum in taxes as his share of Sparta's general accident program. Short of moving out of Sparta, he could not avoid this cost whatever he did. As a result, the comparative costs in Sparta would be $200 per year for the car as contrasted with $250 for train and taxi fares. Chances are Taney would buy the car. In purchasing a second car in Sparta, he is not made to pay the full $400 that it costs society. In fact, he must pay *part* of that cost whether or not he buys one. He will, therefore, buy a car. If he had to carry the full burden of a second car, he would use trains and taxis, spending the money saved on something else—television, or perhaps a rowboat.

For the theory to make some sense there is no need to postulate a world made up of economic men who consciously consider the relative costs of each different good and the relative pleasure derived from each. If the cost of all automobile accidents were suddenly to be paid out of a general social insurance fund, the expense of owning a car would be a good deal lower than it is now since people would no longer need to worry about buying insurance. The result would be that some people would buy more cars. Perhaps they would be teen-agers who can afford $100 for an old jalopy but who cannot afford—or whose fathers cannot afford—the insurance.[3] Or they might be people who could only afford a

3. An example of this may be found in New York State where, with the advent of compulsory insurance (see the Motor Vehicle Financial Security

second car so long as no added insurance was involved.[4] In any event, the demand for cars would increase, and so would the number of cars produced. Indeed, the effect on car purchases would be much the same as if the government suddenly chose to pay the cost of the steel used by automobile manufacturers and to raise the money out of general taxes. In each case the objection would be the same. In each, an economist would say, resources are misallocated in that goods are produced that the consumer would not want if he had to pay the full extent of their cost to society, whether in terms of the physical components of the product or in terms of the expense of accidents associated with its production and use.

As I shall show later, I do not believe resource allocation theory in its extreme or pure form can find much acceptance today, especially as applied to accidents. Its inherent limitations, together with those added by its application to accident costs, are simply too great. But this is far from saying that the theory is useless. It has always had, in fact, a remarkable practical appeal and tenacity. It can even stand substantial modification of its basic ethical postulate—that individuals know what is best for themselves by and large—and still play an important role, albeit a more limited one, in highly welfaristic or socialistic societies. Indeed, it is hard to imagine a society where, somewhere along the line, the market deterrence approach to primary accident cost control would not be significant. All that is needed for the approach to have some influence is acceptance of the notion that *sometimes* people know best for themselves, even if for no other reason than that the

---

Act, New York Vehicle and Traffic Law §§ 310 et seq.), the bottom fell out o the jalopy market.

4. "Afford" is not the proper economic term, though it is the one w would normally use. Technically the question is not whether the teen-ager o his father has or can get the insurance money, but whether he thinks it worth while to spend that much money on a car rather than on other things. "Othe things" would include, of course, the leisure the teen-ager would have to giv up to earn the money.

choices involved arise too frequently for adequate collective decisions. To make the reasons for the appeal of general deterrence even clearer, it may be useful to discuss how it operates to reduce accident costs and how it would do so even in a society not committed to free enterprise.

How Costs Are Reduced by General Deterrence

The general deterrence approach operates in two ways to reduce accident costs. The first and more obvious one is that it creates incentives to engage in safer activities. Some people who would engage in a relatively dangerous activity at prices that did not reflect its accident costs will shift to a safer activity if accident costs *are* reflected in prices. The degree of the shift will depend on the relative difference in accident costs and on how good a substitute the safer activity is. Whatever the shift, however, it will reduce accident costs, since a safer activity will to some degree have been substituted for a dangerous one.

The second and perhaps more important way general deterrence reduces accident costs is that it encourages us to make activities safer. This is no different from the first if every variation in the way an activity is carried out is considered to be a separate activity, but since that is not how the term activity is used in common language, it may be useful to show how general deterrence operates to cause a given activity to become safer. Taney drives a car. His car causes, on the average, $200 per year in accident costs.[5] If a different kind of brake were used in the car, this would be reduced to $100. The new kind of brake costs the equivalent of $50 per year.[6] If the accident costs Taney causes are paid either by the state out of general taxes or by those who are injured, he has no financial incentive to put in the new brake. But if Taney has to pay,

5. This, of course, assumes we know the costs precisely. The $200 accident cost of Taney's operating an automobile can be viewed as the cost of insuring against the accident costs he causes no matter who pays it.

6. The cost of the brakes must be discounted over their effective life in order to arrive at an annual expense figure.

he will certainly put the new brake in. He will thus bear a new cost of $50 per year, but it will be less than the $100 per year in accident costs he will avoid. As a result, the cost of accidents to society will have been reduced by $50.[7]

This example of how general deterrence operates to reduce costs is, of course, highly simplified. It assumes, for instance, that we know that Taney "causes" the $200 in accident costs. It also assumes that the government or the victims, if they bear the losses, cannot cause the brakes to be installed as readily as Taney. Indeed, the assumptions are so simple that they lead one to ask, why we do not simply make all Taneys install the new brakes. Why, in short, do we not specifically deter the "dangerous conduct" instead of bothering with so cumbersome a method as general deterrence?

Mentioning a few more of the many complications inherent in the situation may make clearer why general deterrence is worthwhile. Suppose that Marshall, who uses old-style brakes, has only $25 worth of accidents per year. It is not worth our while to force him to install the new brakes. Indeed, if he were made to install new brakes and if we can assume our measurements of costs to be accurate (a matter calling for a good deal of discussion later), forcing Marshall to install new brakes would add an unnecessary $25 to our cost burden. Yet we would still wish to have Taney install the brakes in order to get his $50 saving. It will be expensive, if not impossible, to make collective decisions distinguishing the Taneys from the Marshalls. It will, in fact, be much easier if we let the distinction be made by Taney and Marshall themselves by letting them choose between paying for the accidents and paying for the new brakes.

Another complication may be even more significant. Suppose we do not yet have the safe brakes, and requiring such brakes is therefore impossible. Placing the cost on cars may still bring about

7. Of course, the $50 brake cost is not an *accident* cost. It is an accident *avoidance* cost. But in terms of primary accident cost avoidance the two are equivalent.

general deterrence in the form of a continuous pressure to develop something—such as new brakes—that would avoid the accident costs and would be cheaper to make and sell than paying the accident costs. General deterrence creates a market for this cost-saving substitute and, therefore, an incentive for someone to develop it and bring about a cost reduction.[8]

GENERAL DETERRENCE IN A
SOCIALIST WORLD

General deterrence would be a useful way of reducing accident costs even in a society where the postulate that by and large people know what is best for themselves is not accepted and where the state—whether in the form of an individual dictator or representatives of the people—is believed to know best. I cannot go into all the theoretical permutations of how the thesis would fit in such societies, or the exact limits under which it would operate, as that would depend largely on who is believed to know best, but a brief outline of general deterrence's usefulness in such situations may serve to point out its widespread applicability.

Let us examine, for example, a situation where virtually everyone admits that broad individual choice has to be restricted: a major war. Most important decisions as to what is to be produced and how are, at such a time, thought to be best decided by a central body; the market is put to one side. It is decided that only so much gasoline and only so much fat are to be allotted for civilian consumption. Likewise, it is decided that only so many civilians are to grow and manufacture general foodstuffs. But once these general decisions are made, there is generally believed to be little use in compelling people, with all their different tastes and habits, to

8. Even in the absence of general deterrence, an inventor may seek to develop safe brakes in hope of governmental action forcing their adoption. But to the usual risk that he may fail to invent safe brakes, this adds the risk that no such collective decision will be made. Alternatively, the government may seek to develop such brakes, but this raises the question of whether governmental decisions as to what is worth inventing should or can replace individual effort.

react in the same way to them. Little is gained by making everyone consume equal quantities of spinach and zucchini, given that some prefer one to the other. The postulate that people know their own tastes best remains. The question becomes how to coordinate these tastes with the collective decisions concerning the total amounts of farm products desired.

During World War II, in fairly broad product areas, the coordination was made through an artificial price system, rationing. Where the collective decision could stand little or no variation (usually where the goods involved had few close substitutes), individual tastes were, by and large, suppressed. People were allowed certain amounts of gasoline and could not get more of it by forgoing something else. As to other goods—such as farm products —enough "money" (blue coupons) was given out so that the demand for these goods in blue coupons would call forth a supply that would approximately use up the scarce resources allocated to farm production. Individuals were then given the right to use their coupons in choosing among these goods, whose coupon prices reflected how much each of them employed the resources whose availability for farm production had been limited by the collective decision. The extent to which these resources were used to produce spinach instead of zucchini still depended on people's preferences.

Unless a society is prepared to say, regarding accidents, that it collectively knows best down to the last detail and can enforce these collective decisions, some room will likewise remain for general deterrence as a method of coordinating general collective decisions about production of goods, given their accident costs, with individual differences in tastes and desires. One can imagine, for instance, a society that decides collectively that only so many automobiles will be allowed because they cause accident costs as well as other costs to such an extent that a greater number is undesirable but which leaves up to the market whether cars have one type or brake or another, are driven by 18-year-olds or 21-year-olds, are driven at night or in the daytime, etc. Similarly, even if a society ruled on automobiles down to the last detail, it still might decide that whether somebody should ride a bicycle or walk was best left to him.

Of course, the more a society makes collectively the broad decisions as to what goods and services it wants, the more likely it is to intervene and seek to influence, by tax or subsidy, the market results regarding even minor production decisions. But it is likely to do this only after it has seen the results general deterrence has brought about. This indicates that the optimal general deterrence result may often be a first step in a collective society—a market gathering of information on the acceptable level of costs for use in reaching collective decisions. The information thus gathered can have a crucial effect.

Assume, for example, that under a free market, general deterrence arrangement, accident costs attributable to minors and people over 70 are so great that very few of them can afford to drive. A welfaristic society may decide not to alter this situation regarding the minors but to reverse it, for collective reasons, for the aged either through a direct subsidy or through an indirect one like compulsory risk pooling. The information the market gathers, however, may well affect the decision whether to give the subsidy to all aged, to aged between 70 and 75, or to aged who use certain safety equipment which reduces accidents somewhat and at a cost that they, given the subsidy, can pay.

In other words, general deterrence is a useful approach even in societies that reject to differing degrees the concept that free market decisions result by and large in a maximization of individual choices and that such maximization leads to the best total societal result. It is a useful approach because it can still serve at least two purposes. It can allow for and give effect to individual differences in tastes, desires, and needs within limits set by broad collective decisions. And it can inform the collective decision-makers of the extent to which individual desires would be limited by any given collective decision.

LIMITATIONS IMPOSED ON GENERAL DETERRENCE BY ITS DEPENDENCE ON RESOURCE ALLOCATION THEORY

As I have suggested, the general deterrence approach has severe limitations. Some of these involve difficulties inherent in resource allocation theory. Others appear when one tries to apply resource allocation theory to the problem of accidents—when, in other words, resource allocation becomes general deterrence. Because of the significance of the latter problems (which come down to the difficulties of deciding what the cost of the accident is and then attributing that cost to an appropriate activity), and because they will be equally important in the analysis of specific deterrence as an approach to primary accident cost avoidance, I have chosen to separate them from the difficulties inherent in resource allocation theory itself and treat them in a separate part of this book. For the moment I limit my discussion to why resource allocation theory provides no basis for pushing general deterrence to extremes. Essentially, this involves a discussion of the problems of monopoly, unemployment, income distribution, and, more generally, the "theory of the second best."

Income Distribution

The problems of income distribution and unemployment seem to trouble economists most. Unless the distribution of income—and therefore of goods and services—is satisfactory, it may be foolish to say that society is best off if all consumers can choose what they want for themselves after seeing what the true costs of their possible choices are. Instead, prices that falsify the costs of various items may actually be preferable if, because they falsify, they lead to a more satisfactory income distribution. Thus, if a society found that the poor were too poor and that they used widgets in great quantities, that society might be better off if widgets were made cheaper (i.e. "subsidized") by not being made to bear their accident costs, than if they bore all their costs in full.

Of course, it can be argued that such a society would still not be as well off as one in which choices were based on full costs and in which the poor, who now had to pay more for widgets or give them up, were "compensated" (perhaps through taxes and grants) by those among the wealthy who were saved from accidents by the decrease in the use of widgets. The classical economist will show *ad nauseam* that those who were made better off by moving to a free market choice system based on full costs could more than compensate those who were made worse off. The problem is that such hypothetical compensation rarely comes about. It may be too expensive; it may be made feasible only through the levying of taxes that misallocate resources grievously; or it may be politically impossible to accomplish. In all such cases, the theoretical desirability of the totally free market approach has little significance in practice.[9]

The same difference between the theory of resource allocation and its practical effects can be stated in a slightly different way. The prime instrument for redistributing income in our society is taxation. One may well feel that the most honest way to accomplish a redistribution of income is through taxes coupled with direct grants to those we wish to help. Those receiving grants might then decide for themselves whether to use the money for widgets or smoked salmon. Hence the classical economist's conclusion that resource allocation theory should stand untroubled by dissatisfactions with income distribution. But very few taxes and grants fail to misallocate resources to some extent, many are politically unfeasible, and all cost money. And it is at least theoretically possible that a system of allocating accident losses could be found that would be politically feasible and would accomplish a desired redistribution of income more cheaply than taxation, or with less misallocation of resources.[10]

9. See generally the brilliant treatment of this problem in Samuelson, *Foundations of Economic Analysis,* at 203–28, 249–53.

10. Cf. Calabresi, "Transaction Costs," esp. at 69.

We must not, however, give too much importance to the notion that poor income distribution might be redressed through accident law. In most instances, the best income distribution is still likely to be obtained directly through taxation. As a result, the significance of the fact that income redistribution is an aim ignored by resource allocation theory is likely to be a negative one. It means that any system of handling accident costs which tends to *aggravate* bad distributions of income is likely to be unacceptable, even if it is very effective from a resource allocation point of view.[11]

Unemployment

The existence of severe unemployment, like unsatisfactory income distribution, would render meaningless the attempt to obtain optimal allocation of resources in a traditional sense and might seem to justify systems of accident law that would alleviate the problem even at the expense of misallocating resources.[12] But this would only be true if there were no more effective means of coping with unemployment. Such means undoubtedly exist, but like those necessary to cure bad income distribution, they cost money, may cause some misallocation of resources, and may not be feasible politically. Again, it is unlikely that these facts would justify using accident law to alleviate unemployment. They may be significant enough, however, to bar any system of accident law that sought to achieve perfect allocation of resources at the cost of increasing unemployment.

11. This is essentially a restatement of the point that cost spreading or secondary cost avoidance limits the degree to which we seek primary accident cost avoidance. Recognition of this factor will serve to keep us from aggravating bad income distribution in a way that would be socially disruptive.

12. This simply means that there are situations in which the predominance of a goal like full employment may cause us *not* to burden an activity with a cost which is properly allocable to it, perhaps because politically it is the easiest way to accomplish the goal. For instance, if housing construction for the poor were considered essential to the creation of full employment, but adequate direct subsidization were not feasible politically, we might, subconsciously or even deliberately, not charge housing construction with its full accident costs. This political necessity assumes a lack of consensus as to our goals, but that is not unusual.

In other words, there are other things that may count more in our society than allocation of resources, and we will often rightly forgo the theoretically best allocation of resources if by doing so some more important policies are served.

Monopoly

The limitations that the existence of monopoly power may impose on resource allocation theory may, at first glance, seem more important than those stemming from unemployment and bad income distribution. Under the theory, choices among goods generally depend on their relative prices. But price will be an accurate reflection of the relative costs of two competing goods only if the ratio of cost to price is the same in both those goods, and this ratio will not be the same where one product is relatively competitive and the other is relatively monopolistic. Sellers in relatively monopolistic industries generally sell at higher price-to-cost ratios than those in relatively competitive industries.[13] As a result, fewer goods are demanded from monopolistic industries than is in fact warranted by their true costs.[14] This is what economists and antitrust lawyers have in mind when they speak of the misallocation of resources caused by monopoly. If, then, we count on people to choose what they want on the basis of a product's total costs to

13. The economist will recognize that I am weaseling on my use of the term "cost." Thus, if the comparison is between a pure competitor and a pure monopoly, what I am saying might be true in terms of accounting costs. But if I am comparing a pure competitor and a seller in an industry that has monopolistic competition, it will be true only in the sense that the price does not properly reflect the optimum costs that would obtain under conditions of pure competition. See generally George J. Stigler, *The Theory of Price* (3d ed. New York, Macmillan, 1967).

14. To say that fewer goods will be demanded is technically no more accurate than to say that fewer goods will be supplied. In the relatively monopolistic industry, the producer maximizes his profits by selling at a price higher than that which would obtain if the industry were competitive. He does so even though he will sell fewer goods at that price and produce less than he would otherwise; at the monopolistic price, consumers will buy less than they would at a lower price. Whether this means that fewer goods are demanded or that fewer goods are supplied is not a meaningful question. Cf. Alfred Marshall, *Principles of Economics* 348–50 (8th ed. New York, Macmillan, 1920).

society, we fool ourselves whenever differing degrees of monopoly power exist.

Economists usually suggest, in addition, that even an economy that had a uniform degree of monopoly power throughout would be less desirable than a fully competitive one. The reasons for this are too complicated to go into here, but they involve the fact that less would be produced in a monopoly economy than under competition—or, as economists put it, the "work-leisure" conditions for an optimal economic organization would be violated. Similar types of "misallocations" are caused by virtually all forms of taxation.[15] As a result, I am concerned less with them than with misallocations among different goods. That is, I am more concerned with whether too many cars are produced relative to televisions and whether both cars and televisions use too much steel relative to aluminum, than I am with the total production of steel, cars, televisions, and fruit knives. In fact, for reasons I shall go into presently,[16] I am principally concerned with the even narrower issue of what kinds of cars relative to one another are produced. In other words, I am more concerned with proper allocation of resources *within* activities than *among* activities, and least concerned with allocations between all activities and leisure.

One can take the same attitude toward monopoly that I have taken toward unemployment and distribution of income and argue that there are better ways of attacking the monopoly problem than by trying to make up for its possible misallocations by rearranging the allocation of tort losses. Or one may take the view normally taken of innovations[17] and contend that ultimately the monopoly

15. See, e.g., Nancy Ruggles, "Recent Developments in the Theory of Marginal Cost Pricing," 17 *Rev. Econ. Stud.* 107, 110–14 (1949); I. M. D. Little, *A Critique of Welfare Economics* (2d ed. Oxford, Clarendon Press, 1957) at 129–65, 294–300.

16. See infra pp. 86–88.

17. In competitive industries that are undergoing rapid changes in technology, it may be true that at a given period in time prices do not reflect the true costs of goods. It seems safe to say, however, that over a long period of time more harm would come from trying to compensate for such temporary

problem is one of time, and that over a long period greater misallocations are likely to come from taking measures within tort law to make up for monopoly's misallocations than monopoly caused in the first place. I am in sympathy with these views, which in effect boil down to the philosophy: "Don't correct one wrong by creating another; you only cause trouble for yourself." Indeed, I think resource allocation finds justification on this basis alone. But since not everyone agrees, some further discussion may be justified.

It might appear that accident costs should be charged to competitive industries in order to induce them to charge more and produce less, and that, to counteract the monopolist's relative underproduction, such costs should not be placed on monopolistic industries. More careful analysis, however, destroys much of even the theoretical validity of making relatively competitive industries bear their accident costs while exempting monopolistic ones from bearing theirs.

Resource allocation theory is of primary importance in situations involving two or more products that can substitute for one another to some significant extent. C. J. Taney is faced with the alternative of using aluminum or steel in making widgets. Suppose that one of these alternatives will result in high accident costs, while the other involves few accidents. Taney's choice between the two metals will be influenced by their relative prices, and these in turn will be influenced by whether or not accident costs are charged to the metal-producing industries.[18] From the standpoint of resource allocation, the fact that both steel and aluminum have a high degree of monopoly power compared with corner hamburger joints is quite irrelevant. The choice is between steel and aluminum, not between these and fried clams. Putting accident costs on corner

---

misstatements of costs through adjustments in tort liability than by treating such industries in the same way as all other competitive industries.

18. For purposes of the example, it makes no difference whatsoever whether the accident cost of widget manufacturing is viewed as stemming from injuries to the workers in widget factories, to consumers of widgets, or to both.

hamburger joints and not on steel and aluminum plants might help counter a minor misallocation of purchases between metals and clams. But such exclusion of accident costs would almost certainly create a major resource misallocation between steel and aluminum.

In America, industries producing goods that can to some degree substitute for one another have, by and large, similar degrees of monopoly power.[19] Hence charging all industries with their accident costs would probably be desirable from the standpoint of resource allocation, even though monopoly power differs greatly in the economy as a whole.

This is especially likely to be so since very often the effect of charging accident costs is to alter the goods produced within one industry. Thus in contrasting first-party insurance plans with third-party insurance plans, I commented that the choice would affect the relative costs of the Juggernaut Eight and the Foreign Fly, both products of the automobile industry. From the standpoint of encouraging intelligent choices between these two types of cars, proper allocation of accident costs might well be crucial whether or not the automotive industry were monopolistic in relation either to the economy as a whole or to some competing industries.

Even in those instances in which the latter industries do not have the same relative degree of monopoly power, and in which internal changes in type of production are unimportant, quirks in the price-setting process may in some cases promote favorable resource allocation. Unfortunately, an explanation of how this would come about requires some tedious discussion of how added costs are reflected in prices. The instances of favorable resource allocation as a result of pricing quirks are not very important, and since I have treated them at length elsewhere there is no need to discuss them here.[20] The conclusion I reached can be quickly stated.

—
19. See, e.g., G. Warren Nutter, "The Extent and Growth of Enterprise Monopoly," in William D. Grampp and Emanuel T. Weiler, eds. *Economic Policy* (Homewood, Ill., Richard D. Irwin, Inc., 1953), 141–46.

20. See Calabresi, "Risk Distribution," at 508–12.

First, there are many situations—probably the most significant ones—where allocation of resources would remain a valid basis for the general deterrence approach to accidents despite varying degrees of monopoly power. This would be particularly true where industries producing close substitutes have essentially similar degrees of monopoly power. But it would also be true in some situations where competitive industries produce goods that are reasonably close substitutes for the products of relatively monopolistic industries.

Second, there are also situations where putting accident costs on the activities that cause them would result in no resource allocation effect at all. Such a situation might be one in which industries producing rough substitutes were each oligopolistic and failed to change price and output as a result of increased costs and in which all firms in the industries involved were making sufficient extra profits to survive the loss in profits entailed by such an unshiftable cost item.

Third, in some cases the general deterrence approach will work against the proper allocation of resources. These are all cases in which the misallocations caused by the failure to make industries bear their accident costs would tend to cancel other, preexisting misallocations—in other words, cases where two wrongs make a right. Such a situation might exist if (1) a competitive industry produced goods that were relatively close substitutes for the products of a monopolistic industry; (2) the monopolistic industry had higher accident costs than the competitive one; (3) the monopolistic industry reacted to a cost rise by raising prices and decreasing output; and (4) changes in total product of the two industries were more important from the standpoint of resource allocations than accident-avoiding alternatives within each industry.

Fourth, while instances do exist where the general deterrence approach hampers proper resource allocation, it is fair to say that cases where it enhances proper resource allocation greatly predominate.

Theory of the Second Best

Since the article just summarized was written, a point of view toward welfare economics called "the theory of the second best" has become quite popular among a group of economists.[21] This point of view in effect generalizes the problems the existence of monopoly brings to resource allocation theory. In its broadest terms, it takes the position that if some of the conditions needed for optimal resource allocation are not being met, one cannot show that meeting the other conditions will be a good thing in terms of resource allocation.[22] Indeed, one can describe various situations where apparent steps toward better resource allocations will actually bring about greater misallocations. Since all the conditions of perfect resource allocation cannot be met everywhere in our society, the theory stated in these all-encompassing terms may be taken to suggest that we can never be sure that any action does, in fact, promote economic efficiency.

21. The principal source of the current discussion is R. G. Lipsey and Kelvin Lancaster, "The General Theory of Second Best," 24 *Rev. Econ. Stud.* 11 (1956). Among the recent writings on the subject are P. Bohm, "On The Theory of 'Second Best,' " 34 *Rev. Econ. Stud.* 301 (1967); Takashi Negishi, "The Perceived Demand Curve in the Theory of Second Best," 34 *Rev. Econ Stud.* 315 (1967); M. McManus, "Private and Social Costs in the Theory of Second Best," 34 *Rev. Econ. Stud.* 317 (1967); O. A. Davis and A. B. Whinston, "Piecemeal Policy in the Theory of Second Best," 34 *Rev. Econ Stud.* 323 (1967); Davis and Whinston, "Welfare Economics and the Theory of Second Best," 32 *Rev. Econ. Stud.* 1 (1965); Albert Fishlow and Paul A David, "Optimal Resource Allocation in an Imperfect Market Setting," 69 *Journal of Pol. Eco.* 529 (1961); Lipsey and Lancaster, "McManus on Second Best," 26 *Rev. Econ. Stud.* 225 (1958–59); McManus, "Comments on the General Theory of Second Best," 26 *Rev. Econ. Stud.* 209 (1958–59). For earlier approaches to the same problem see, e.g., Samuelson, *Foundations of Economic Analysis,* at 252–53, and J. M. Clark, "Toward a Concept of Workable Competition," 30 *Am. Econ. Rev.* 241 (1940).

22. Compare, e.g., Lipsey and Lancaster, "The General Theory of Second Best," at 11–13, 17–18, with, e.g., Davis and Whinston, "Welfare Economics and the Theory of Second Best," at 1, 12; Davis and Whinston, "Piecemeal Policy in the Theory of Second Best," at 323–26, 330–31; and Fishlow and David, "Optimal Resource Allocation in an Imperfect Market Setting," at 529–30, 542–44.

If one steps back from the purely theoretical position, however, the effect of the theory of the second best becomes less destructive. In practical terms, the point of view it espouses suggests simply that the broader the changes sought in the name of economic efficiency, the less likely we are to be sure that improved efficiency will in fact follow. Ultimately, the theory does no great damage to the notion that, if a car without a special kind of brake "causes" $100 in accident costs and a car with the brakes "causes" no such accident costs, it is probably worthwhile to install the brakes if they cost less than $100. Even this cannot, according to the theory, be proven mathematically, for it will depend in part on the general effects that increasing production of brakes in relation to other goods will have, and this in turn may be good or bad, depending on what other misallocations exist in the society. But since, by and large, no very great reordering of the economy is likely as a result of putting these accident costs on the car manufacturer or driver (except for the installation of the brakes), as lawyers or even as political economists, we can fairly safely assume that such an allocation is beneficial.

In effect, the question becomes the same as that asked with respect to steel, aluminum, and corner hamburger joints in the example I used when discussing monopolies: is more to be gained in curing (or exerting pressure to cure) an immediate significant misallocation than may be lost as a result of failing to compensate for preexisting, more general misallocations? The more we think of general deterrence as operating to encourage safer equipment by placing the accident costs of unsafe equipment in direct confrontation with the costs of the safer equipment, or as operating to reduce particularly accident-prone subcategories of activities by indicating how much safer and hence less expensive slightly different variations of the same activity would be, the more we are likely to make correct decisions, even given the theory of the second best. The more we think of the benefits of general deterrence as accruing through the diminution of a whole broad activity, such as driving in general, relative to other activities, the more we are likely to be uncertain that we have actually improved matters. It is particularly useful to keep this limitation on resource allocation theory in mind when we examine how we should decide which activities should bear the costs of which accidents, for this limitation will enable us to ascribe much more importance to what are often described as "short-run" changes, than to "long-run" ones.[23]

While the limitations on resource allocation theory inherent in such problems as income distribution, unemployment, and monopoly, which are described more generally in the theory of the second best, do not, as we have just seen, invalidate the general deterrence approach to accidents, they make a *perfect* world of general deterrence undesirable. Furthermore, like the problems that arise in the application of resource allocation theory to accidents (determination of the costs of accidents and of who causes them), and like doubts about the validity of the basic postulate that people know best for themselves, these limitations suggest that general deterrence cannot be our sole approach to accident law. To see this more clearly, we need to discuss what a world of perfect general deterrence implies.

THE WORLD OF PERFECT
GENERAL DETERRENCE

To describe a world of perfect general deterrence is to refute its possibility. In the extreme, general deterrence would consider the problem of accident costs to be precisely one of market decisions to buy and sell goods, and accident costs would give rise to *no* collective decisions regarding whether activities were worthwhile. If an activity could pay for the accidents it caused and make a go of it, it would be considered worthwhile; if it could not pay such costs, it would be priced out of the market. But for this to work properly, activities would have to be able to "buy" willing victims. Just as the potential injurer would have to decide whether the accident was worth its costs to him, so the victim would have to

23. See discussion infra pp. 138–39.

decide whether the payment to be received in compensation made the accident worthwhile from his point of view. The costs of accidents would then be determined freely by the market, and there would be no need for collective intervention.

Obviously this is a highly improbable situation. In the extreme, it presupposes such perfect knowledge that all "accidents" would become intentional killings, mayhems, or taking of property by the injurer; and suicides or sales of person or property by the victim. Short of the extreme, it presupposes at least a *statistical* intention to injure and a *statistical* willingness to be injured (for a price) that does not and cannot represent the attitudes of actual injurers and victims in our society. An examination of each of these "theoretical" worlds of general deterrence will disclose what an actual world of optimal general deterrence would look like.

The first of these theoretical worlds requires perfect knowledge, so that both the victim and the injurer would know that a particular act performed at a particular time in a particular way would result in a particular injury. Victim and injurer could then bargain without collective intervention for an appropriate price to be paid for the injury. But it is virtually inconceivable that with such perfect knowledge the parties would not find it cheaper to act in a slightly different way and avoid the injury. In other words, with such perfect knowledge there would be no "accidents" and virtually no injuries—general deterrence would work perfectly. The few injuries that would remain would be acts of madmen, and intolerable—or perfect martyrdoms, and divine.

It might be thought that even without perfect knowledge, pure general deterrence, requiring no collective determination of accident costs, could exist so long as we have statistically certain injurers and victims. People willing to take a risk for a price would form a supply of victims, and people willing to pay the price in order to undertake activities which injure would form a demand side for the victims. A price representing the market value of the injury costs would be established. And risky activities would be undertaken only so long as they could "pay" that price.

Activities which it is reasonably certain will cause close to a certain number of injuries each year and which are willing to pay for these injuries clearly exist. Can we properly speak, however, even in a statistical sense, of a supply of willing victims?

It may appear that potential victims do undertake some risky enterprises in exchange for payments that compensate them for the risk of being injured. Thus it may seem that both the supply and the demand sides of an injury market exist, and that no collective decisions are necessary to the determination of the costs of accidents. Closer examination, however, casts severe doubt on the feasibility of this statistical world of pure general deterrence.

It depends on market bargains—establishing the value of accident costs—between *potential* injurers and *potential* victims *before the accident*. In practice this presupposes that the potential victims are already in a bargaining relationship with the potential injurers *before* the accident and can therefore ask for payment for being potential victims. Market determination of accident costs is not meaningful in any practical sense in situations where the injuring party has no bargaining relationship with the potential victims before the accident. For example, while it may appear that coal miners receive, and mine owners pay, wages that reflect the costs of mine accidents as estimated by both sides, it is hard to see how a similar bargain could be struck between drivers and pedestrians. In theory, drivers might seek out all the pedestrians whom they could conceivably injure, offer them an amount of money in exchange for taking the risk, receive counteroffers from them, and ultimately strike bargains establishing market values for the costs of car-pedestrian accidents. But such bargains are inconceivable in reality.

Even in the case where potential victims *are* in a bargaining relationship with potential injurers before the accident, it is usually unrealistic to treat market determination of the value of accident costs as adequate.

In the first place, adequate market determination of accident costs requires freedom on the part of victims to refuse the bargain and thus avoid the risk of injury. If the organization of our society is such that the only alternative work available to coal miners is the almost equally dangerous occupation of lumberjacking, it is hard to accept the valuation of accident costs arrived at through the "free" bargains between miners and mine owners as a satisfactory estimate of the accident costs involved.

In the second place, free market determination of the value of accident costs will lead to an acceptable result only if the potential injurers and victims are reasonably aware of and take account of the risks, i.e. only if they have adequate statistical knowledge of the risks involved and act on that knowledge. Injurers may often obtain and act on such knowledge, but as we have seen in our discussion of why private insurance is not likely to bring about adequate loss spreading, victims are unlikely to do either. Virtually all the arguments made there apply here: it may be very expensive for potential victims to obtain adequate knowledge of what the risk is; they may be psychologically incapable of viewing themselves as *actual* victims; they may suffer from the Faust complex and inevitably choose the good life now and regret it later; and they may not be the only ones to bear the costs when they occur.

In the third place, statistical willingness to take risks does not give an adequate value for what an accident costs if it actually occurs. This is because the value individuals give to a particular accident depends on the likelihood of its occurring. A man may take $1,000 for one chance in a thousand of being killed, thus seeming to value his life at $1,000,000, and still require much more than $10,000 for one chance in a hundred of being killed. And if he accepted $50,000 for one chance in a hundred, thus valuing his life at $5,000,000, this would be no indication that he would accept $2,500,000 for one chance in two of being killed, or $5,000,000 in exchange for the certainty of death. As we shall see later, this does not mean we should not try to give values to lives and limbs, but especially when coupled with the other factors I have just mentioned, it makes any purely market determination of the costs of accidents entirely inadequate.

For all these reasons, even a society that is basically committed to the general notion that individuals know best for themselves, and hence to general deterrence, will not leave valuations of accident costs to the free market. Some of the problems with free market determination of the value of accident costs will be mitigated in situations where the bargaining on the part of potential victims is carried out by representatives (such as unions) who presumably are aware of the risks and do not suffer from the same psychological disadvantages. But this mitigation will occur, at best, only in some of the bargaining situations, which themselves are only a part of the world of accident costs.[24]

Like it or not, we must conclude that accident costs cannot be determined adequately in the free market and that we therefore cannot have a total absence of collective decision-making in the context of accident law. We must either decide collectively which activities are worthwhile (i.e. decide collectively both the value of the accident to the victim and the value of the accident-causing activity to the doer, which is what we do in specific or collective deterrence); or we must decide collectively how much accidents cost victims in some objective sense and leave for market determination the value of the accident-causing activity to the doer (which is as close to perfect general deterrence as is feasible, and which can be described as "optimal general deterrence"). Potential victims might, of course, still be left some freedom to set their own prices through individual bargains.

The crucial question in the world of optimal general deterrence is how to decide collectively how much accidents cost victims. Only if that question is decided properly can we possibly assume that accident-causing activities will take place in the ways and to the extent we want. As we shall see later, this question—which I call

24. There are many nonemployment bargaining situations, the most notable probably being that of the personal consumer. In buying a power mower, or a car, one does not ordinarily take cognizance of all the factors a disinterested analyst would presumably find important, nor is all the pertinent information generally available.

"what is the cost"—is immensely complicated and by itself would keep us from accepting general deterrence as anything more than one of several goals for accident law. For the present it is sufficient to say two things: (1) A collective valuation of accident costs should, for general deterrence purposes, be made in as individualistic a way as is possible, since the notion that individuals know best for themselves remains the basic postulate; therefore the aim of the cost valuation will be to come as close as possible to what individuals would find the cost to be if they could do so in an open market. (2) Since a collective "objective" decision of what an accident costs a victim can only be an approximation, there is no reason to believe that the world of optimal general deterrence is, even on its own premises, what we want.

Thus, *one* of the reasons why we say that a drunken driver should not be allowed to drive, even if he likes drunken driving so much that he is willing to give his victims our objectively determined compensation, is that we do not feel that our objective determination can be accurate. If we do not allow eminent domain to individuals even where the objectively determined value goes to property interests that can be valued with some degree of accuracy, we surely cannot allow individual eminent domain over human lives to become the sole basis of our accident law.[25] Yet that is what optimal general deterrence on its own premises would come to.

Of course, even if we thought that the problems with free market accident cost determination could all be overcome, we might still find a world of total general deterrence not to our liking. The allocation of losses necessary in such a world might result in intolerable concentrations of losses, the administrative costs of establishing and running this world might be too high, and our "moral" sense might be offended by activities that could pay their

25. Eminent domain is the right of the government to take property for a public purpose and with compensation. While in some instances the government has been allowed to give this power to individuals, e.g. to railroad companies in the 19th century, a showing that a public purpose underlies such grants has always been required.

way under such a system. As a result, collective judgments would still be required. In other words, a world of total general deterrence might not be desirable because it does not allow room for our other goals.

There is obviously a conflict between desires to have a free market determination of the value of an accident-causing activity on the basis of what it is worth to the doer—given its objectively determined costs to victims—and desires to have a collective determination of its value on the basis of broader considerations of the activity's worth to society and its relationship to the general moral context of the society. There is also a tension, as we have seen, between achieving the desired degree of primary accident cost reduction through general deterrence and minimizing the secondary costs of accidents through perfect loss spreading. Finally, there is tension between each of these and the aim of achieving these goals as cheaply as possible—tertiary cost reduction. We cannot have all our goals for accident law perfectly met. This is not to say, however, that at any given time we may not be able to improve the *existing* system in a way that brings us closer to all of these goals. To say that the goals are ultimately inconsistent with one another is far from saying that a change cannot further all of them somewhat, especially if the change is from a system that developed haphazardly, with none of these goals specifically in mind.

CHAPTER 6

Primary Accident Cost Avoidance:
The Specific Deterrence Approach

DEFINITION

I call the second approach to primary accident cost reduction specific or collective deterrence. At its extreme specific deterrence suggests that all decisions as to accident costs should be made collectively, through a political process. All the benefits and all the costs, including accident costs, of every activity would be evaluated together and a collective decision would be made regarding both how much of each activity should be allowed and the way in which each should be performed. (No one actually considers such a collective view of society either desirable or feasible, just as no one could accept a world of total general deterrence.)

General deterrence, although it cannot avoid collective valuation of accident costs, seeks to value accident costs on as individual a basis as possible. Specific deterrence would occasionally be forced to use the market, but ideally it would rely on the market only as a basis for broader collective judgments. Similarly, it might need to use the market to enforce its decisions, but it would do this only in as limited a way as possible.

In practice, specific deterrence takes a number of forms. It can be seen in a relatively pure form in decisions to bar certain acts or activities altogether. But the approach can be seen to operate even in many situations where no out-and-out bans on activities are imposed. Indeed, whenever accident costs are valued in relation to which activity causes them, a collective decision is implied, not only as to the value of the accident costs to the victim but also as to the value of the "cost-causing" activity or the way in which it was performed. In other words, activities are being collectively judged to be desirable or undesirable and are being subsidized or penalized accordingly. As we shall see, such penalties or subsidies would never be necessary in perfect specific deterrence and imply some use of the market, and hence of general deterrence notions. But they are a long way from the minimal degree of collective decisions that general deterrence, taken as a sole approach, would allow.

BASES OF SPECIFIC DETERRENCE

There are five major bases for specific deterrence as a goal of accident law.[1] Not all of them would be accepted by everyone, but virtually everyone would accept at least one. The first is simply the antithesis of the basic postulate of general deterrence: individuals do *not* know best for themselves. The second, similar but more limited, is the notion that in deciding how many accident-causing activities we want, comparisons of nonmonetizable "costs" and "benefits" which the market cannot handle must be made. The third is that in making a decision for or against accidents we are not concerned solely with costs, however broadly defined, but must consider moral concepts. The fourth is that the inherent limitations in resource allocation theory, whether described in terms of income distribution, monopoly, or theory of the second best, require some collective decisions. The last is that general deterrence cannot efficiently reach some categories of activities and can almost never reach those very small subcategories of activities that we call acts, and that to reach these in an economically efficient way, collective action is needed.

Individuals Do Not Know Best for Themselves

There is no need to go into this at length. I have already mentioned it in analyzing why voluntary private insurance is not likely

1. For an excellent economic analysis of some of the bases for specific deterrence, see Lester B. Lave, "Safety in Transportation: The Role of Government," 33 *L. & Cont. Probs.* 512 (1968).

to be adequate. I have also pointed out that this is more likely to be true in the area of accidents than in other areas because of psychological difficulties individuals have in imagining themselves as victims. To justify specific deterrence, however, the notion must refer to an inability to judge the desirability of an activity for oneself, even given an already collectively decided valuation of accident costs. (Such a collective valuation of accident costs is, as we have seen, unavoidable under general deterrence.)[2] The notion presupposes, for example, that a *collective* judgment on whether cars of a particular type are desirable is better than a series of individual judgments to buy or not to buy that kind of car, even where the price of the car includes an appropriate share of the collectively valued accident costs that kind of car "caused."

Obviously this basis can be as broad or as narrow as one cares to make it. One can assume that individuals know best on the production side—how goods are made—but not on the consumption side—which goods are wanted. One can assume that they know best as to luxury goods but not necessities, or vice versa. But in whatever area one assumes that there exists a better way of evaluating acts or activities than through a tallying of individual market choices, a need for specific deterrence is implied.

Accidents Involve Nonmonetizable Costs

The second basis for specific deterrence is that a market choice between accident-causing activities is bound to be misleading because accidents involve costs that cannot be reduced to money and hence cannot be made the basis of a free market choice. This basis can be viewed as a more limited case of the previous one. The argument is that even if the marketplace could make the best choice among acts and activities given an accurate monetary valuation of accident costs, such a valuation is impossible because many "costs" of accidents, such as lives and pain and suffering, cannot be measured in purely monetary terms. Given this impossibility, collective

2. There might be room for difference as to precisely how collective this valuation of costs should be. See infra pp. 199–214.

political decisions as to acts and activities are deemed better than pure market ones.

However, if we have done the best we can to give collectively a money value to accident costs—and if we accept the notion that people generally do know best for themselves—does it not follow, despite nonmonetizable costs, that the best feasible mix of activities is derived through a free market? What does one gain by compounding the weakness of our collective decision as to what an accident costs with another weak collective decision as to what the activity causing it is worth? The answer, according to this argument, lies in the notion that where significant judgments involving nonmonetizable costs are to be made, a collective decision that takes into account all possible nonmonetizable costs and benefits is preferable to a market decision that seeks to monetize some costs but ignores others, and is even preferable to one that seeks to monetize all costs. Thus it is held that if cars, apart from their nonmonetizable accident costs, cause some nonmonetizable benefits by increasing the mobility of society and some nonmonetizable costs by increasing air pollution, the best decision as to cars would be one that considered all the values involved collectively, in nonmoney terms, and reached a political judgment. The problem of cars would be treated politically, as are the problems of war and peace, parks, and public housing, and for the same reasons.

One reason may be that the cost of evaluating the nonmonetizable costs and introducing them into the market is not worth the benefits market judgment would bring.[3] Or it could be no more than a feeling that political decisions as to nonmonetizable costs and benefits are more likely to reflect our desires than market ones. It would be pointless to object that such political judgments are likely to be inaccurate because they evaluate unmeasurables, since virtually all our political judgments are of that nature. They are decisions regarding goals, principles, and ideas—choices among unmeasurables.

3. See Calabresi, "Transaction Costs."

This is far from saying, however, that the existence of non-monetizable costs is a good argument for specific deterrence in all instances. Even if we accepted the notion that informed political decisions are always desirable when nonmoney costs are involved, it would be impossible for us to make such political decisions in all the myriad situations where a choice among accident-causing activities has to be made. There are too many, and they are too detailed. At most, this basis for the specific deterrence approach suggests that where different activities involve substantial and substantially different degrees of nonmonetizable benefits, and when they cause accidents involving substantially different degrees of nonmonetizable costs, a strong argument for collective decisions exists. But since there are too many such situations, large areas exist where no collective judgments as to such costs and benefits are worthwhile and where general deterrence approaches are therefore likely to be used.

A society may well decide that an accident-avoiding device is worthwhile because adopting it has little impact on the non-monetizable benefits derived from the industry—such as widget manufacturing—that would have to use the device, while the non-monetary accident costs avoided by the device are substantial. The society might therefore require the device, making a typical collective or specific deterrence type of judgment. That same society might still decide, however, that a choice between widget manufacturing and other activities, or a judgment as to the amount of widgets desired, is best left to the market on the basis of its monetary costs (including a monetized value of its accidents) and its desirability as valued in the market by widget buyers. The reason for the different decisions might be no more than that for a particular accident-saving device it was possible to make a judgment on the relative desirability of nonmonetary items, while for the activity in general no basis for such a political judgment was found, or no incentive strong enough to bring about a political judgment existed. The reverse may also be true. A whole activity may be barred because its nonmonetized costs are collectively deemed too great in view of its nonmonetizable benefits. But were the activity allowed, judgments as to particular safety devices might still be best left to the market because their nonmonetizable effects were too uncertain or too detailed to be worth evaluating politically.

Moral Judgments Are Involved

Like the first two, the third basis for specific deterrence is grounded in doubts as to an individual's capacity to judge best for himself. But while the first reflects these doubts even for judgments involving monetizable costs, and the second reflects doubts as to cost and benefit items that are not readily monetizable, the third reflects doubts that individual judgments will adequately reflect moral imperatives, which can hardly be termed costs or benefits at all. Thus specific deterrence is needed because there are some things we do not want in our society regardless of costs. Prostitution and murder should be barred even if they can pay their way a thousandfold because—and the answer is self-evident as well as self-serving—they are immoral.

It does not matter that some of our taboos originated from what was thought to be an evaluation of nonmonetizable costs and benefits or even from monetizable costs. They now have a force and a weight of their own, regardless of costs, and they must be enforced. It is, of course, the nature of moral imperatives that if they are truly accepted by a society, their observance is not left up to individual taste and judgment. As a result, a collective judgment of the specific deterrence type is to be expected when such moral considerations are involved.

Even when we are not dealing with an absolute moral taboo, our moral framework forms a basis for specific deterrence. I have said that specific deterrence differs from general deterrence in that all evaluations of accident costs under specific deterrence consider the value of the activity causing those costs, and that the specific deterrence approach tends to lump accident costs and the activity causing them together in evaluating activities. This evaluation may be influenced by the nonmoney costs and benefits involved on each side. But it may also be influenced, and often is, by moral judgments as to the activity involved. For example, while we may not require people to go to church, we may still decide collectively that even if going to church is an activity that causes many accidents, it ought to be permitted and encouraged. Accordingly, churchgoers may be charged less than the usual rate for the injuries they cause by going to church. Similarly, we may not absolutely bar drunkenness and yet feel that drunkenness is so immoral that we should absolutely bar drunken driving even to those more than willing to pay for the accident costs they "cause." Alternatively, we may make drunken drivers pay more for their accidents than little old lady drivers.[4]

In all these cases, we again could describe the decision in terms of the nonmoney benefits of churchgoing, or the nonmoney costs of drunkenness. And to do so would point out the similarities between these situations and those involved in the second basis for specific deterrence. In fact, the differences among all the bases discussed could be viewed as differences of degree. Yet to describe the decision in this way would obscure the fact that while the previous basis for specific deterrence involves trying to balance items close to what we usually think of as costs but inadequately expressed in money terms, here, as in absolute taboo situations, we are dealing with situations where to speak of cost or benefit in even a vague sense seems inappropriate or even blasphemous. We are, in short, speaking of things which, regardless of their original relation to costs, now carry a moral value or opprobrium apart from costs. That they do not become absolute taboos may be due to conflicts with other moral principles or attitudes ("people should not be compelled to go to church," or "when individuals harm only

---

4. Such overvaluations or undervaluations of costs would not exist under a system of total specific deterrence; it would simply be decided to *bar* an undesirable activity, or perhaps to draft people into one considered socially desirable. We are speaking here of less than total specific deterrence. See infra p. 111–13.

themselves it is by and large their own business"). But they carry enough weight so that we do not want individual decisions regarding them to be made on the basis of a neutral or objectively determined money cost of accidents. When strong moral values with respect to the accident-causing activity are involved, we feel more confident if the decision is made through a conscious collective choice involving both the accident costs and the activity causing them. That is, we prefer some specific deterrence.

This basis for specific deterrence could be made broad enough to encompass justice within it. After all, if collective decisions as to the desirable level of accident-causing activities take into account the moral value of the activities as well as the monetary and non-monetary costs involved, the decisions must also consider the fairness of the result. And any system of accident law that relies substantially on the specific deterrence approach would certainly take into account general considerations of justice as well as of secondary cost avoidance and administrative efficiency in collective determinations of which activities should be allowed. For analytical purposes, however, I have not defined specific deterrence this broadly. The division between moral considerations that I include as part of the specific deterrence approach, and broader ones that will be treated under the general goal of justice is of course ultimately arbitrary. But it does help us to distinguish the issue of what is involved in a collective rather than a market decision regarding which activities are worth their accident costs, from the more general and more difficult question of what makes any of several possible accident law systems seem fair.

Inherent Limitations of Resource Allocation Theory

The fourth basis for collective deterrence is a restatement of the collective belief that the resource allocation basis of market deterrence has both inherent and practical limitations. If, for example, income distribution in a society is collectively deemed undesirable in some way, and if one way to improve the situation is to have more of certain accident-causing activities (e.g. driving b the poor), we may well decide collectively to have more of those activities than the market would allow. And it is not sufficient to object that it would be better to redistribute income in other ways and then employ market deterrence. First, it may be politically impossible to accomplish this redistribution in other ways, and second, other ways of redistributing income may involve greater administrative costs or even greater injury to the market resource allocation ideal than would the redistribution effectuated through the use of specific deterrence.

The same analysis applies to other limitations of market deterrence. For example, in terms of the theory of the second best, if some significant misallocation of resources exists in a society, the economically most efficient or politically most feasible way of countering the misallocation might be to have more (or less) of an accident-causing activity than market deterrence would give us. Whenever this is so, a basis would exist for specific deterrence, that is, for a collective decision as to the amount of that activity we should have.

General Deterrence Cannot Effectively Reach Some Categories of Activities, Especially Acts

The fifth basis for specific deterrence is totally practical. It is grounded in the notion that even if people can decide best for themselves whether or not to perform an activity and bear its costs, this judgment will in practice affect only fairly broad modes of behavior, not individual acts. General deterrence, the argument runs, works well only if the individual compares the costs of accidents with the costs of forgoing or altering the accident-causing activity. This will occur only if all individuals are made to pay the costs of the accidents they "cause" and are able to estimate accurately the risk before an accident occurs. But often this is not the case. If individuals do not insure, odds are that they cannot convert the risk they bear into the proper money terms, so that the choice they make between the activity and its substitutes is not based on sound information.

Actually, many individuals fear the secondary costs of making lump sum accident cost payments and therefore insure against accidents, and when they do not do so voluntarily, society often compels them to, since it fears the secondary costs more than they do. If individuals insure, the risk is properly converted into money terms. But by the very nature of insurance, it is not converted into money terms that reflect the risks of the smallest subcategories of activities performed by each individual (what we call acts). That would be too expensive. Instead the risk is pooled with other risks. Indeed, it is only because insurance involves pooling of risks that it accomplishes loss spreading. Yet this very spreading means that each individual no longer faces a choice between an act and its accident costs, but faces instead a choice between what we may call a group of acts, or an activity, and its accident costs.

The individual who might decide not to run a yellow light if he knew it increased accident risks by $100 does not have that information before him when he comes to the light. He will have paid his insurance premium, which will reflect the fact that a man of his age, with his kind of car, driving as much as he does, "causes" certain accident costs on the average, including some resulting from running lights. On the basis of these facts, reflected in his premiums, he may abstain from driving or change the make of his car, but he will probably not alter his behavior once he has decided to drive and arrives at the stoplight. Of course, if his insurance category is also based on his accident record, he will be somewhat affected, since he knows that if he has an accident his rates will go up. But the money value of the risk of thus going into a higher insurance category as a result of running the light is not the same as the money value of the risk of accident costs to society caused by running the light. And unless the money risk the driver faces is equal to the money risk of accident costs to society, he will not make an adequate general deterrence choice in deciding whether to run the light.[5]

5. Even if the two risks were equal, before he could make an adequate general deterrence choice he would be required to evaluate correctly the risk of the higher premium at the time he decided to run the light. That he would do so is unlikely.

It follows from all this that while general deterrence may give individuals free market choices among competing activities, it will do so only as long as these activities are broad enough to be efficient insurance categories. This sets the stage for specific deterrence. If we believe that individuals on the whole would not run lights if they were made to face the costs light-running causes society, we are totally justified (even if people know best for themselves) in specifically deterring light-running. Even if we do not know what individuals would do if they knew the appropriate costs, we may be justified in barring light-running since we cannot learn, in the market, what individuals do desire here, and *must* decide collectively, one way or the other.

Of course, any such collective decision tends to destroy individual differences in tastes. It usually applies the same rule to those who have much to gain from running lights (truckers on a fixed schedule) and to those who really do not care. But then, the general deterrence approach does no better, because—*ex hypothesis*—light-running cannot be made an adequate insurance category. Indeed, it can be argued that in dealing with such acts, specific deterrence can give more individual choice, either by varying the rules for different groups (on the basis of a collective judgment that the act is good for one group and bad for another), or by imposing noninsurable fines which those who really need to run the light can risk. The first, however, may cause some inefficiency and injustice, while the second may involve us in spreading or secondary cost problems.

The same analysis of the practical limitations of general deterrence in dealing with acts applies to certain broader subcategories of activities. Suppose it is decided that car-pedestrian accidents are a cost of driving.[6] The question still remains: are they a cost of the way cars are made or of how people drive? Let us assume that they are in some sense a cost of both. In theory, if the cost of such accidents is put on drivers, insurance rates will reflect not only

---

6. For how we go about reaching this decision, see infra pp. 133–73.

the difference in accident-proneness of different categories of drivers (teen-age drivers, city drivers, extra-mileage drivers, etc.), but also the safety of the cars they drive (old cars, cars with special brakes, cars with seat belts, etc.). Conversely, if such accident costs are put on automobile manufacturers or dealers, car prices should reflect not only the safety features of the cars (seat belts, special brakes, etc.), but also the accident-proneness of the category of the buyer who will drive the car (age, place of residence, etc.).[7] In practice, however, the decision to put such accident costs on drivers makes any substantial categorization by type of car too expensive, and the decision to put the costs on the manufacturers or dealers makes categorization by type of driver too expensive.

This means that in most instances general deterrence will give adequate cost choices only for categories of drivers or only for categories of cars, depending on which category is held liable. As for the other categories, sufficient categorization to give adequate market deterrence choices will, in practice, be too expensive. Exactly the same problem will exist that did with respect to acts, and the solution will be the same. If costs are allocated to drivers, some collective rules governing how cars are made are likely to be necessary. If costs are allocated to manufacturers or dealers, collective rules controlling drivers become almost inevitable. Analogously, if first-party insurance plans such as Keeton-O'Connell are adopted, collective regulation of cars that protect passengers but tend to injure third parties may become necessary. And if third-party insurance remains the rule, more collective requirements of passenger safety devices such as seat belts are likely. The reason, again precisely the same as the one for using specific deterrence in dealing with acts, is that collective rules are the most economically efficient way of reaching these particular categories

7. See Calabresi, "Does The Fault System Optimally Control Primary Accident Costs?" 33 *L. & Cont. Probs.* 429, 460 n. 44 (1968) (cited hereafter as Calabresi, "The Fault System"), and Calabresi, "Views and Overviews," 1967 *U. Ill. L.F.* 600, 606, n. 4 (1967) (cited hereafter as Calabresi "Views and Overviews").

once costs have been allocated so as to get the best general deterrence control of the other categories.[8]

Once more, the use of specific deterrence tends to destroy individual differences in tastes, but it may be the best we can do. A full discussion of all this must wait until we see how we decide who should bear the cost of which accidents. And in one sense it must wait even further until we consider how mixed systems accomplish our complex mixture of goals. For now, it is sufficient to note that specific deterrence may by fiat bring about primary accident cost reductions that general deterrence cannot encourage because of costs of subcategorization and because of desires to spread losses. Specific deterrence will do this by controlling acts, for example, which we cannot (for efficiency reasons) or do not (for spreading reasons) wish to isolate in insurance categories. Needless to say, the more significant the risks these acts involve and the greater the difference in desires among individuals to perform these acts, the more likely it will be that they will be the bases of insurance categories and that general deterrence will be able to affect them, and conversely, the smaller will be this practical justification for specific deterrence. I would guess, however, that for all the importance of the first four bases of specific deterrence, this one, since it is acceptable to even the most devout believers in the market, remains as significant as any.

Of course, where the first four bases cause some doubts as to market judgments, situations that from the standpoint of the fifth basis are borderline will more likely be decided in favor of specific deterrence collective judgments.

LIMITS ON SPECIFIC DETERRENCE: THE WORLD OF TOTAL SPECIFIC DETERRENCE

Aside from the difficulty of deciding which activity causes which cost (this will be discussed in a separate chapter because it concerns general deterrence as well), the principal limits on specific deterrence are (1) the impossibility of making political judg-

8. Cf. Calabresi, "Transaction Costs," at 71–72.

ments in regard to every decision involving choices for or against accidents; (2) the fact that individuals cannot control each individual act; and (3) the limits imposed by our other goals.

Impossibility of Total Political Decision-Making

The notion that it is impossible to decide collectively all choices for or against accidents is in a sense the reverse of the fifth basis for specific deterrence, the idea that general deterrence cannot effectively reach some categories, especially acts. Specific deterrence can reach some acts, as we have seen, but how many? Every decision we make regarding what we do, how we do it, what goods we use, how and by whom they should be made, involves a choice between a safer and a more accident prone way. It should be obvious that we cannot make all of these decisions collectively or politically. In the first place, the fact-finding necessary to determine the relative merits of each of these choices and their accident cost potential would be impossibly expensive—the market is often by far the cheapest fact-finding device available. In the second place, even if these tertiary costs were not totally out of proportion to the benefits gained, it would be impossible to gear ourselves to make such minute decisions politically or collectively.

The collective process lends itself to dramatic choices (war or peace, legal prostitution or not), even when fairly detailed behavior (drunken driving or not, seat belts or not) is involved. It does not lend itself to such prosaic choices as those between one type of shoe and another, or between driving 20 miles a day and 40 miles a day. Only in the rare instances when choices become dramatized are people willing and able to think enough about them to make an intelligent collective judgment—a judgment that has some chance of achieving a better result than what would follow from letting individuals decide for themselves on the basis of prices that reflect relative accident costs.

Sometimes this individual decision-making—the general deterrence approach—brings about dramatically undesirable results. Attention is focused on the fact that too many people are dying because too many people fail to use seat belts, or because too many people are running lights, or because there are too many teen-age drivers. Each of these statements suggests a lack of satisfaction with the general deterrence result, arising from one or more of the specific deterrence bases. When such dissatisfaction arises, even very small subcategories of activities may be subjected to collective judgment. But it would be unrealistic to suppose that because specific deterrence can reach some of these, it is a workable approach to all or even many of them.

The fascinating thing is that while specific deterrence can achieve primary loss reduction by reaching more *detailed* activities than general deterrence can reach in practice, it can only be effective for a very limited number of such acts or activities. Thus both the general deterrence and specific deterrence approaches are ultimately limited in the degree to which they can accomplish primary accident cost reduction without either violating other goals (like justice) or causing undue secondary (spreading) or tertiary (efficiency) costs. But these limits are not the same for each, and one may effectively reach where the other cannot or ought not.

Individuals Cannot Control All Their Acts

A limit to specific deterrence of a somewhat different type arises from the fact that individuals cannot control all their acts. We saw that specific deterrence may at times be more effective than general deterrence as an approach to primary accident cost reduction because it can reach individual acts that general deterrence, given the desire to spread losses and the expense of subcategorizing, often cannot. We also saw, however, that specific deterrence cannot effectively decide the worth of all accident related acts and is best employed only in a limited number of instances. In deciding what these instances are, it is very important to consider the degree to which people can control their behavior.

It may seem, for example, that it would be very good to forbid people from absentmindedly taking their eyes off the road while driving. A general deterrence category could never be drawn that gave people the choice between the costs of such absentmindedness and its worth; one could not make such absentedminded drivers into an insurance category. If we made a political judgment that this absentmindedness was undesirable, specific deterrence might seem appropriate. And yet unless a decision to bar absentmindedness could be effective, that is, unless people had a substantial degree of control, conscious or unconscious, which could be affected by forbidding this act, specific deterrence would be useless.

Even if the penalty for the act were very severe, if people could not control their behavior the penalty would simply cause them to abstain from the category of acts—i.e. the activity—that might give rise to the proscribed act. This would certainly reduce the frequency with which the act occurred. But if the effect of specific deterrence is not to bar the individual act (which general deterrence could not reach), but to discourage a broader activity that gives rise to the act, we must ask whether general deterrence could not reach that activity equally well. That is, the fifth basis for specific deterrence might no longer be applicable, for general deterrence could reach as far. And whether general or specific deterrence would be preferred would depend on whether one preferred individual or collective judgments as to the relative desirability of the activity giving rise to the act, not on the purely practical consideration as to whether general or specific deterrence reached further in an efficient way.

The same practical inability of specific deterrence to reach individual acts would arise if, in order to cause people to abandon the *specific* act or subconsciously avoid it, we needed a penalty so severe that we would not tolerate its imposition. In effect, such a case is analogous to the situation where if general deterrence were to subcategorize to the level of the specific act, the resulting unspread burden and secondary losses would be too great. Since an effective specific deterrence penalty would be intolerable, primary cost deterrence would be possible only at the broader activity level where a lesser penalty might be effective, but where general deterrence might also reach. Once again, specific deterrence may, like general deterrence, be limited in the degree to which it can individualize and deter dangerous subcategories, but the limitation may apply to different acts than the limitation on general deterrence. Thus, in practice specific deterrence may be effective as to some small subcategories where general deterrence is not, and vice versa.

The World of Total Specific Deterrence

The limits on specific deterrence are highlighted by an examination of what a world of total specific deterrence would look like. In this theoretical world, every decision regarding each act of each individual would be made collectively. A collective decision would be made as to whether it was better for him to wear one kind of shoe or another, drive at one time or another, and so forth. Each activity-cost relation would be subdivided into its smallest subcomponent—the doing of the particular thing, in the particular way, at the particular time, by the particular person—and a collective decision as to its merit would be reached.[9] Obviously such a world would be not only impossible, for the reasons already given, but intolerable as well.

Most of the reasons why it would be intolerable are obvious and need not be discussed. There is one, however, that merits further attention, i.e. the conflict between total specific deterrence and spreading.

While the world of total specific deterrence would not involve secondary accident costs—unspread accident burdens—in quite the same way total general deterrence would, it would involve analogous problems and analogous conflicts. People would be barred from doing certain acts; other acts that caused accident costs would be allowed. These accident costs could presumably be met to the desired degree out of a social insurance fund and hence

9. The *total* specific deterrence objective would rule out the use of any type of pressure, in attempting to obtain compliance with the decisions reached, which gave people a choice between compliance and a penalty. Financial pressure would obviously be inadequate, but no type of pressure could be entirely adequate.

cause only the optimal degree of secondary losses. But what of the losses caused by barring people from doing certain acts? Unless the man for whom driving were exceedingly valuable—even if only in his own judgment—were compensated for the collective decision to bar him from driving, he would suffer something very much akin to the normal secondary losses of accidents. Similarly, when a factory is closed as a result of a collective decision that it is undesirable (given its primary accident costs), unless all the workers put out of work, their families, and all those who could no longer get its products were compensated for their losses, substantial secondary costs would exist.

Of course, compensation of these "losers" is theoretically possible through collective governmental funds under specific deterrence, while it may not be under general deterrence (since under general deterrence it may be the very lack of compensation that forces people to make individual choices for or against accident-causing activities). But this only begs the question. If cost pressures are not used because government compensation is given, what pressures *will* be used to bring about the world of total specific deterrence?

The answer is penalties, fines, jail, and so forth. But this simply poses the problem of secondary losses in a different way. Are the primary cost savings achieved by the prevention of specific acts through such penalties as jail, fines, the whip, the gallows, etc., worth the cost of imposing those penalties? We would usually view this question in terms of justice and answer that some of these methods are not just in dealing with accidents. But what we are talking about here is, in fact, closely analogous to what we are talking about when we say that the unspread burdens of accident costs in general deterrence may cause too great secondary losses for the primary accident costs they seek to avoid. Thus in both cases we will have to decide whether the secondary costs (of unspread economic burdens in one case and direct compulsion in the other) are worth the primary accident cost reduction they bring

What can be accomplished in the way of primary accident cost reduction without violating imperatives of secondary cost reduction may be greater if specific and general deterrence are both used than if one is used to the exclusion of the other. Thus while secondary costs might make intolerable the many unspread accident costs general deterrence as a sole approach would entail and the many penalties specific deterrence as a sole approach would need, the existence of *some* penalties and *some* unspread cost burdens might still bring about primary accident cost reduction in a less offensive way than if only one or the other could be used. In this sense then, specific and general deterrence, theoretically irreconcilable though they may be, may yet find a practical, peaceful coexistence.

Specific Deterrence and the Market: Some Mixed Systems

There are many different ways in which a specific deterrence approach can coexist with a substantial degree of market control of accidents. The most obvious is when a decision is made to prohibit some activities altogether, while controlling other activities through the market. More complex mixtures, resulting in a combination of market and collective control being used on the same activity, are also available. Whenever a collective decision is made to encourage or discourage an activity through a subsidy or a tax, a mixed approach to primary cost reduction is being used. Such mixtures are, in fact, very similar to the use of general deterrence in a socialist world, for in effect they all employ individual or market reactions to effectuate collective decisions of differing degrees of specificity. Such mixed systems, to which I now turn, range from the most collective to those that make substantial use of the market.

Prohibition and Restriction

The purest ways of achieving specific deterrence I call prohibition and restriction. These are really the same thing on different levels of generality. I speak of prohibiting an activity (banning the sale of firecrackers or all driving), or alternatively of restricting it (allowing firecrackers only in limited circumstances or barring driving at speeds of over 80 miles per hour). When we restrict an activity, we are simply prohibiting one of its subcategories. Thus, both restriction and prohibition require totally collective judgments balancing the desirability of acts or activities against the effect prohibiting them would have on accidents. It follows that restrictions and prohibitions are mixed systems only in that what is not restricted or prohibited is left to other systems of control.

Obviously we will rarely *prohibit* what we customarily think of as activities. It is seldom that such broad categories are so undesirable that we want to bar them altogether, since a broad category usually has too few acceptable substitutes. We are more likely to *restrict* activities, that is, to decide that a *way* of doing them (a subcategory) is not worth *its* accident costs and hence should be prohibited. We are, for instance, more likely to prohibit cars without brakes than to prohibit cars altogether. But whether the choice is to prohibit or to restrict, some effect will be felt in other activities as a result, for as we shall see, even the purest specific deterrence cannot avoid some market reactions. If the prohibition is effective, however, its major effect will be on the activity or act we collectively sought to bar. Right or wrong, we will have eliminated it as a cause of accident costs—and that is the prime aim of pure specific deterrence.

Limitation of Activities

For the reasons already discussed, we will not always want or be able to use such pure specific deterrence in controlling activities. If we do not wish to prohibit a broad activity because it is too useful, and have no criterion for restricting it that satisfies us collectively, we may decide to *limit* it. A simple limitation implies a decision that we want no more than a given amount of the activity, but that collectively we are indifferent as to who engages in it or how it is performed. (Any *collective* decision as to who should perform it or how it should be performed would be a restriction, i.e. a prohibition of certain subcategories of the activity.) The decision regarding who will engage in an activity we have decided to limit can be made in one of three ways. We can determine who engages in the activity (1) by lot; (2) according to willingness to bear a nonmoney burden imposed on those who engage in the activity, such as standing in line or first-come, first-served; or (3) according to willingness to pay a money burden imposed on the activity.

The first of these is rather peculiar. It implies a collective decision that although the collective deciders have no adequate reason for preferring that the activity be done by some people rather than by others (otherwise they would instead restrict the activity) they expressly do not want to allow individuals to choose for themselves whether or not to do it. The collective decision to use chance prohibits individuals from sorting themselves out according to their willingness to pay (in money or other ways) for the right to engage in the activity. It suggests that collectively we want only a certain limited amount of an activity, but that we do not have (or do not wish to exercise) collective preferences as to who should engage in it, and cannot (for rather special reasons) tolerate market determination of who should take part. The arguments concerning a draft lottery in time of war suggest the type of situation where this may be the case. Doubts about how collective decisions are made and how income distribution affects market decisions suggest, to some people at least, that a totally arbitrary choice (like a lottery) is more desirable where lives are so obviously at stake.[10]

The second and third ways of limiting activities are very similar. They both imply market-type decisions regarding who should engage in the limited activity. The collective deciders have determined how much of the activity is wanted (given its desirability and accident-causing propensity), but they have left up to the

---

10. How people are selected for special medical treatment not yet generally available (e.g. kidney dialysis and heart transplants) affords an example of the different approaches taken in different hospitals to a similar problem.

market the question of who shall engage in the activity. The only difference between the two is that since one uses money payments it is necessarily dependent on our system of income distribution, while the other is linked to the distribution of ease of meeting the burdens it imposes.[11] Since our society normally uses money burdens[12] where it desires market reactions, I will consider only money limitations in further detail.

The most familiar type of money limitation is taxation of an activity regardless of the number of times it is involved in accidents. Nearly as common is subsidization of substitute activities. What distinguishes such systems as taxation from prohibition or restriction of an activity is, as we have seen, the allowance of individual choice as to whether to engage in the activity. If an activity is taxed, those who most prefer the activity will engage in it, and the market will determine the level of frequency at which it occurs. The number of people who will pay the tax and engage in the activity will depend, of course, on the magnitude of the tax and the availability of adequate substitute activities. These facts will also determine the degree to which the tax is shifted to other activities and the effect the limitation has on activities not limited directly. The level of frequency at which the activity occurs will

11. For example, it may be decided that ice-skating at the local rink will not be charged for, but that the safe capacity of the rink is one hundred persons. The first hundred will be admitted, and the others will wait until sufficient numbers leave during the course of the permitted skating period to allow them to enter. A burden is imposed: those who do not wish either to wait in line or to arrive early enough not to wait in line are excluded; as the waiting time increases, more people are excluded, and some may conceivably wait throughout the entire period and not be satisfied. Even so, the objective of the system —safety and the absence of a direct monetary burden—will have been achieved.

Somewhat the same kind of system is adopted during wartime, when rationing becomes necessary. Aside from the black market, money will not avail someone who wishes to purchase a rationed item without the proper ration stamp or coupon; the distribution of stamps thus replaces the normal income distribution.

12. Except, of course, in time of war (cf. supra note 11, Chapter 6).

be determined in an analogous way when subsidization of substitute activities is used. Again the result will be that those who most prefer the limited activity will stay with it; others will shift to the alternative activities made cheaper by subsidization.[13]

A decision to limit an activity implies some lack of confidence in collective decisions or in the feasibility of enforcing them. But limitation retains significant elements of specific deterrence. The tax we have postulated, for instance, would be fixed on individuals regardless of their accident involvement. Individuals would therefore be given no incentive to seek out ways in which they thought accident costs could be reduced further. This necessarily implies that the collective deciders believe they can make this choice better than individuals can and is typical of the specific deterrence approach. Were a tax imposed on the basis of accident involvement rather than on a fixed basis, the market would operate to seek out ways of avoiding accident costs as well as to determine who would engage in the activity. The result would be very close indeed to general deterrence. It is, in fact, the least pure system of specific deterrence discussed here.

We are much more likely to limit broadly defined activities than narrowly defined ones, as we will generally have more confidence in collective decisions dealing with the value of the latter to individuals than of the former. Just as we are more likely to prohibit cars without brakes than to prohibit cars altogether, we are more likely to tax cars generally than to tax cars without brakes. Limitation seems an inadequate control for a narrowly defined activity

13. The extent to which an individual has effective choice will depend, however, on the distribution of income; as far as engaging in the taxed activity is concerned, the rich have more choice than the poor. It should also be noted that in terms of income distribution, the effect of taxing an activity may be very different from that of subsidizing its substitutes. Subsidization has the effect of increasing the income of those who shift, and thus may well involve a progressive redistribution of income; whereas taxation will probably mean a regressive redistribution (assuming that most indirect taxes are regressive). This different income distribution effect may alter the degree of shift from the activity to the substitutes, at least to the extent that the *income* elasticity of the activity and the substitute differ.

that has adequate substitutes and, we are relatively sure, causes substantial accidents costs. (Conversely, prohibiting a very desirable activity with few substitutes seems rash, however many accident costs it may cause.) Limitation of narrowly defined activities is also likely to be impractical. Since they and their subcategories are often relatively hard to detect, the expense needed to detect them for purposes of taxation or other limitations is often not worthwhile, whereas the benefit gained from prohibiting them may justify the costs of detection.

It is impossible to draw a fine line between limitation and prohibition in every case, and something very close to limitation will also occur to control some narrowly defined acts or activities. Even if the doers of the proscribed act or activity were always caught, prohibitions or restrictions would not be fully effective if the penalty for violation of the prohibition were not severe enough. The result in such cases will be very close to a limitation of the penalized act or activity.[14] The effect of such an inadequate penalty is to burden the would-be doers of the act or activity with the penalty. To the extent that some choose the act knowing they will be penalized, they make the same choice made by those who engage in a taxed activity. Of course, the greater the penalty and the more substitutes available, the closer the limitation will come to outright prohibition. In practice, almost no penalty is severe enough to prohibit any act or activity altogether, and so prohibitions and limitations merge.[15] But we may nonetheless distinguish some penalties, which in terms of the activities affected are severe

14. For the effect of ineffectiveness due to a less-than-perfect ability to catch violators, see discussion infra pp. 120–23, and esp. note 16.

15. There is an additional effect where the penalty is of a criminal type: most penalized criminal activities are considered criminal because they are thought to carry a certain moral opprobrium (although this is debatable in some instances, especially of certain so-called white-collar crimes). The less the moralistic flavor attached to the penalty in question, the more it partakes of the characteristics of a limit rather than of a prohibition. Thus a trucking firm will undoubtedly be more willing to risk $1,000 in speeding fines than a $1,000 fine for fraud. The latter carries more moral opprobrium—i.e. a greater nonmoney penalty.

enough or carry sufficient moral opprobrium so that the result may properly be termed prohibition, from others so mild that the result is best considered a limitation. Actually, since *no* penalty catches the wrongdoer *all* of the time, this analysis is incomplete. The actual effect is a merging of a pressure to avoid being caught with a limitation type of burden on the penalized act. The size of the burden is the magnitude of the penalty times the risk of capture.

To summarize, limitation of an activity (whether directly or through inadequate penalties) will be used to control activities that we wish to discourage without deciding collectively who is to be discouraged and without providing incentives for individuals to find better ways of reducing accident costs than can be collectively imposed. If our objective is simply to limit the number of cars, we will tax all cars equally until the desired amount of traffic is reached. In effect, this is deciding the costs and benefits of the activity to society, but letting the market decide its desirability to individuals. If we make a specific deterrence choice as to who should be discouraged, the effect is totally different. We will then be prohibiting various subcategories of the activity, thus restricting it. We may, of course, wish both to limit and to restrict an activity: we might tax all drivers to discourage driving generally, while prohibiting some subcategory of driving like driving at excessive speeds. But this only means that we wish to make pure specific deterrence decisions regarding some subcategories of an activity, while preferring some element of market choice as to the rest.

Penalties on an Involvement Basis: Activities Defined before an Accident

So far we have concerned ourselves with relatively pure systems of specific deterrence. When we prohibit or restrict an activity, we imply that the collective choice as to how accident costs are to be reduced is the best possible one. When we limit an activity we imply the same thing, except that if the limitation is effectuated not through chance but through taxation or like means, we allow individual or market decisions regarding which individuals will engage in the limited activities. Sometimes, however, specific deterrence cannot use such pure devices. At times it is impossible to define—other than vaguely—the conduct (the act or activity) we wish to prohibit before an accident occurs. At other times it may be possible to define and forbid the conduct before the accident, but practically impossible to catch the doer unless he is involved in an accident. Both of these situations give rise to penalties that, either by design or necessity, are imposed only on an involvement basis.

The situation where we can define beforehand precisely the act or activity we want to prohibit but cannot detect it except on an accident involvement basis is the easier of the two to deal with. In this case, the collective decision-makers can still be assumed to know best which acts or activities should be stopped; but in practice—presumably for reasons of efficiency—they can only discover and penalize the activities when they result in accidents. Since the object is to deter the activity, and the individual accident is nothing more than the event that brings the proscribed activity to light, the penalty will not vary with the damages.

In such situations, those who wish to engage in the proscribed act or activity have a substantial incentive to avoid accidents in order to avoid triggering the penalty.[16] There will be notable differences, however, between this market pressure against accidents and that brought about by general deterrence. Here the pressure will be exerted against accidents rather than accident costs be-

16. This case is closely analogous to the situation in which an act or activity is prohibited, but can be detected and penalized only part of the time. The effect of this type of prohibition can be analyzed in exactly the same way as prohibitions in which accident involvement triggers the penalty. The only difference is, of course, that ways of doing the act will be sought out that minimize the occurrence of whatever results in being detected while committing the prohibited act, rather than the occurrence of accidents. All such "incomplete" penalties will result in something like a limitation effect because some who wish to do the act will feel that the *risk* of getting caught and paying the penalty is worth taking.

cause the penalty is constant. Thus devices that prevent accidents will be introduced if they are cheaper than the risk of bearing the penalty (however this latter is computed). And they will be introduced just as readily if the accidents they avoid cause minimal damages as if they cause catastrophic ones. The pressure to avoid accidents will be determined by the size and type of penalty imposed, not by the amount of accident costs the activity incurs.

It should be remembered that even though the activity can only be detected when it results in an accident, the specific deterrence goal is to proscribe the activity. It is not to give individuals a choice between accident costs and the costs of avoiding them, or even to induce a market pressure against accidents. But since some of those who wish to engage in the activity will take a chance if they believe that by modifying the activity in certain ways, accidents—and hence the penalty—can be avoided, penalization by involvement does not result in the same control of an activity as purer specific deterrence systems do. Instead, it will result to some extent in modification of that activity.[17]

There will also be some modification of *other* activities (not specifically controlled by the collective deciders) if those who engage in the proscribed activity can, by inducing such modifications, reduce the chances of an accident's occurring and therefore of being penalized. The collective deciders must be aware, therefore, that when they decide to bar an activity on an involvement basis[18] and set the size of penalties to enforce that prohibition, they will cause market-determined ripples of effects to reach other activities[19] which, though they may diminish accidents, are inconsistent with the specific deterrence goal.

17. Modification is the same thing as elimination of some subcategories—those that would give rise to the accident and hence to the penalty.

18. Or an analogous basis; see supra note 16.

19. One can even imagine a limiting case where accidents can be totally avoided by altering acts or activities other than those proscribed. In this case, if the proscribed act is desirable enough on the market, if the fine or penalty is great enough, and if the nonproscribed acts or activities which can avoid accidents are sufficiently amenable to bargaining or to bribing (see infra note 2,

It is impossible to determine theoretically the degree to which an involvement prohibition will affect both nonproscribed and proscribed activities; this depends on the size and type of the penalty, the relative abilities of each activity to avoid accidents, and the feasibility of inducing change in the nonproscribed activity.[20] All we can say is that to the extent that the collective deciders are *sure* of what they want to bar, they must keep the possibility of such effects in mind, as well as the possibility that in some instances these effects will diminish the pressure on the activity they sought to proscribe. This is not to say that in practice they can always avoid these possibilities. They may, however, be able to reduce them by barring bribes designed to induce changes in nonproscribed activities, by prohibiting insurance against the penalties, and perhaps by setting nonmoney penalties. None of these devices forecloses the possibility of such effects, but they may serve to keep the pressure on the proscribed activity as great as possible.[21]

One may summarize the situations where a penalty is assessed on an involvement basis in the following way. A specific act or activity is limited through assessment of penalties. The size of the burden and hence the stringency of the limitation will depend both on the size of the penalties and on the risk of detection, i.e. the risk of an accident occurring. This will depend in turn on the abil-

---

Chapter 7), the only effect of the involvement basis proscription will be to cause the *other* acts or activities to be "bribed" out of business, and the proscribed act will continue to occur merrily, never caught and never penalized because no accidents will occur. As we shall see later, infra pp. 135–38, this would mean that the activity bribed out of business would be likely to be the cheapest avoider of the accidents. The general deterrence goal might be met by its exclusion; the specific deterrence goal, since it was directed at exclusion of another activity, regardless of market desirability, would not.

20. See discussion of bribing, infra pp. 150–52.

21. If wrongdoers could be caught 100% of the time, there would be no need to bar insurance. Every individual would then be, in effect, his own insurance category, and the only aid insurance could be would be as an intertemporal spreader—i.e. essentially a savings account. This would raise no problems, as the burden would still be imposed exclusively on the wrongdoer

ity of those who wish to engage in the act or activity to avoid accidents by modifying their behavior or causing others to modify theirs. Thus market-type decisions occur that not only let individuals decide whether to engage in the act or activity given the burden imposed (given, in other words, the chance of being in an accident and having to pay the penalty), but also let individuals who would engage in the act seek out ways to avoid accidents.[22]

Penalties on an Involvement Basis: Activities Defined after an Accident

More difficult is the case where penalties are assessed on an involvement basis because the collective deciders, although they have a general idea of what they seek to prevent, cannot define it precisely before an accident. If it can be assumed that charging a penalty after an accident will in the future deter the doer and others like him from other acts that would *ex post* be collectively deemed undesirable, then it may not be irrational to have such after-the-fact penalizations. For this assumption to be valid, however, the collective deciders must be able to give some general indication of what will be penalized. Vague descriptions, such as "careless conduct," will suffice so long as the potential doers of the acts or activities involved understand in some way the general content of the phrase *before* any accident occurs. At the very least, they must be able to apply the phrase to specific situations immediately before an accident may occur in a way that approximates

22. See supra pp. 120 ff. The reader can readily identify the additional market effects which would be forthcoming if the collective deciders chose to make the penalty greater when the wrongful act results in serious damage than when it does not. Such an approach would presumably be based on the judgment that very harmful wrongful acts are more likely than relatively harmless wrongful acts to be the result of serious wrongful intentions and could even be made into a justification for assessing some specific deterrence penalties on an involvement basis quite apart from practicality. Whatever the merits of such a justification, which is analogous to criminal law differentiation between attempted and completed crimes, it cannot be stretched into justifying specific deterrence penalties equal to the damages "caused," let alone insurance against such penalties. See generally the discussion infra pp. 125–28, 266–73.

the intent of the collective deciders. Then such postaccident penalizations may result in deterrence of some conduct that the collective deciders would decide to bar if they had available to them all the facts of the preaccident situation available to the individual involved.

There are many problems with this type of specific deterrence. In the first place, it must be assumed that the act or activity can be controlled by the individual at the moment it becomes apparent to him that it is "undesirable," i.e. that it involves conduct the collective deciders would penalize. And this assumption often, though not always, requires swallowing a whale. In the second place, the very uncertainty and vagueness of the prohibition makes us hesitate, by reason of our sense of justice, to use certain types of penalties. In the third place, this same uncertainty and the possibility that the individual may guess wrong as to what will be deemed undesirable after an accident make it likely, if the penalty is serious enough, that individuals will abstain from broad activities that might put them in the position of having to make this difficult guess. This is undesirable unless the collective deciders want to limit or restrict these broad activities and choose this rather roundabout and expensive device (involving, as it does, much individual, market-type choice) to do it.

Finally, because the penalty is necessarily imposed on an involvement basis, all the general problems that arise when involvement penalties are used arise here too. The collective deciders must take into account the fact that the penalties imposed will, because of their involvement basis, tend to affect acts other than those they are attempting to bar. But their very lack of certainty before an accident may cause them to worry less about this than they do in the situation where they are sure of what they wish to stop. Presumably, however, their lack of certainty does not extend to total neutrality. If it did, they would employ general deterrence. Thus the collective deciders cannot avoid considering whether the conduct they have collectively decided to deter *is* being deterred, or whether some other acts or activities, to which they have no objection, are in fact being discouraged. This consideration will again affect the choice of penalties.

All these factors suggest that penalization of conduct defined *ex post* must be used gingerly. They do not, however, suggest that it should play no role. If nonmoney penalties seem too severe for such cases, money penalties may be used. As with any penalties assessed only on an involvement basis, the collective element in the decision can be strengthened by forbidding attempts to induce modifications in activities not collectively penalized but whose modification would lessen the occurrence of the accidents that do trigger the penalties. Insurance and indemnification contracts covering the fines or penalties imposed would likewise be barred. While the reason for this may seem obvious, the analysis is actually rather complex, and the problem deserves separate attention.

Individuals who wish to engage in activities in ways that might, if an accident resulted, be penalized under an *ex post* judgment, would in many instances seek to insure against the penalty. Anyone who insured against such penalties would be grouped together with others who were actuarially as likely to perform an act that would lead to an accident and, after the accident, be collectively deemed undesirable and hence subject to penalty. Each group would be charged an insurance fee. This would have the same effect as a licensing fee for each group. Once this fee was paid, the individual members of each group would not need to concern themselves about whether an accident occurred in ways that would result in penalization.[23]

But this result is the equivalent of making a specific deterrence decision that (1) any activity in which an accident and an *ex post* undesirable act might occur should be divided into subactivities

23. This assumes, of course, that the penalty insured against is the only one imposed. It also assumes that an individual's involvement in penalized accidents would not affect the cost of his insuring against the penalty. But even this risk of going into a higher risk actuarial subcategory by reason of accident involvement could conceivably be insured against, much in the manner in which one purchases a guaranteed insurability option in life insurance.

(each subactivity being the activity as performed by an actuarial group whose members have approximately the same risk of accidents involving an *ex post* undesirable act); and (2) that each subactivity be limited (taxed) through a fee that would vary according to the actuarial chance that a member of the group would have an accident in which his conduct would, after the accident, be deemed subject to penalty. If this were the aim of the collective deciders, they could accomplish their aim much more efficiently by imposing such limitations directly.

In fact, of course, this is not the aim. The aim of penalizing conduct defined after the accident is to influence behavior more specifically, i.e. *immediately* before any accident. The notion behind such *ex post* allocations of fines has to be that individuals can at the last minute before an accident estimate what would be penalized better than insurance companies can when, long before the accident, they make up actuarial groups and set rates for them. For if insurance companies can do as good a job as individuals can, then so can the collective deciders. And this is impossible *ex hypothesis*. To assert it is to deny our original assumption that individuals can, at the last minute, give greater meaning to such vague phrases as "careless conduct" than can be given them by collective deciders before an accident actually occurs.

The point of this is not really as difficult as the analysis. Collective deciders can have as much information as insurance companies. If they decide that the best way to decrease certain types of accident costs is to charge a certain amount to those people who actuarially have a certain likelihood of having accidents as a result of conduct the collective deciders would say *ex post* was undesirable, they can do so directly and efficiently. This would be the same as putting a limitation on the category of which these people are members. But where penalization of conduct defined specifically only after an accident is used, the collective deciders have not chosen merely to limit an actuarial group's engaging in an activity. They have sought instead to penalize individuals in order to make *them* decide at the last minute (but still before the accident) whether or not to do some particular act. This necessarily implies the belief that keeping such last minute pressure on individuals is a better way of avoiding accident costs than limiting the actuarial group. The collective deciders would, therefore, be irrational if they allowed insurance, since this would convert the last minute pressure into limitation of an actuarial group, the very device they had rejected.[24]

Needless to say, the size of the uninsurable penalty would have to be carefully controlled. This is not only because our sense of justice would forbid large money penalties (as it would most non-money penalties) where the criteria for responsibility are vague, but also because if the money penalty is too large many individuals would refuse to be put in the situation where they would have to make a last-minute choice. They would prefer to avoid the activity which gives rise to acts which might be severely penalized. This would *ex hypothesis* result in a combination of acts and activities different from what the collective deciders want. The penalty—called an uninsurable tort fine—would therefore have to be large enough to induce individuals to try to avoid it by avoiding (before an accident occurs) the specific if somewhat vaguely defined acts that *ex post* would be penalized, but small enough to forestall inducing any substantial number of people to abandon

24. Contrast the general deterrence approach, where forbidding insurance would be irrational. If general deterrence puts the accident costs of specific acts on individuals and forbids insurance, this implies an assumption that the individual, choosing at the last minute, can make the best choice as to whether the act contemplated is worth the accident costs it would cause. But this assumption, unlike the specific deterrence assumption that individuals in specific situations can give concrete meaning to general guidelines of behavior, is impractical. The noninsurable risk on the individual actor would be so great as to cause him to avoid the broader activity that gave rise to the possibility of an accident occurring—i.e. he would make his choice at a level where the costs and benefits of his actions were more certain. This would be undesirable, since the objective is to deter the act, not the broader activity. See supra, pp. 103–07.

broader activities the collective deciders would not wish to have curbed.[25]

We may summarize this fourth mixed system of specific and market deterrence as follows. Penalties are put on acts or activities on an accident involvement basis. As a result, the market will operate both in deciding who performs the acts or activities and in seeking out ways to avoid accidents.[26] (This is true of the third method as well.) In addition, since the acts or activities are defined only in general terms before an accident occurs, individuals will, in deciding what acts or activities to engage in, estimate what is likely to be penalized if an accident does occur, and the acts or activities deterred will depend on this estimate. To this extent, which acts or activities are actually limited will be left to individual choices as circumscribed by the vague guidelines imposed by the collective deciders.

The Residue of General Deterrence

One further important point remains to be made with regard to specific deterrence. Unless the specific deterrence approach results in a total elimination of accidents, the question of the market effect of the costs of those accidents still occurring will have to be faced. In fact, since we do not wish to abolish accidents at all costs, accidents will continue to occur under a specific deterrence approach. And since they occur, the question of how people will react in the market to the accident costs is unavoidable. In this sense then, all systems of specific deterrence are mixed systems. If the costs are left on victims, the activities that tend to produce vic-

25. One of the factors that might go into determining the appropriate size of the tort fine might be the income level of the wrongdoer. The collective deciders might seek a penalty which would deter all individuals to the same degree regardless of income. This is not the place to discuss possible administrative difficulties with such an approach. The point is only that—to the extent we deem it worthwhile to do so—noninsurable tort fines can be molded to achieve our collective ends regardless of the wealth of the wrongdoer. See also infra note 5, Chapter 11.

26. Once again, this means avoiding accidents, not accident *costs*.

tims will be more expensive than if the costs are placed on non-victims, and a general deterrence reduction in these activities will result. If they are shifted to other activities involved in the accident, these activities will bear a general deterrence burden and react accordingly. If they are placed on unrelated activities, these will react in the same way as if they had been burdened with an indirect tax.[27] It follows that it is not enough for the collective deciders simply to decide on penalties to be placed on certain acts and activities. They must consider not only what is collectively desired and what penalties will tend to accomplish this, but also how the allocation of those accident costs that are not prevented by specific deterrence prohibitions will affect this collective decision. As we shall see, this makes a specific deterrence decision on what activities to proscribe very hard. That decision, like the analogous one under the general deterrence approach (i.e. which activities should bear which costs), is one of the two fundamental problems facing any system of primary accident cost control. We must now direct our attention to those two problems.

27. That is to say, an indirect tax the effect of which can be lessened by a reduction in the number of accidents. Therefore, these unrelated activities will try to bribe accident "causers" to change, given the assumption that the bribery is cheaper than payment of the costs imposed.

PART III

Two Major Problems in Reducing Primary Accident Costs

Any system of accident law that seeks to achieve primary cost reduction must provide a basis for making two very complicated decisions: (1) the extent to which each of the activities combining to cause an accident is responsible for the accident costs, which for the sake of brevity I call "what-is-a-cost-of-what," and (2) the proper valuation of the cost of accidents, which I call "what-is-the-cost." These decisions must be made whether the accident cost reduction is to be accomplished through specific deterrence, general deterrence, or some mixed approach. Indeed, these decisions will be made even when in fact primary accident cost reduction is not considered a major goal, although the decisions become more difficult when primary accident cost avoidance is sought.

These decisions are inevitably made in every accident case because even leaving accident burdens where they happen to fall is an implicit decision of what an accident costs and which act or activity ought to bear the costs. But they need not be made on the basis of the particular facts of any individual accident. They may, for efficiency or other reasons, be made on the basis of general rules derived from particular accidents and still serve the purposes of primary cost reduction. To the extent that primary cost reduction is not our aim, these decisions may also be made on the basis of the other goals we seek to accomplish.

An accident occurs in which an aged man, driving a new blue car, is injured when his car collides with an old car driven by a young steelworker. The road is hilly; several bicyclists and pedestrians were on the road; a plane was flying overhead; the steelworker was hurrying to work; and the aged man had to file a tax return in three days. What portion of the costs resulting from this accident is properly attributable to drivers, to pedestrians, to bicycles, to planes, to hilly roads, to steel, to age, to youth, to new cars, to blue cars, to old cars, and to taxes? That is what must be answered under the general deterrence approach. The question under the specific deterrence approach is a similar one. Should we prohibit or otherwise regulate driving, walking on highways, bicycling on highways, driving old cars, driving new cars, driving when taxes are due—or a little of each? While the effect of the decision allocating responsibility, as well as the way the decision is made, may be different depending on whether general or specific deterrence is used, a decision must be reached in either case.

As we have seen, no practical system of accident law can accomplish primary cost reduction through general or specific deterrence alone; any realistic system is likely to decide the issue of what-is-a-cost-of-what with reference to both specific and general deterrence criteria. Fault combined with insurance, i.e. the fault system, decides this (as well as the cost of an accident) on the basis of a very specific mixture of the market and the collective approaches. As such it must be compared to other mixed systems with regard to how well it achieves both primary accident cost control and the other goals of accident law.

Before we can evaluate mixed systems, however, we need to know how the pure specific deterrence and the pure general deterrence methods would go about making this decision. Under general deterrence, we must determine which activity or groups of activities can reduce accident costs most cheaply in terms of market values, since only if costs are allocated to these activities can there be a proper general deterrence choice for or against accident costs. The analogous problem for specific deterrence is to determine which activities can reduce accident costs "best" from a collective point of view. Obviously these statements need substantial elucidation and discussion.

CHAPTER 7

Which Activities Cause Which
Accident Costs: The General Deterrence Approach

A pure market approach to primary accident cost avoidance would require allocation of accident costs to those acts or activities (or combinations of them) which could avoid the accident costs most cheaply.[1] This is the same as saying that the system would allocate the costs to those acts or activities that an arbitrary initial bearer of accident costs would (in the absence of transaction and information costs) find it most worthwhile to "bribe" in order to obtain that modification of behavior which would lessen accident costs most.[2]

This formulation implies several things. If there were no transaction or information costs associated with paying people to alter their behavior, it would not matter (in terms of market control of accidents) who bore the accident costs initially. Regardless of who was initially liable, there would be bribes or transactions bringing about any change in the behavior of any individual that would cause a greater reduction in accident costs than in pleasure.[3] Since

1. McKean, in "Products Liability: Trends and Implications," uses a somewhat different terminology. What I call the cheapest or easiest cost avoider, he calls the party that has the greatest comparative advantage in producing safety or injury reduction. See id. at 45–49. Our goals are the same. His terminology has many advantages; for instance, it makes clear the comparative nature of the choice (which may be inadequately emphasized even by such terms as easi*est* or cheap*est*). It may have the disadvantage that by analogizing safety to a product, it may lead some readers to forget that the abstention from acts or activities may be the cheapest way to "produce" safety.

2. "Bribe" as used throughout this book implies no moral turpitude or corruption by either party but rather an open, legitimate inducement.

3. See generally R. H. Coase, "The Problem of Social Cost," 3 *J. L. & Econ.* (1960). On these assumptions no misallocations of costs would ever be pos-

in reality transactions are often terribly expensive, it is often not worthwhile spending both the cost of the transaction and the amount needed to bribe someone else to diminish the accident causing behavior. As a result, the accident cost is not avoided by society, while another allocation that could eliminate or lessen the transaction cost is available and would result in the avoidance of the accident cost. The aim of the pure market determination of which activity to hold liable is to find this other allocation.

An overly simple example may be in order. Suppose car-pedestrian accidents currently cost $100. Suppose also that if cars had spongy bumpers the total accident costs would only be $10. Suppose finally that spongy bumpers cost $50 more than the present bumpers. Assuming no transaction costs, spongy bumpers would become established regardless of who was held responsible for car-pedestrian accidents. If car manufacturers were liable the would prefer to spend $50 for the new bumpers plus $10 in accident damages, instead of $100 for accident damages. If pedestrians were held responsible and could foresee the costs, the would prefer to bribe the car manufacturers $50 to put in spongy bumpers and bear $10 in damages, rather than bear $100 in damages. Exactly the same result would occur if an arbitrary third party, e.g. television manufacturers, were held liable initially; the too could lessen costs to themselves by bribing car manufacturer to put in spongy bumpers. The result is the same simply because the cost of avoiding the accident is in all instances smaller than the cost of compensating for it. Wherever this is so, and wherever costs nothing to bribe (and people have the necessary knowledge the market will seek the cheapest way and avoid the accident.

Now let us alter the example to add transaction costs. Assume that any allocation other than leaving the cost where it falls (i.e. on the pedestrian) entails $5 in administrative costs. Assume also

---

sible. See Calabresi, "Transaction Costs." In fact, information costs are real part of transaction costs, and hereafter when I use the term transaction costs, include them.

that for pedestrians to bribe anyone is very expensive, e.g. $65. (This is because it is costly to gather pedestrians together to bargain and to handle the problem of would-be free-loaders.[4]) Assume finally that it would cost television manufacturers $30 to bribe. What would happen in our example?

If car manufacturers were held liable, they would bear $100 in accident costs plus perhaps the $5 allocation cost. They could avoid this in the future by putting in spongy bumpers at $50, paying $10 in damages, and perhaps the same $5 in administrative costs (assuming for the sake of simplicity that these remained constant). Clearly they would install spongy bumpers.

If pedestrians were held liable, they would bear $100 in accident costs. But to get spongy bumpers installed would cost them $50 (bribe) plus $65 (transaction costs), and they would still bear $10 in accident costs. Since $125 is more than $100, a change to spongy bumpers would not seem worth the expense. But the absence of spongy bumpers would in fact entail an unnecessary cost to society of the difference between $100 (accident costs when borne by pedestrians) and $65 (the cost to society when car manufacturers are held liable).

If television manufacturers were held liable, the figures would be $100 plus $5 with no spongy bumpers, compared with $50 (bribe) plus $30 (transaction costs) plus $10 (remaining accident costs) plus perhaps $5 (administrative costs). Since $95 is less than

4. The free-loader is the person who refuses to be inoculated against small-pox because given the fact that almost everyone else is inoculated, the risk of smallpox to him is less than the risk of harm from the inoculation. If enough people are free-loaders it becomes necessary to compel inoculation to avoid smallpox epidemics. The free-loader is also the person who refuses to join a union because the fact that most other workers are union members assures him of the benefits of unionization without the cost. The use of compulsion in these areas suggests that the problem of free-loaders is crucial whenever many people must agree to bear a cost in order to bring about a change favorable to all of them. It would not be crucial if nonpayers could be excluded from the benefits of the change, but such exclusion is often extremely expensive. It is precisely that expense which justifies compulsion. Cf. Calabresi, "Transaction Costs."

$105, spongy bumpers would probably be installed. But this result would have been achieved in a more expensive, less efficient way than if car manufacturers had been liable, for $30 in unnecessary transaction costs would have been imposed on society.

Clearly then, on the basis of our initial assumptions, it would be best to make automobile manufacturers liable.

Throughout these examples I have ignored the question of long-run changes in the level of the activities discussed. I have assumed that the only effect of the different liability rules proposed would be to influence the decision to install spongy bumpers.[5] In fact, liability rules can have a broader, long-run effect. They can change the relative profits of the activities involved and thus affect the relative number of car manufacturers, cars, pedestrians, and television manufacturers in my examples.[6]

This presents no particular theoretical problems. If there are no transaction costs, the same kind of transactions which occur to cure short-run misallocations will occur to cure long-run ones. Thus whatever reductions in cars, pedestrians, and television sets cost least in forgone pleasure will become established.[7] If one assumes transaction costs, as one must, the theoretical problem remains the same as in the short-run case, namely allocating costs to the cheapest (long-run) cost avoider so as to make worthwhile changes likely and at the same time avoid unnecessary transaction costs.

In practice, the problem is more difficult. Transactions to alter the long-run level of activities are almost always prohibitively costly, as they would require, for example, large groups of potential buyers to agree to bribe a manufacturer to produce more, or to agree to subsidize the entry of new manufacturers into an industry. And judgments as to who is likely to be the cheapest long-run cost avoider (i.e. as to the relative desirability in the market of a few more cars as against a few more pedestrians) are harder to

5. Cf. Coase, "The Problem of Social Cost."
6. See Calabresi, "Transaction Costs."
7. See Calabresi, "Transaction Costs," correcting Calabresi, "The Decision for Accidents," at 730 n. 28, 731 n. 30; and Calabresi, "The Wonderful World," at 231 n. 28. See also Nutter, "The Coase Theorem on Social Cost: A Footnote," 11 *J. L. & Econ.* 503 (1968).

make than judgments as to short-run cost avoiders (i.e. as to who is likely to be in the best position to determine whether spongy bumpers are worth their costs).[8] This means that in many situations we may as well ignore the long-run judgment, as one guess is as good as another, and that concentrating on the short-run judgment is the best we can do.

A more complicated situation occurs, however, when we can guess which activity is likely to be the cheapest long-run cost avoider and that activity is *not* the cheapest short-run cost avoider. Suppose we believe that reducing pedestrianism is the cheapest long-run cost avoider, but that introducing spongy bumpers in some kinds of cars is the cheapest short-run change. How can we achieve both? Sometimes we may not be able to and then we must choose whatever cost avoidance seems most important and the cost avoider we are most sure of. At other times we can achieve both by combining market devices (such as allocation of liability to car manufacturers) to induce use of spongy bumpers where they are desirable, with collective inducements or controls (such as fixed subsidies to car manufacturers paid out of fixed taxes on pedestrians) to increase the number of cars relative to pedestrians.[9] The permutations are almost infinite, but the practical decisions are no more difficult than they would be if we sought to achieve primary cost control mainly through collective decisions.

The question for a pure market approach is, then, how we should determine who, in practice, is the cheapest cost avoider, i.e. how we should determine who is in the position of the car manufacturer in the example for each category of accidents. In almost every area we can make some rough guesses, based on intuitive notions or on undifferentiated and unanalyzed experiences, as to who is clearly not the cheapest cost avoider and who may be. These could be further refined by controlled experiments, but such experiments are unlikely to be carried out because they cost too much. There are, however, guidelines which can be used for finding

8. Cf. the discussion of the theory of second best, supra notes 21, 22, Chapter 5, and accompanying text.
9. See Calabresi, "Transaction Costs," at 71–72.

out who, in the absence of more information, is likely to be the cheapest cost avoider. If even the guidelines give no satisfactory indications, a market approach can either make a guess, divide the costs equally among the activities not excluded by the rough guess or the guidelines, or be "indifferent" as to who should bear costs in these extreme cases and allocate them on the basis of approaches and goals other than market reduction of primary accident costs.

I will first discuss the rough guess, then consider each of the guidelines individually (so that they can later be contrasted with the criteria used by the specific deterrence approach, as well as with those used by various mixed systems like the fault system), and then examine the situation where even the guidelines give no clear indications. Finally, I shall examine the possible forums and methods that are likely to make the decisions the market approach requires in the most intelligent way.[10]

THE INITIAL ROUGH GUESS

The general deterrence rough guess must be guided by market considerations. It is essentially a collective guess, but one concerning individuals' market valuations. It will be limited to ruling out as potential loss bearers those activities that could reduce the costs being allocated only at what would *obviously* be too great an expense.[11] The cost of reducing accident costs by reduction in or modification of a given activity will depend both on its market desirability (how much people want it and how many substitutes it has) and on the relation it bears (in some causal sense) to the accident costs under consideration. For example, although the costs of car-pedestrian accidents could probably be reduced substantially by reductions and modifications of pedestrian activity, such cost reduction might be too expensive if pedestrianism is

10. By forum I mean the body which should make these decisions, e.g. a jury, a court, an administrative agency, or a legislature. By methods I mean both the devices such a body would use and the level of generality at which they would make their decisions, e.g. case-by-case versus category determinations, schedules of damages versus individual valuations.

11. Activities which would find it impossible to reduce costs would be a subset of those that could reduce such costs only at too great an expense.

viewed as a fixed activity, i.e. one without ready substitutes. Similarly, placing the costs of car-pedestrian accidents on leather shoes would be silly even though leather shoes have close substitutes, e.g. rubber shoes, because a shift to such substitutes would have virtually no effect on the costs of car-pedestrian accidents.

Thus the general deterrence rough guess must be made with special reference to the relative desirability and uniqueness of activities (as expressed in the market) and to their relation to the costs being allocated. Of course, in practice even a general deterrence rough guess may have reference to specific deterrence criteria. Some activities might be excluded because politically (and regardless of the market) we wished them to be left unaffected and fixed, despite the effect placing part of accident losses on them would have on accident costs.

The rough guess, then, is designed to exclude from consideration as potential loss bearers all those activities that could reduce costs only by causing losses which are clearly much greater, in terms of meeting individuals' desires as expressed in the market, than would result if one achieved the equivalent or greater reduction in accident costs by burdening other activities. Needless to say, all collective judgments as to relative abilities of different activities to achieve primary cost reduction, and as to relative costs at which these could be achieved, are very hard to make and very tenuous. They always involve a guess as to which activities can avoid accidents most easily (at the least expense) by reduction of the activity or by the introduction of safety devices. And even worse, they involve guesses as to what *combinations* of activities can achieve cost reductions most cheaply, for often the optimal reduction in accident costs would be achieved by dividing them among a number of activities. They are not, however, any harder than the equivalent rough guess that must be made under specific deterrence. And at the rough guess stage, where only activities that clearly cannot avoid the accident costs relatively cheaply are excluded, it may not be so hard in practice to make reasonably satisfactory decisions.

For example, the accident involving the old man and young

steelworker had many "causes," including several I did not even mention. My failure to mention them was a type of rough guess, reflecting my judgment that burdening the activities not mentioned with some or all of the costs of this accident would have virtually no effect on accident costs, or would have an effect only in a much more roundabout and expensive manner than burdening some of the activities mentioned would. In addition, even some of the activities mentioned could be ruled out through a rough guess. Unless such accidents frequently occurred near airports or in areas where planes often fly low, it is unlikely that burdening planes with part of the cost would affect such accidents much. Even if the airplane was a distraction in this case, the odds are that another distraction would have taken its place if it had not been there. Furthermore, the elimination of *all* possible distractions would not occur even if they were burdened with all the costs of such accidents. And even if such a burden would eliminate or substantially reduce the distractions, the resulting reduction in accident costs could almost certainly have been achieved at a lower social cost (with a lesser deviation from people's desires) by burdening some of the other involved activities. A rough guess to ignore the plane would almost certainly be justified.

The methodology of the rough guess has a very close analogy in the traditional resource allocation theory of economics. In most situations we are not troubled with deciding what-is-a-cost-of-what. This is so because most cost allocations are made among a limited number of parties who are dealing with one another, such as buyers and sellers of steel. In such situations, the problem of who should bear what portions of the various costs involved in making steel does not normally seem to require any rough guess. The only situation in traditional economics where the problem comes up is where external costs or benefits are involved, such as when the manufacture or sale of steel has an effect, good or bad, on parties outside the buying-selling relationship. Then the question of the extent to which this cost or benefit is attributable to the party outside the relationship and the extent to which it is attributable to either the steel seller or the buyer (the parties within the relationship) is crucial.

But how do we know that in most traditional resource allocation situations no such external effects are present? Why do we decide to ignore and not attribute to the steel seller-buyer combination all sorts of costs and benefits to third parties that could be attributed to the presence of steel? We do it—whether or not we think about it—in the same way in which we make the accident cost rough guess. We look at the same kind of cost avoidance factors and conclude that little is to be gained by allocating these outside costs or benefits to the steel seller-buyer combination for the same reasons we concluded, in my accident example, that there was little to be gained by allocating the accident costs to the airplane flying by. Where we have doubts, we designate the situation as one where some external effects of steel manufacturing may exist, but we do not mention all the other possible external effects that we have easily discounted.

The allocation of accident costs is different only in that in accident situations significant problems of allocation among independent parties are common, and therefore external effects are more frequent. But even in accident situations we should not waste much time before eliminating by a rough guess those parties that have no more relation to the accident than selling or buying steel has to the great run of possible external effects which are always ignored. We should concentrate instead on the difficult allocation problems—on the allocation of costs among those parties that may be significant avoiders of the accident costs and on the criteria relevant to making that allocation.

A GUIDELINE: RELATIONSHIP BETWEEN AVOIDANCE AND ADMINISTRATIVE COSTS

The first guideline for picking the cheapest cost avoider is to seek the optimal relationship between avoidance costs and administrative costs. This simply means that if finding (or allocating costs to) the cheapest cost avoider is very expensive, it may lower total costs to allocate costs to a slightly more expensive cost avoider. Any cost savings achieved by the seemingly better allocation may not be worth the costs borne to find it. If placing accident costs on drivers according to miles driven results in nearly as much car-pedestrian accident cost avoidance as a charge on drivers according to age and accident involvement, and if the latter costs much more to administer, in practice the cheapest cost avoidance may well be achieved by the first method. In this sense, the relative administrative costs of first-party insurance plans like Keeton-O'Connell and third-party plans like the Blum and Kalven stopgap plan clearly become relevant, but to what extent depends on the accident cost avoidance each kind of plan would give.

A GUIDELINE: AVOIDING EXTERNALIZATION

The second guideline is to seek the maximum degree of internalization of costs consistent with the first guideline. This is a bit of economic jargon for a fairly simple concept. I have said that while we often do not know with certainty which allocation of costs would in theory accomplish the cheapest cost avoidance, in most cases we can rule out a great many allocations as almost certainly being no good. We may not know whether pedestrians or drivers are the cheapest cost avoiders of car-pedestrian accidents, but we may nonetheless be sure that either is better than taxpayers in general or television manufacturers. Therefore we should rule out any allocation that externalizes costs from pedestrians or drivers to taxpayers in general unless this allocation of costs is so much cheaper administratively that administrative savings make up for the lack of accident cost savings. It is precisely this unexplained externalization to taxpayers that makes the Blum and Kalven stopgap plan so puzzling—more puzzling, indeed, than social insurance plans, since these rely expressly on administrative cost savings and goals other than primary accident cost reduction to justify the externalization they entail.

Externalization occurs in three ways. I call the first externalization due to insufficient subcategorization, the second, externalization due to transfer, and the third, externalization as a result of inadequate knowledge.

Externalization due to Insufficient Subcategorization

Allocation of car-pedestrian accident costs to driving in general (through a fixed tax on all drivers) might be an example of externalization due to insufficient subcategorization. If it turned out that teen-age drivers were responsible for a disproportionate number of car-pedestrian accident costs, the allocation described would result in externalizing some of the cost from this subcategory of driving to the broader category of driving in general. Had the accident costs been allocated to drivers by accident involvement according to age group, the result would be that *all* drivers would bear a portion of the cost, but teen-age driving would bear a greater share.

A broader example of externalization due to inadequate subcategorization would occur if the costs of car-pedestrian accidents were treated as general costs of living (the broadest category) and paid out of general taxes. If this were the case, accident costs might, in theory, affect whether people lived in America or in Argentina (assuming that these accident costs and the taxes based on them were different in the two countries). But once people decided to live in America, these costs would not affect their decisions to drive or walk. People would be in a position to make the proper choice for or against accidents at the "where shall we live" level but not at the "driving-walking" level. Thus only a very attenuated general deterrence pressure would exist. Of course, car-pedestrian accidents *are* general costs of living in America. But putting the cost on cars or on pedestrians will affect not only the decision to drive or walk (the subcategory) but—if the cost is significant enough—the decision to move to Argentina as well (the category).

Subcategorizing, moreover, is fairly immune from the *post hoc ergo propter hoc* fallacy, at least after a period of time. Suppose that car accident costs are put on drivers and that drivers of red cars bear more of the costs than drivers of blue cars, not because red cars are inherently more dangerous, nor because drivers of red cars tend to drive more dangerously, but because of a coincidence, a statistical quirk. The cost pressure now borne by red cars will cause some drivers to switch to blue cars temporarily. But over time the quirk will disappear and the accident cost records of the two colors will tend to be equalized. If, surprisingly, the quirk persists, not because red cars are more dangerous than blue cars but because people who prefer red cars are more accident prone, some cost pressure in favor of blue cars will also persist. The ultimate equilibrium reached between red and blue car accident costs will depend on the extent to which preferring red cars is in fact linked to dangerous driving. Since there will be some drivers who prefer red cars and do not drive dangerously, the subcategorization will almost certainly not be as good as a further one which found a more direct criterion for identifying accident-prone drivers than driving red cars. But this does not mean that the subcategorization that took place was undesirable. To the extent that driving red cars and dangerous driving were simply connected by coincidence no harm was done, while to the extent that some real, even if subconscious link existed, a roundabout general deterrence pressure would have been achieved.

Since subcategorization is expensive, it will be cheaper at some point to have externalization to a broader category than to subcategorize indefinitely. That is why the guideline is the greatest internalization possible consistent with the optimal level of administrative costs.

There are three types of cost associated with subcategorization: the cost of gathering the facts necessary for subcategorization, the cost of analyzing the facts gathered and converting them into actuarially significant data, and the cost of assigning accident costs to increasingly smaller subcategories. If these costs are substantial, we might not be willing to spend the money to define some actuarially significant subcategories, even though their definition is possible, or to allocate accident costs on the basis of some of the actuarially significant subcategories we have actually defined. But this is simply another way of saying that sooner or later the point is reached where the cost of further subclassification is greater than the value in primary cost avoidance subclassification is likely to give.

The problem of how far to subcategorize in practice, however, is not an unduly complex one. It is in fact quite similar to the problem faced today by insurance companies when they subclassify for fault-proneness. They find it worth their while to charge higher rates for unmarried male drivers under 25 than for females, married males, or unmarried males over 25. But they do not break this down further and charge different rates for unmarried male drivers of 22 and 7 months as against unmarried male drivers of 22 and 8 months. The expected difference in accident-proneness—even if it could be measured—is not worth the cost of the subclassification.

The fact that the costs of subclassification limit the desirability of such subcategorization suggests that at times it may not be worth categorizing at all. If the reduction in primary accident costs achieved through general deterrence were minimal and the costs of employing that approach—the costs of categorizing—were too great, it might well be that social insurance paid out of general taxes would be the best solution. In effect, this would be placing the cost on the broadest category—living in a given country—of which all other classifications are subcategories. It seems unlikely, however, in view of insurance company actuarial practices, that no subclassification would be worthwhile in those areas where accidents and accident costs are a significant problem.[12]

Externalization due to Transfer

Allocation of car-pedestrian accident costs to pedestrians is one of many possible examples of externalization due to transfer. If the

12. In practice, the existence of subcategorization costs has a further effect. It should cause us to allocate losses in a way that makes least expensive that kind of subcategorization which we guess is likely to be important. For further discussion see infra pp. 170–71.

result of this allocation is that society picks up the tab through social insurance paid out of general taxes because most pedestrians are inadequately covered, what looks like a decision to put the costs on pedestrians rather than drivers actually results in neither bearing the costs. Under these circumstances, who should bear the costs depends on whether drivers or taxpayers are likely to be the cheapest cost avoiders, since the practical effect of allocating costs to pedestrians is to make taxpayers bear the costs.

There are many reasons why externalization due to transfer may occur, some practical and some political. Many of these will be discussed later when we compare how the fault system and the pure market approach would allocate the same costs. Here it is sufficient to note that the search for the cheapest cost avoider requires a comparison of the cost avoidance potential of those who will actually bear the accident costs after transfers, rather than of the initial loss bearers. Wherever one of the posttransfer loss bearers could be ruled out on either rough guess, subcategorization, or other grounds, it follows that the other loss bearer is the cheapest cost avoider.

Externalization due to Inadequate Knowledge

Externalization due to inadequate knowledge would occur if pedestrians to whom car-pedestrian accident costs were allocated could not, because of inadequate knowledge or for psychological reasons, accurately foresee the risk of bearing accident costs involved in walking. We are assuming that pedestrians would be the cheapest cost avoiders if they could accurately convert into money the risk they take by walking. But if they cannot, because of inadequate knowledge, putting the cost on them would not affect their behavior and would have as little effect on accident control as scattering the cost would.[13] It follows here too that

---

13. A slightly different but equally undesirable result would occur if pedestrians overestimated the risk involved in walking. In such situations, too much pressure to alter or abstain from walking would be exerted.

whatever division between drivers and pedestrians were desirable in theory, allocation to drivers would give the cheapest cost avoidance in practice, assuming, of course, that they had adequate knowledge.

Avoiding Externalization: An Example

It may not be readily apparent why, when we do not know how to divide car-pedestrian accident costs between pedestrians and cars, it is better, from a general deterrence point of view, for cars to bear all the costs than for cars to bear part and for the rest to be externalized and removed from both cars and pedestrians.

An example may help explain this. Let us make the basic assumption that a rough guess has excluded all activities other than walking and driving as cheapest cost avoiders of car-pedestrian accidents. Let us also assume that the cheapest way of reducing car-pedestrian accident costs would be to affect both cars and walking somewhat, but that we do not know how much we should try to affect each. We do know, however, that together they cost society a certain amount. We can therefore say that from a resource allocation or general deterrence point of view we are always better off if we reduce or alter the combined activities (jointly or severally) up to the point where people would rather pay for the accident costs than bear the costs of a further reduction or alteration. Up to that point, the change "costs" people less than the accidents avoided and so is worthwhile. This is so, moreover, even if the change is entirely at the expense of one activity and even if a cheaper change could be accomplished *in theory* by affecting both. This last premise does not deny that the original change "cost" people less than it saved them; all it shows is that a theoretically better change was possible. But under our basic assumption, this theoretically better change is not available in practice. The situation we are examining is one where whatever part of the accident costs is not put on cars is removed from both cars and pedestrians and borne in a way that affects neither. Instead of the theoretically better combined effect on both activities, the result of dividing the costs is no change in walking and some in driving, when *ex hypothesis* a still greater change in driving would save more than it would cost.

A GUIDELINE: THE BEST BRIBER

The third guideline for picking the cheapest cost avoider is rather different from the first two. It is to allocate accident costs in such a way as to maximize the likelihood that errors in allocation will be corrected in the market. This criterion assumes that despite transaction costs, a tendency exists for the market to find the cheapest cost avoider and influence him by bribes. It therefore urges us, to the extent we are unsure of who the cheapest cost avoider is, to charge accident costs to that loss bearer who can enter into transactions most cheaply. This means that if the initial loss bearer chosen is not in fact the cheapest cost avoider, we have minimized the obstacle transaction costs impose on the market's finding and influencing the behavior of the cheapest cost avoider. Obviously this criterion does not suggest picking a party that clearly is not the cheapest cost avoider simply because he can bribe easily. It suggests that to the extent we are unsure of our choice among possible cheapest cost avoiders, the best briber in the group is our best bet.

In practice, finding the best briber is somewhat more complicated than might appear. The requirement that this be the activity that can most cheaply enter into transactions with other potential cost causers hides within it several other requirements.

The first has to do with awareness of the risk. No matter how cheaply an activity can enter into transactions, it is not the best briber if those who engage in the activity are not sufficiently aware of the risks of accident costs involved. Without this awareness they would not know enough to try to enter into transactions to reduce their cost burden, and allocation of the costs to them would therefore not result in the market seeking out the cheapest cost avoider.

The second requirement involves the ease with which different activities can discover whom to bribe. In effect this simply means that one of the costs of entering into transactions is the cost of learning whom it is most advantageous to transact with. The use of the best briber guideline implies that we do not know collectively who the cheapest cost avoider is, since if we did we would have allocated the costs to him in the beginning. It also implies that we believe that market trial and error offers the best way of locating the cheapest cost avoider. It is not true, however, that such trial and error techniques are equally cheap for all the activities we might consider charging. Accordingly, we should charge that activity which can minimize all the costs of entering into transactions, including these information costs.

Finally, the cheapest way of entering into transactions may, in some situations, involve coercion of some potential free-loaders. Coercion in our society is costly, but this does not mean that it always costs more than it is worth.[14] The best briber may therefore be the activity that can enter into transactions with the least use of coercion, or, if coercion is cheaper than other devices, which can call forth at the least cost that degree of coercion needed to bring along the would-be free-loaders and establish the transaction.

In other words, the loss bearer who can enter into transactions most cheaply must be chosen with *all* the cost elements involved in entering into transactions in mind, and these include not only the most obvious transaction costs, but also costs of risk, information, and even coercion where it is the cheapest device available.

Allocating costs to the best briber assumes that when the two other guidelines are insufficient, the cheapest cost avoider is more likely to be identified by the market than through a collective decision. This assumption is based on the usual reasons for preferring the market: market decisions automatically involve a great number of experiments by individual parties, changes in conditions do not require new collective decisions, mistakes will affect only the individual businessman, and so forth. Not all of these reasons, however, always apply. For example, if transactions can

14. See Calabresi, "Transaction Costs," at 70–73.

only be entered into by coercing nearly everyone involved in an activity to join in the bargain, the advantages of experimentation and flexibility do not exist. Where this is the case, burdening the best coercer results in something closely analogous to a societal determination of the cheapest cost avoider, except that the determination will be made by the burdened party rather than by the forum we would normally use to make such a societal decision. In these situations, where the myriad of individual choices usually contemplated in market decisions is unavailable, we may well decide that a societal decision made on an experimental basis (for society can also experiment to a limited extent) would be more likely to determine the cheapest cost avoider than the market.

THE HARD CASE

All this suggests that while the guidelines I have discussed will often indicate which activities should be charged with accident costs, there will be some areas in which they will be insufficient. In such areas the general deterrence approach can operate in three ways. It can make a guess about which activity is likely to be the cheapest cost avoider and then test it experimentally; it can divide costs among all the activities the choice has narrowed down to; or it can allocate losses in accordance with guidelines derived from approaches other than the market.

The Educated Guess

The methodology of making an educated guess or intuitive judgment as to which activity is likely to be the cheapest cost avoider is precisely the same as that employed in making the initial rough guess; the only difference is that the choices are less obvious. This does not mean that we can have no valid judgment on who is most likely to be the cheapest cost avoider, or that we cannot test that judgment empirically. But the judgment will often be difficult to explain in precise terms and it will often be based on hunches. This may justify identifying the difficulties inherent in making it in the hard case.

The principal difficulties with finding this cheapest cost avoider stem from the fact that "ease of avoidance" (the relative ability to reduce accident costs cheaply) depends on a variety of unknowns. In the first place, it depends on the relative market desirability of the activities we are considering as possible loss bearers. For example, if the choice is between avoiding certain accident costs by decreasing by x amount the number of cars on the road and avoiding them by decreasing by y amount the number of pedestrians on the road, ease of avoidance would require us to estimate whether it would "cost" less (i.e. would hurt the people involved less) for y number of pedestrians not to be able to walk or for x number of drivers not to be able to drive. Obviously this is not something we are likely to be able to determine with any certainty.

The matter is made more difficult by the fact that the best solution, i.e. the cheapest way of avoiding the cost, is often a reduction of *both* activities, walking and driving. And if it is hard to know whether people would give higher value to the walking that would have to be eliminated or to the driving that would have to be eliminated, it is even harder to compare each of these with the values people would give to the various *combinations* of walking and driving that would have to be eliminated to accomplish the same result. Yet it is just these relative values which we would have to know to divide accident costs optimally between walking and driving, at least to the extent the guidelines already discussed have not resolved the problem for us.

Moreover, the problem is not merely one of reduction of activities. More often it is one of changing ways of doing the activities, perhaps by introducing safety devices. And this refers not only to existing alternatives and safety devices, but also to those that might come into being. Thus we are not just deciding whether it is cheaper to avoid accident costs by reducing walking or reducing driving, but whether putting costs on walking will—through some reduction in walking and some alteration in the way or time takes place—tend to reduce car-pedestrian accident costs more cheaply than would putting the cost on driving, given that driving, like walking, might be reduced and altered if it bore the costs. In addition, we must compare both of these with the various permutations that charging, for example, 60 percent of the costs to walking and 40 percent to driving, or 50 percent to each, or 75 percent to one and 25 percent to the other, would bring about.

Stated slightly differently, the educated guess is complicated by the fact that each of the activities among which we are choosing is comprised of an infinite number of subactivities or subcategories. We have seen that in theory, placing costs on a subcategory of one activity will affect both that subcategory and the category to which it belongs. Therefore we normally do not worry about the proper degree of subcategorization, but seek instead the smallest subcategory that can be reached efficiently. This is satisfactory where we consider allocation between a category and its subcategories; it is not quite so simple when we are deciding between cars driven by 20-year-olds and blond pedestrians as possible loss bearers. Within each category (cars and pedestrians) we may have no problem. But in deciding which of the categories to burden, or in what proportion to burden each, we must be aware of their possible subcategories, because the ability of each category to avoid the cost cheaply depends in part on the extent of subcategorization that can be made efficiently in each category.

For example, whether cars or pedestrians can avoid certain accident costs more cheaply will be decided one way if it is found that when costs are put on cars, i.e. on their smallest efficiently reached subcategories, most of the burden ends up on cars more than ten years old, with the result that they are almost priced out of the market and accident costs are reduced drastically, whereas putting costs on pedestrians can reduce accident costs to a similar extent only by keeping *all* people from walking. It would be decided another way if charging pedestrians by *their* smallest subcategories put most of the cost on people who walked at dusk without a flashlight and that at a cost of $.50 per person per year this subcategory could avoid the accidents, whereas putting costs on subcategories of cars would indicate no special accident-proneness for most sub-categories of cars and *all* driving at dusk would have to be eliminated to accomplish any significant primary accident cost reduction.

The reader will readily recognize the analogy between this example and one of the questions that must be faced in choosing between first-party insurance plans like Keeton-O'Connell and the American Insurance Association proposals, and third-party plans like the nongovernmental part of the Blum and Kalven stopgap plan. If the choice among these plans depended entirely on general deterrence, and not on the collective desirability of teenage driving as against family-man driving, we would have to consider whether subcategorization emphasizing passenger safety was more likely to give cheap cost avoidance than subcategorization emphasizing third-party safety.

In other words, the search for the cheapest avoider of accident costs is the search for that activity which has most readily available a substitute activity that is substantially safer. It is a search for that degree of alteration or reduction in activities which will bring about primary accident cost reduction most cheaply. This search necessarily involves a comparison not only of activities with one another, but also of the subcategories of the various activities with one another because it is likely that the best alternative will be found by alteration or elimination of a subcategory.

I should reemphasize that the aim of the search is *not* the elimination of primary accident costs. The best available combination of allocations of accident costs will almost certainly still result in a market choice for some accident costs rather than for the alteration in behavior that would avoid them. It may still be true that the cheapest alternative to some accidents is more expensive than the accidents, and at some point this will certainly be true given our lack of total knowledge. But the point of the search is to let the decision for accidents be based on the cheapest alternative, i.e. to enable a comparison between what accidents cost us and what the cheapest way of avoiding them costs us.

Finally, the search for the cheapest cost avoider must take into account the fact that the same factor may be involved in different categories of accidents involving different activities. Assume, for example, that all car-pedestrian accidents involve cars with a certain type of brake and 80-year-old pedestrians. Assume also that charging the entire costs of such accidents to 80-year-old pedestrians is optimal in terms of reduction of those costs because elimination of walking by 80-year-olds would cost less than changing to another type of brake. If this were our universe, general deterrence (unhampered by spreading notions) would charge the pedestrians.

Now assume that all car-bicycle accidents involve cars with the same brake problem and bicycles ridden by youths under 21, and assume that charging car-bicycle accident costs entirely to cyclists is optimal in terms of reduction of such costs because it is cheaper to eliminate cycling by adolescents than to change brakes on cars. It would seem that general deterrence would require cyclists to bear the accident costs. But now consider car-pedestrian and car-bicycle accidents together, and make the assumption (entirely consistent with the preceding ones) that charging car-pedestrian *and* car-bicycle accident costs entirely to cars is optimal in terms of reducing such costs because changing brakes on cars is cheaper than eliminating cycling by adolescents *and* walking by 80-year-olds. Despite our initial impressions, cars should be charged with the costs of both types of accidents.

The very simplicity of this example highlights the difficulty it demonstrates. Because the interaction among activities is complex, accident cost allocations made only on the basis of the cheapest cost avoidance in each accident case or only on the basis of cheapest cost avoidance in each *type* of accident case may not *in sum* be optimal in terms of total reduction of such accident costs. As a result, our search for the cheapest cost avoider cannot consider each accident situation in a vacuum. In one way this makes the search a great deal harder, but as we shall see, it also simplifies it in another way once we accept the fact that perfection is neither possible nor very important.

The search for the cheapest cost avoider may seem to be so difficult that we might despair of making intelligent decisions. But desperation is actually quite unwarranted. All the various plans discussed in the first chapter of this book make precisely such decisions, though they often make them only implicitly. Similarly, under the current fault system we make choices of at least equal difficulty. Of course, just as we are often wrong in deciding whether a party was reasonably prudent, we may well often be wrong in deciding who or what combination of changes in activities could have avoided accident costs more easily. The point of trying to make ease of avoidance decisions is not that they must always be correct to be of value, but that to the extent that we explicitly try to divide accident costs among parties with ease of avoidance in mind, we are more likely to achieve a division of costs that approaches the general deterrence optimum than if we divide costs with other objectives in mind or without any clear notion of what our objectives are.

We should remember, moreover, that the educated guess comes into play after our problem has been considerably simplified. The original rough guess (really a simple ease-of-avoidance test for eliminating clearly irrelevant activities) will have reduced our range of choices to manageable proportions. And the three guidelines already discussed will have narrowed the choice still further. The activities among which we must make a hard ease-of-avoidance choice are thus a limited group. It is not unreasonable to believe that in many situations we will have adequate ground for intuitive choices among them and that we will be able to test our choices empirically. If we cannot make intelligent intuitive choices, this simply means that from the general deterrence or market point of view we have no grounds for believing one of the remaining parties to be a better loss bearer than the others, and any division, whether based on chance, economy, or goals other than general deterrence, may be equally good *so long as it does not violate our earlier general deterrence guidelines.* Furthermore, we know that if we make a grievous enough mistake, the activity charged will attempt to mitigate the effect of our mistake by entering into transactions and paying the activities that can avoid costs more cheaply to do so. The more egregious the error, the more worthwhile such transactions will be despite the costs of entering into them.

Allocation by Involvement

If we have no adequate intuitive grounds on which to base an educated guess and if we do not wish to allocate costs in accordance with criteria derived either from the collective approach or from nonprimary accident cost reduction goals, we can simply divide the costs among the activities the choice has narrowed down to. The result of such a division would be actuarial categories reflecting the relative frequency with which each of the activities charged was involved in accidents.

This division, however, is desirable only if we have no better ground for allocating losses, that is, if all other possible grounds are too inaccurate or too expensive. Its weakness can be seen in the following example. Assume that an accident involving two activities costs $80 each time it occurs. Assume also that such an accident could always be avoided by either activity through the installation of a safety device costing $60 per accident prevented. An involvement test would charge each of the activities $40 per accident. At first, neither activity would install the safety device. Either might eventually do so as a result of transactions with the other. But if the cost of entering into such transactions was more than $20 per accident, no transactions would take place and the accidents would not be avoided, even though if *either* party were originally charged with the full costs of the accident the safety device would be installed, as it should be. Lest this situation seem worse than it is, the exact opposite result would be reached if, instead of the situation posited, we posit the case where the only way to avoid the accident is if *both* activities modify their behavior somewhat, e.g. by installing a $30 safety device.

In any area where we would be tempted to allocate costs on an involvement basis, we would not, of course, know who the easiest cost avoider was. Given our lack of knowledge, we would have to ask: (1) Would the actuarial categories be more likely to reflect ease of avoidance accurately if we made a far-out guess as to ease of avoidance and divided costs accordingly than if we divided the cost equally in each instance without attempting a guess? (2) Even assuming that division of costs on the basis of a far-out ease of avoidance test gave us better results, would these results be sufficiently better to warrant their administrative cost?

The answers to these questions will depend in part on the relative costs of making guesses and making equal divisions. They will also depend, however, on the applicability of a theory of statistical probabilities. In the absence of any indication of who the cheapest cost avoider is, dividing accident costs equally among the activities involved in each accident will maximize the chances of achieving the cheapest cost avoidance if the costs of any misallocation increase at a faster rate than the deviance between the actual allocation and the best possible allocation.[15] To put it another way, if, as the difference between a proper allocation and a misallocation of accident costs increases in size, the bad effects of the misallocation increase more rapidly, then—in conditions of ignorance—the chances of minimizing bad effects are greatest if accident costs are divided evenly. This is not unlikely in view of the way supply and demand curves are normally drawn. Involvement may therefore be a good way of dividing accident costs from the standpoint of market deterrence where we have no grounds for allocating accident costs differently.[16]

15. If absence of indications of who the cheapest cost avoider is can be taken as an indication that causative factors are divided according to a normal probability distribution, then equal division is best even if the social costs of misallocations do not increase faster than the deviance. But if absence of indications suggests total agnosticism, i.e. a rectangular distribution, equal division is clearly preferable only where social costs of misallocations increase faster than the deviance from the optimal allocation. Equal division under a rectangular distribution eliminates the greatest possible deviances, but it doubles the chances of deviances of half the size.

16. Contrast Blum and Kalven, in *Public Law Perspectives,* at 68–69, where they state that there is no way of knowing whether charging motorists 50%

Use of Other Goals

If none of the guidelines discussed indicate who should bear the costs of accidents in a particular area, if the involvement test is also unlikely to increase the chances of allocating costs to the cheapest cost avoider, and if we believe that any further guessing and experimentation to identify the cheapest cost avoider would not be worth its costs, then we can say that even the purest general deterrence approach is indifferent as to who among the remaining possible loss bearers should be burdened. But we may not be indifferent to who bears the losses in terms of either the collective approach to primary cost reduction or other goals such as spreading, and these may, therefore, determine the allocation. Thus if we can make no intelligent determination of whether first- or third-party insurance plans allocate losses to the optimal general deterrence loss bearers, we may, without infringing on general deterrence, choose third-party plans because they favor small cars which collectively we may prefer, or first-party plans because they, let us assume, lead to better cost spreading. Indeed, long before we reach this point, the demands of other approaches and goals will have made themselves felt since the pure market approach to primary accident cost reduction which I have been describing is clearly not what we desire.

Forum and Method

All this leads us to what is perhaps the most important single requirement for picking the cheapest cost avoider. A forum and method must be chosen that are best suited to take the previous criteria into account and to examine which party can most cheaply modify its behavior so as to avoid accidents. In other words, we must entrust the choice of cheapest cost avoider to a forum which is capable of (1) ruling out all those activities that by a kind of

---

of the loss brings about more or less of a distortion than would charging them nothing or charging them everything.

rough guess we would readily agree cannot be the cheapest cost avoiders of a category of accidents; (2) considering which allocation leads to maximum internalization at any given administrative cost level; (3) ruling out allocations that cost more to bring about than they are worth; (4) identifying the cheapest briber among loss bearers; (5) making the best intuitive guess of the activity likely to be the cheapest cost avoider (to the extent previous guidelines do not settle the issue) and testing that guess through controlled experiments or statistical record-keeping; and (6) doing all this without introducing other, extraneous factors.[17]

Since in practice we will never want pure general deterrence, it is not worthwhile discussing at length which forum and method are most likely to accomplish it. The basic issue resolves itself into two questions: (1) Can the cheapest cost avoider be found more easily through case-by-case decisions of who could avoid costs most cheaply in each accident or by deciding directly which insurance categories or activities could avoid various categories of accidents most cheaply? (2) What body is likely to make each of these types of decisions best? My own conclusions are that if finding the cheapest cost avoider is our aim, case-by-case decisions are not desirable, in which case a body like the jury is very unlikely to be suitable for selecting the cheapest cost avoiders. The reasons for these conclusions are many, and are best discussed later when we compare the fault system with the general deterrence approach.

THE BARGAINING CASE—A DETOUR

This would conclude discussion of what-is-a-cost-of-what under the general deterrence approach were it not often asserted that there is one area where it makes no difference (from the standpoint of general deterrence) who bears accident losses. I believe this to

17. A typical extraneous factor would be collective moral judgments regarding the desirability of the activities involved. This factor is extraneous to finding the cheapest cost avoider if we are seeking a predominantly market system of accident cost control. If we want a mixed system it may not be extraneous, and the question becomes whether the forum used is the one best suited to introduce collective moral judgments into the system.

be incorrect, and that distinguishing this area—the bargaining case—only serves to confuse matters in practice. A short detour will suffice to show why.

It is often asserted that where two parties stand in a bargaining relationship with each other it does not matter which one is initially charged with accident losses arising out of that relationship because the market will allocate the losses in the best way possible regardless of initial allocations. Thus, to use an example from most basic torts books, it is said that ultimately it makes no difference whether the dock owners or the shipowners in a situation like *Vincent v. Lake Erie Transp. Co.*[18] are held liable for damage to docks caused by unexpected storms. If shipowners are liable, dockage fees will be less; if dock owners are liable, dockage fees will be more. In either case, the extent to which each activity ultimately bears the loss depends essentially on how easily the other can find a cheaper (because less accident-prone) substitute. If the loss is put on ships, the ships will tend to minimize their losses by going to safer docks until owners of unsafe docks have cut their prices sufficiently—or installed sufficient safety devices—to make using their docks and bearing accident costs as cheap as using other docks. If the owners of unsafe docks initially bear the loss they will minimize it by installing safety devices until it becomes cheaper to pay for the accidents than to install more safety devices and they will charge shipowners for the accident and safety device costs until the charges are so high that it becomes cheaper for ships to use other docks. The same analysis will apply in reverse if the cheapest way to avoid the loss is to make ships safer. In any event the least expensive way to minimize the loss will be sought out and used, and the loss and the cost of minimizing it will be shared between the parties in the same proportion, whichever party is initially liable.

This kind of argument can be made with varying degrees of

18. 109 Minn. 456, 124 N.W. 221 (1910). (Shipowner responsible for damage done by ship to dock during violent storm despite holding that ship's master acted without negligence in keeping ship tied to dock.)

realism in any bargaining situation. Should the cost of industrial accidents be put on workers or on their employers? Should the accident costs of rotary lawn mowers be borne by manufacturers or users? Theoreticians such as Blum and Kalven insist that in terms of general deterrence of accident-prone activities it should make no difference either way.[19] But as we have seen, in theory it would make no difference who bears accident costs even among parties that do *not* stand in a bargaining relationship with each other. In reality, of course, it can make a great deal of difference in the bargaining situation, just as it does in the nonbargaining one. And the reasons it does make a difference are merely concrete examples of the guidelines for picking the cheapest cost avoider I have already outlined.

The first reason for the difference is that one of the two parties may, in practice, be far more able than the other to evaluate the accident risk, i.e. the expected accident costs. And if this is the case, his activity is better suited (in terms of deterrence of accident-prone activities) to bear the initial loss. If individual purchasers are made to bear the costs of rotary mower accidents and invariably underestimate their likelihood, they will tend not to purchase a substitute mower that seems to be more expensive but is relatively cheaper if accident costs are adequately taken into account. Presumably the rotary mower industry knows more accurately the expected cost of using mowers in any given year; and if the cost is put directly on the industry, individuals will be made aware of these costs through the prices of mowers and be better able to make the appropriate choice for or against accidents. To the extent that they choose against accidents (against the now higher priced mowers, reflecting the accident costs), pressure will exist on the mower companies to develop safer mowers. Conversely, if we are dealing with allergies that result from eating strawberries, it may well be true that the consumer is in the best position to value the risk. The same may not be true, however, of any allergy that causes death the first time it appears in any individual. Thus, quite apart from

19. See Blum and Kalven, *Public Law Perspectives,* at 58–59.

spreading motives, a reason may exist for making distinctions between these situations in products liability cases. This reason is, in fact, simply a concrete case of the guideline that externalization due to inadequate knowledge should be avoided.

The second reason is that it may not cost the two parties the same amount to insure against the loss. If the loss is placed on the party for whom insurance is less available or more expensive, a false cost —the excess cost of his insuring—will in effect be made a part of the price of the goods. The possibility of self-insurance does not affect this; it only suggests that occasionally one of the parties is sufficiently large so that noninsurance is the cheapest alternative. Once again, the choice of loss bearers depends on which of the two parties to the bargain can inject the cost into the price of the goods or service most cheaply. This is a more specific example of the guideline that unnecessary avoidance costs should be avoided.[20]

The third reason is nothing more than externalization by transfer. If placing the loss on one of the two parties to the bargain results in all or part of the loss being removed from both of the parties and placed on unrelated parties that would be excluded from loss bearing under any of our general deterrence criteria such a placement is undesirable. For example, if placing the cost of rotary mower accidents on the users ultimately resulted, for political or social reasons based on a desire to compensate, in the loss being paid for by the government out of general social insurance, such a loss allocation would tend to prevent the appropriate choice for or against rotary mowers. If placing the loss on the mower company instead did not result in such an externalization, there would be a clear reason for placing the loss on the mower company.

The classic example of this is industrial accidents, although product liability law provides nearly as classic an instance. It did make a difference in terms of accident deterrence (despite the analysis of theoreticians at the time) whether industrial accidents were initially charged to workers or to industry. This was not because industr

20. For further discussion see infra pp. 251–53.

always was more the "cause" of the accidents than workers, but because industry could insure more cheaply than the workers and was better informed on what the costs of accidents would be, and because placing the loss on the workers was most likely to result in externalizing part of it from both workers and industry. Therefore placing the loss on industry better enabled us to minimize accident losses by an appropriate choice for or against accidents.

All this would seem fairly obvious and perhaps not worth spending time on but for the fact that Blum and Kalven have recently argued that while generally economic theory shows that it makes no difference which of two bargaining parties initially bears accident costs, there is one, and only one, reason why the theory does not work perfectly.[21] Their reason is a little different from any of my three arguments. Both the implicit rejection of my suggestions and the proposal of another criterion warrant additional discussion.

Their argument is as follows: "Placing liability on the [manufacturer rather than the consumer-victim in a product liability or other bargaining case] is tantamount to compelling [potential victims] to buy insurance against the loss through paying a higher price."[22] Moreover, this insurance necessarily fails to take into account the different degrees of accident-proneness of different potential victims and therefore makes the safe consumer pay as much as the unsafe one. At first glance this argument seems compelling. But it turns out that the first point, on compulsory insurance, is false, strictly speaking; and the second, while it does suggest a valid guideline for determining the better loss bearer in a bargaining situation, names it as the exclusive guideline, when it is actually only one of the same type and general significance as the three I have suggested. (It is a specific example of externalization due to insufficient subcategorization.)

21. See Blum and Kalven, *Public Law Perspectives,* at 59. But see Blum and Kalven, "The Empty Cabinet," at 248, n. 23, modifying their original position. The argument, however, continues to be made from time to time in various forms. See, e.g., Buchanan, "In Defense of *Caveat Emptor.*"
22. Ibid.

It is true that if we make manufacturers of a product com-
pulsorily liable with no right to "opt out" (exculpate themselves)
for a price discount, the user will, in effect, be forced to insure
against accidents. Part of the cost of all accidents will be included
in the price he pays, and he will be covered if he is injured. That is
what insurance is. But it is equally true that if manufacturers are
not liable and have no right to "opt in" to liability for a higher
price (indemnify the injured user), then *manufacturers* will, in
effect, be forced to insure against liability for accidents, and users
will be the insurers.[23] The manufacturer (according to the theory)
will have to charge less for the product than if he were liable, since
users will be aware of the risk they take in buying the product.
This reduction in price represents the cost of the compulsory liability insurance to the manufacturer.

The case in which manufacturers cannot assume liability strikes
us as unlikely, and in practice perhaps it is. We do not usually
think of manufacturing situations where we would not allow the
seller to agree to indemnify the buyer. The typical manufacturing
situation, however, is just one instance of the bargaining problem.
Consider instead a large number of small farmers selling wheat
(which occasionally explodes) to a gigantic milling company, or
more realistically, small parts manufacturers selling to a large industrial user.[24] In these cases the notion of forbidding the seller
from opting into liability (i.e. agreeing to a form indemnification
contract), with the resulting compulsory insurance of the seller,

23. The users could, of course, farm out the risk by insuring with parties
outside the bargain, i.e. insurance companies. Similarly, if the manufacturer
were initially held liable, he too could farm out the risk. These facts in no way
affect the analysis in the text, for in either case the insured is compelled to be
insured. The possibility of farming out the risk only means that the original
insurer is not compelled to be a *final* insurer. It is still true, however, that the
cost of avoiding the position of final insurer, i.e. the cost of farming out the
risk instead of self-insuring or taking a lump loss, is, and ought to be, an
important factor in deciding who the better risk bearer is.

24. Cf. U.S. v. New York Great A & P Tea Co., 173 F.2d 79 (7th Cir. 1949)
(company held to have abused its mass buying power in a monopsonistic
situation).

seems quite plausible. The cases of the farmers and the small parts manufacturers are, in fact, exactly the same as those given by Blum and Kalven, but with buyers and sellers reversed. The only difference is that in my examples we may want to make insurance of the seller compulsory, while in their example we seem to want to make insurance of the buyer compulsory. In either case it is our decision to exclude contractual arrangements designed to shift the initial loss from one bargainer to the other that makes the insurance compulsory, *not* the fact that the loss is originally placed by the law on one or the other.[25]

The fact of the matter is simply that whenever we determine which of two bargaining parties will bear the initial undivided cost of an accident and forbid the shifting of that liability to the other in exchange for a fee, we are compelling the party not held liable to insure against the loss with the party that is liable.[26] This is not to say that we are indifferent as to which party we wish to compel to insure or as to whether we wish to compel insurance at all or to make it optional by allowing exculpatory or indemnificatory clauses. The point is simply that the argument about compulsory insurance is false, for whether compulsory insurance results from a liability scheme depends not on which party is held lia-

25. Opting in may be different from opting out, for it might seem that where one party opts into liability, he has a greater awareness of what he is doing than when he allows the other party to opt out of liability. But imagine the giant milling company using a form contract requiring opting into liability. In any case, this difference is but another illustration that knowledge or awareness of risk may affect the choice of whom we wish to hold initially liable and whether we wish to allow such a party to exculpate himself.

26. Strictly speaking, "held liable" is not used in the normal sense. I am using the term to identify the party that under the law bears the initial undivided loss, whether that party is the one who is originally injured or the one who through a legal judgment must compensate the injured party and thereby become the financially injured party. I use the term this way to emphasize the fact that whether the original injured party or some other party is made to bear the undivided loss is in the first instance the result of a legal judgment, a "holding liable," and not of metaphysics. Failure to recognize this fact easily leads to the error of thinking that compulsory insurance in this area is a one-way street.

ble in the first instance, but on whether once we decide to hold one party liable we let that party exculpate itself by shifting the risk of undivided loss to the other for a price. Nor does the fact that we are more likely to let one party exculpate itself than the other change the point at all. This fact merely suggests that other reasons for assigning liability in a bargaining situation (such as unequal awareness of risks) are sufficiently strong to impel compulsory insurance of the nonliable party.

This leaves unanswered, however, the point that the insurance that comes about in a bargaining situation is a particularly noxious one since it charges all those who are insured the same premium. All users of Brand X (which occasionally explodes) will, it is said, pay the same additional amount for the product once it is decided that Brand X will compensate the injured buyer, even though people over 45 are more likely to suffer serious injury than nimble 29-year-olds. But why would all parties pay the same amount for this insurance? In the wonderful world of pure theory, where all parties know and evaluate all risks equally well and insurance costs stand in the same proportion to risk for all parties, there would be no such equality.[27] The manufacturer of Brand X would charge different users different prices depending on their accident-proneness, in effect charging them different insurance premiums according to their risk categories. The fact that the manufacturer does not distinguish among his purchasers in this way is simply a sign that in practice the distinction is not worth the cost, which is not unusual in insurance. Indeed, if Brand X were used in making toilet paper (hardly any explosive potential) and airplane bodies (very high explosive potential), and if the maker of Brand X were the party held liable, we can be sure that the prices charged to the two types of buyers would be very different and would reflect the different accident-proneness of the users.

27. Indeed, in the world of pure theory, those who are troubled at the lack of differentiation in premiums should be dismayed at the very existence of insurance. See Calabresi, "The Wonderful World," at 228–29 n. 24.

The reverse is similarly true. If users of goods are uncompensated for injuries—that is, if manufacturers are "forced" to insure with their buyers—and if different manufacturers have different accident records, they may or may not be able to command different prices for their goods. This ability will depend on how significantly different their accident records are and on the feasibility of having a price structure with differing prices. If the manufacturers can command different prices, then the case is like Brand X toilet paper and airplanes reversed. If they cannot, then it is like the "horror" posed by those who argue that we are imposing an especially evil type of compulsory insurance, except that here it is the safe manufacturer instead of the safe user who is forced to pay the same insurance premium as the accident-prone one.

Having said all this, I must admit that Blum and Kalven do have a point. It is certainly true in *fact*, although not in the pure theory they claim to be discussing, that in most bargaining situations one of the parties is better able to differentiate than the other. It may be more difficult or expensive for manufacturers who are held liable to charge different prices to users in accordance with the latters' accident-proneness than it is for users who are held liable to command different prices from manufacturers according to the manufacturers' accident-proneness.[28] If this difference exists in

---

28. This is not unlikely in what we think of as the normal situation with respect to manufacturers and users, because of the numbers involved (it may be easier for many users to inform themselves about the products of a few manufacturers than it is for the manufacturers to inform themselves about the habits of each user), and perhaps because it may be easier to determine characteristics of products than to determine habits of individuals. But manufacturing cases are only one instance of the bargaining situation. And especially in nonmanufacturing cases, the person we think of as the user may be in the opposite position. See, for example, Vincent v. Lake Erie Transp. Co., supra note 18, where the dock owners could probably estimate with relative ease the damage a given boat would inflict to a dock during a violent storm, while shipowners might find it difficult to say which dock would most likely be hit by a violent storm.

The passage of time may affect our estimate. Whereas it was once easier for

fact, then an argument (based on general deterrence) exists for user rather than manufacturer liability. But it exists despite the theory which says it makes no difference who is held liable, as the argument is of exactly the same nature as the three arguments I suggested previously for deciding who ought to bear the loss in a bargaining situation. For surely, knowing whether the various manufacturers are more aware than the users of the accident risks involved in their products is as important as knowing whether they can distinguish the accident-proneness of users more easily than the users can distinguish the accident-proneness of manufacturers.

The combination of these two factors is perhaps best expressed as one aspect of our externalization by insufficient subcategorization guideline. Since subcategorization is highly desirable from the standpoint of general deterrence but costs money, it is better in bargaining situations—other things being equal—to put the initial loss on that party whose liability will most cheaply result in important subcategorizations on both sides of the bargain.

For example, it appears to make no difference in theory whether automobile accident costs are initially put on car manufacturers or on drivers. The reasons for this are the reasons why, in theory, it would make no difference whether shipowners or dock owners were held liable in *Vincent v. Lake Erie* situations. In practice, however, it may make a great deal of difference in terms of subcategorization whether car drivers or car manufacturers are initially held liable. Putting losses initially on the manufacturers emphasizes and facilitates subclassifications based on make and design of car, while putting losses initially on drivers emphasizes subclassifications based on characteristics of drivers. Car manufacturers, if held liable, could *in theory* charge different prices to different car buyers depending on their accident records and char-

---

the employer (held liable for injuries to employees) to adjust the wages of the employee according to his safety record than it was for the employee (made to bear the cost of his injuries) to command higher wages from more accident-prone employers, today in industries where labor unions are strong the reverse may be true. Cf. Calabresi, "The Decision for Accidents," at 728 n. 22.

acteristics. Conversely, car drivers, if held liable, could in theory command different prices from manufacturers according to accident-cost proneness of various models.[29] And in an economist's perfect world this would surely happen, and we would get the same degree of subclassification regardless of which of the bargainers bore the loss initially. In the real world, however, we must accept the fact that we will have different subclassification or differentiation effects depending on which of the two categories is picked for liability. We are, in short, back to the very same kind of problem posed by the choice between first-party insurance plans like Keeton-O'Connell and third-party plans like the nongovernmental part of Blum and Kalven's own stopgap proposal.

Thus the criterion for liability between bargaining parties which we have been discussing would once again seem to be no more than a concrete instance of a guideline we derived for accident cost avoidance generally: namely to make liable the party whose liability results most readily in significant subclassification within the party and differentiation—i.e. subclassification—in its dealings with the other bargaining party. If placing the loss on drivers results in significant subclassifications by characteristics of drivers and, reasonably cheaply, in price distinctions among cars driven, then a general deterrence argument exists for saying that drivers are the better loss bearers. This is so unless placing the loss on manufacturers results in much more subcategorization by car characteristics than would the alternative allocation, and this further subcategorization is deemed much more important than some subcategorization by characteristics of drivers.

We may summarize this detour as follows: while it makes no difference in theory for general deterrence which of two parties to a bargain bears accident costs arising out of the bargain, in practice it may make a great deal of difference. The reasons for the

29. Car manufacturers held liable could write insurance for drivers who purchase their cars, as liability insurers do now, differentiating by indicia of accident-proneness; or, conversely, drivers could buy insurance, the premiums for which varied with the make of car driven, the effect being in theory to vary the price of each make with its accident-proneness.

difference and the guidelines for deciding who should bear the loss when it does make a difference are simply specific instances of the general guidelines used for finding the cheapest cost avoider whether the situation involves bargainers or not. Indeed, the only difference between the bargaining and the nonbargaining situations is that some of the principal transaction costs which hamper the market in nonbargaining situations (such as the cost of handling would-be free-loaders) are absent in bargaining situations.

This means that the market can more often correct errors and find the cheapest cost avoider efficiently. It does not mean that it can always do so. In practice, the situations where it is most likely to be able to do so are those in which the bargainers are of approximately equal size, number, expertise, and wealth. And in these situations, conscious allocation of losses among bargainers may be quite unnecessary and wasteful.

It is hard to visualize many nonbargaining situations where we also do not care, from the standpoint of general deterrence, who bears accident costs initially. *Some* transaction costs seem inevitable in virtually all nonbargaining situations (especially since long-run transactions to cure long-run misallocation of accident costs would seem to be needed). Hence it will make a difference whether we allocate costs *immediately* to the cheapest cost avoider. If, however, we do not know enough to be able to decide which activity would be the cheapest long-run cost avoider, or if (for reasons like those suggested by the theory of the second best) we are concerned only with short-run general deterrence, then we may conclude even in some nonbargaining situations that where we allocate costs is not going to matter. These situations would be very much like the bargaining ones in which we were indifferent, i.e. situations involving parties of approximately equal size, number, expertise, and wealth. But they would also be situations where the costs of entering into transactions with the other party would be virtually nil, no matter which party was initially burdened. This last condition is what may, in practice, make loss allocation among nonbargainers more important than among bargainers.

In any event, in the bulk of cases, the market or general deterrence approach will require a decision as to who is the most desirable loss bearer regardless of whether bargainers or nonbargainers are involved, and that decision must be made according to the same criteria in either case.

CHAPTER 8

Which Activities Cause Which Accident Costs: The Specific Deterrence Approach

Any approach to primary accident cost reduction must decide which activities are responsible for which accident costs. Without such decisions—which are inevitably collective—it is meaningless to speak of reducing the costs of accidents by reducing accident-causing behavior. Under the general deterrence approach, this decision should result in allocation of accident costs among activities so as to bring about market choices which reduce or alter those activities that can most cheaply avoid accident costs up to the point where the accident costs are cheaper, in terms of market valuations, than the change in behavior necessary to avoid them.

The specific deterrence approach attacks the same problem in a somewhat different way. The question again is the extent to which we wish accident costs reduced, given that we must give up otherwise desirable behavior to avoid accidents. But instead of letting the market determine this, specific deterrence would determine it collectively. This implies not only collective decisions as to which acts or activities are responsible for accidents, but also collective decisions regarding the tolerable level of accident costs in light of the activities that must be given up to reduce accident costs. And these decisions will be based not on market valuations of the desirability of the acts or activities, but on collective judgments as to their desirability. Since this desirability would not be determined by the market, it need not be limited, as it is under general deterrence, to what can be stated in money terms. Thus specific deterrence can and must evaluate the "moral"[1] as well as the "eco-

---

1. "Moral" here includes all nonmoney values.

nomic" value of various acts or activities whose reduction or alteration would reduce accident costs.[2] For this reason the question of
which activities should be held responsible for which costs should
be phrased differently for specific deterrence than for general deterrence. While general deterrence seeks the "cheapest" way of
reducing accident costs, specific deterrence may be said to seek the
"best" way of reducing them.

I am, however, using the phrase "best cost avoider" in a very
particular way. I am using it to mean that reduction or alteration
in activities which gives us the optimal *primary* accident cost avoidance; I do not include all the other possible goals of accident law
here. Allocation of costs to the best specific deterrence cost avoider
may thus entail spreading or administrative costs that are too great.
More important, effectively barring a particular activity may violate our sense of justice. In other words, the word "best" allows
introduction of those moral factors that may cause us collectively
to prefer one activity to another, but it is not meant to include *all*
the factors that may cause us to prefer one system of accident law
to another. I indicated earlier that one could define specific deterrence so that it did include everything but that to do so would
make analysis more difficult.

At first glance, the specific deterrence decision of which activities
to hold responsible for accidents may seem to be relatively easy.
It is, after all, very similar to political decisions we make all the
time. To the contrary, it is very difficult, because it involves decisions far more detailed than we are accustomed to making through
the political process, and because even if the specific deterrence
decision-makers are always correct as to the desirability (apart
from accidents) of various activities, they would still be guessing
when they attempt to determine which activities to alter in which
ways in order to reduce particular accident costs. Thus, even if a

2. Specific deterrence will also value the accident costs in both economic
and moral terms, whereas general deterrence, relying as it does on individual
market choices among activities, must express those costs entirely in economic
terms. See infra pp. 230–31.

collective determination that drinking is bad were easy, we could not make an intelligent specific deterrence judgment about barring drinking unless we knew the relationship between drinking and accident costs. In fact, as that "Noble Experiment" prohibition showed, a collective determination that drinking is bad is not simple either, and that makes things all the more difficult.

Making decisions may actually be more difficult under a pure specific deterrence approach than under general deterrence because, as we shall see, some of the guidelines for choosing among activities used under general deterrence are essentially market guidelines, so that rejection of the market as a means of evaluating desirability and effectuating decisions renders them useless. The specific deterrence choice would not, of course, be made in a step-by-step manner any more than the general deterrence decision would. Nevertheless, a step-by-step analysis of what-is-a-cost-of-what for specific deterrence paralleling the analysis used under general deterrence will be helpful.

THE INITIAL ROUGH GUESS

The specific deterrence approach, like general deterrence, must begin the determination of which activities are responsible for any given costs by excluding a number of activities that clearly should not be deemed responsible. But the criteria for such exclusion under specific deterrence differ somewhat from those under general deterrence. Rather than excluding just those activities that can reduce the given costs only at too great an expense, specific deterrence would also exclude activities collectively deemed so desirable that it would be pointless to call them responsible for accident costs.

For example, consider the aged man–young steelworker accident described earlier. The specific deterrence approach would probably exclude the airplane as a cause of the accident for reasons similar to those for which general deterrence would exclude it. No matter how much we regulated airplanes (or under general deterrence made airplanes bear such accident costs), automobile accidents would be affected very little. But unlike general deterrence, specific deterrence might also exclude driving by aged men as a cause of the accident if driving by aged men were collectively thought to be so desirable that it should not be regulated or curtailed in any way. The extent to which driving by aged men could pay its way if it had to pay some of the costs of the type of accident being considered (i.e. the desirability of the activity determined individualistically in the market), a key question under general deterrence, would be irrelevant under a pure specific deterrence approach.

Just as a relatively desirable activity would be likely to be excluded by the specific deterrence rough guess, an activity believed to be only slightly responsible for certain accident costs in a causal sense might not be excluded if it was otherwise deemed quite undesirable. Thus if airplanes were deemed relatively undesirable because Pullman cars, which they might render obsolete, are a great part of the American heritage, the fact that planes were occasionally noticed as distractions in automobile accidents might be taken into account more seriously in deciding whether and how to regulate them. Likewise, if airplanes were somehow considered immoral, their possible relation to automobile accidents (distant though it may be) would more likely be taken into account in regulating them. The undesirability and immorality would be collectively determined under specific deterrence, not based on a judgment as to the value the market would give to the activity.

The specific deterrence rough guess therefore involves striking a balance between the desirability of an activity and the effect regulating or curtailing the activity would have on the accident costs being considered, with the weights on both sides collectively determined. It should be clear that the more difficult it is to balance an activity's desirability against its relationship to given accident costs, the more the decision whether to exclude a particular activity is a hard choice rather than a rough guess. Actually, since specific deterrence decisions would not be made in a step-by-step fashion, the distinction between rough guess and hard case would not be likely to be made. I make the distinction only because it enables us to examine the differences and similarities between the specific and general deterrence approaches.

RELATIONSHIP BETWEEN AVOIDANCE AND ADMINISTRATIVE COSTS

Just as the general deterrence approach must consider how much it costs to reach an intelligent decision regarding whom to charge with the costs of certain accidents, so the specific deterrence approach must always be aware that more money may be spent in deciding whom to regulate than the effects of the regulation justify. The point is precisely the same for both approaches and need not be considered further except to note that a difficult (and therefore expensive) decision under general deterrence guidelines may be easy if specific deterrence criteria are considered as well. (Thus it may be very hard to decide under general deterrence guidelines between allocating automobile accident costs on a first- or third-party insurance basis. But consideration of collective criteria, such as the social desirability of driving by teen-agers, may make the choice easy.) And the reverse is equally true. Accordingly, a strong argument can be made solely on efficiency grounds for a mixed system of primary cost avoidance.

EXTERNALIZATION

The externalization of costs under general deterrence has close analogies under specific deterrence. We have already seen that attempts to prohibit or control a particular act or activity specifically may, in practice, result in decisions by individuals to forgo a broader activity.[3] If this is so, and if the broader activity is a desirable one (i.e. one that even a specific deterrence rough guess would exclude), the accident costs under consideration can probably be better reduced by regulation of another activity that "causes" them. In effect, this kind of externalization is analogous

3. Supra p. 110.

to the general deterrence externalization which would result from a practical inability to make accident costs affect a particular activity because it was not sufficiently organized so that it could be reached efficiently by market pressures. We want to avoid this kind of externalization of specific deterrence regulation, just as we want to avoid the similar externalization of costs under general deterrence.

Equally analogous to externalization of costs is the situation where a specific act or activity that is not excluded from regulation by the specific deterrence rough guess (i.e. one that bears some relationship to the accident costs under consideration and is not deemed so desirable as to require its exclusion) could be regulated, but only by enacting penalties which we refuse to enforce because we think them too harsh. It would be pointless to hold such an activity responsible for accident costs because the measures necessary to control it would not be taken. This is like the general deterrence case where the placing of accident costs on an activity causes such large secondary costs that externalization follows. In both cases, society could not tolerate the secondary effects necessary to bring about primary cost reduction by affecting that particular activity, and this externalization analysis would suggest that the activity was neither the cheapest nor the best cost avoider.

Of course, the specific deterrence choice is not really a step-by-step one, and this externalization situation could be viewed as very similar to the rough guess situation described in the preceding section, in which an activity is considered so desirable that it should not be burdened with *any* penalties, harsh or otherwise. Just as a balance must be struck between an activity's desirability and its relation to accident costs, so we must balance the apparent need to regulate an activity against the penalties necessary for its effective regulation. This does not weaken the analogy to general deterrence. It merely points out that specific deterrence decisions are more likely, because they are broader, to be made in one step which considers together all the factors that general deterrence might consider separately.

Both the examples of externalization just discussed involve externalization by transfer. Without going into the matter at length, it should be clear that externalization due to inadequate knowledge is also a danger under specific deterrence. Regulation of undesirable acts or activities will be ineffective if those who would engage in the regulated activities do not realize the regulation is aimed at them. Since, however, the penalty for engaging in the activity is more likely to be definite under specific deterrence than under general deterrence (where, without insurance, the "penalty," i.e. the accident costs, are unknown until after the accident),[4] the problem is likely to be less severe for specific deterrence. In effect, therefore, one aspect of inadequate knowledge—unknown costs—and the externalization attendant on it can be remedied more efficiently under specific deterrence than under general deterrence.

As we shall soon see, externalization by inadequate subcategorization unfortunately poses a greater problem for specific than for general deterrence. All this indicates a point crucial to all types of externalization: while externalization may occur under both specific and general deterrence, activities that cannot be charged with accident costs under the general deterrence approach because the costs would be externalized may nonetheless be successfully regulated, without externalization, through specific deterrence; conversely, activities that cannot be effectively regulated through specific deterrence may be charged with accident costs and reduced through general deterrence. In other words, while practical limitations exist for both approaches and while secondary effects under both approaches would preclude holding certain activities responsible, the practical difficulties and secondary effects caused by each approach do not necessarily impinge on the same activities. As a result, a mixed system which used both specific and general deterrence approaches would probably be able to reach more acts or activities than either general or specific deterrence could reach

---

4. Insurance under general deterrence may bring externalization by transfer instead, if the activity is not one whose accident costs can be insured against separately. See infra pp. 246–49.

alone. For this very practical reason, as well as the more theoretical ones already discussed, any system of accident law is likely to seek primary cost reduction through use of both specific and general deterrence.

SUBCATEGORIZATION AND TRANSACTIONS

I have mentioned that the choice of what-is-a-cost-of-what may in some ways be more difficult under specific deterrence than under general deterrence because some general deterrence guidelines for choosing among activities are not useful under specific deterrence. These are guidelines that relate to some types of externalization by insufficient subcategorization and to charging the best briber. The reason they are not useful is quite simple: they are guidelines designed for aiding the market, and pure specific deterrence rejects market evaluations and market means of effectuating the choices it makes.

Regulation or prohibition of the most narrowly defined act or activity (the smallest subcategory) responsible for accident costs is as desirable for specific deterrence as allocation of costs to the smallest subcategory is for general deterrence. It is obviously better, for instance, to bar drunken driving (the subcategory) than to bar all driving (the category) if drunken driving is responsible for all or even most automobile accidents. But while under general deterrence we can simply put the costs of accidents on the smallest practical subcategories, confident that the market will properly allocate the costs among the subcategories and the category according to ease of avoidance, we can do no such thing under specific deterrence. When we decide to bar an act or activity under specific deterrence, we do not significantly affect the broader category of which it is a part. And since we do not, our choice to bar a subcategory implies a collective decision that the accident costs involved are best avoided by barring *that* particular subcategory rather than another subcategory or the category of which both are a part. In other words, a specific deterrence decision to bar a subcategory implies an exact decision as to which act or activity can best avoid the accident costs. By contrast, under general deterrence, the placing of costs on the smallest subcategory of an activity involved in an accident is simply a device for letting the market allocate the costs properly among the category and its sub-categories. Accordingly, no difficult what-is-a-cost-of-what decision is needed.

For example, if having decided under general deterrence that automobile accidents are a cost of driving, we place the costs of an accident on the 33-year-old driver who was involved in it, no harm will be done if 33-year-old drivers (the subcategory) are in fact involved in no more accidents than other drivers. In other accidents other age drivers (other subcategories) will be burdened, and the effect of our allocation, at least over time, will be to put pressure on all drivers (the category of which 33-year-old drivers are a part). If, instead, 33-year-old drivers *are* involved in more accidents than other age drivers, to that extent a greater portion of the cost burden will remain on them and only a smaller por-tion will burden driving generally. But under specific deterrence, we must decide collectively whether 33-year-old drivers should be restricted because of their accident-cost proneness. And if we de-cide that they should and it turns out that 33-year-olds are no more accident prone than other age drivers, we will have made the wrong choice with harmful consequences. There will be fewer 33-year-old drivers on the road but at least as many equally acci-dent-cost prone drivers of other ages as before. We will have re-stricted the subcategory when actually the restriction, if desired, should have been at the category level. And it would take another collective decision to correct our error.

I am not, of course, suggesting that because general deterrence is free from this problem it is necessarily superior to specific deter-rence. It avoids the problem because it relies on the market, and the market has its limitations as well as advantages (e.g. it can only handle money costs). I am only saying that there are some decisions that need not be made under general deterrence because of its reliance on the market, and these decisions, which must be made collectively under specific deterrence, involve the hard choice of whom to hold responsible for accident costs.[5]

The same reasons that limit the usefulness of subcategorization for specific deterrence preclude reliance on transactions and bargains under pure specific deterrence. These transactions work through the market to seek out the cheapest cost avoider. To the extent that specific deterrence rejects the market in controlling the best cost avoiders, it is barred from benefiting from the existence or the possible creation of bargaining relationships designed to lessen accident costs. This does not mean that the market will have no effect under specific deterrence. It only means that if the specific deterrence collective decision was in fact the one that was collectively desired, any market effect must be a deviation from what was originally desired and therefore bad *ex hypothesis.*

By and large a decision to bar or restrict an act or activity and to penalize it heavily whenever it occurs cannot be modified by the existence of actual or potential bargaining relationships. Bargaining or similar transactions can cause other activities to be affected (e.g. by increasing the demand for substitutes), and the specific deterrence deciders must take this into account. But even where bargaining relationships exist or can be entered into cheaply, an activity subject to this kind of penalty will not normally have any incentive to seek out the cheapest cost avoider.

Once we decide, for instance, that rotary lawn mowers will be forbidden, no market modification will result even if most mower accidents could be avoided by selling mowers only to users who

---

5. In a mixed system, we are likely to see the use of general deterrence subcategorization precisely in the areas where we are least confident as to the accuracy of a specific deterrence hard choice among a category and its subcategories.

Specific deterrence penalization by accident involvement might have an effect analogous to that of general deterrence subcategorization, assuming that each subcategory's members would become aware of the subcategory's accident involvement record and that the penalty did not carry much .stigma. See supra pp. 123–24.

will wear boots. The mower companies would have nothing to gain by offering a discount to booted users or by offering boots to buyers. They would still be barred from selling rotary mowers. All they can do is try to show the collective deciders that the specific deterrence decision was wrong. For this purpose the continued existence and spread of mower accidents involving unbooted users and nonrotary mowers may actually help! But the fact that under general deterrence mower companies could—and would—exert a cost pressure for wearing boots will be irrelevant. The hard choice decision to forbid rotary mowers rather than to require boots will have already been made collectively. If it was correct, fine, but if it was wrong it can only be corrected by another collective decision. There is an enormous difference between this and the placing of accident costs on either the users or the sellers of all mowers and letting the market decide whether altering mowers or wearing boots is the best way to avoid mower accidents. It is, in fact, the difference between pure specific deterrence and pure general deterrence.

When less than pure specific deterrence is used and devices like limitations or penalties assessed on an accident involvement basis are employed, some modification of the specific deterrence decision may result through transactions. If, for example, it was decided to affect the use of rotary mowers by penalizing mower manufacturers every time a rotary mower was involved in an accident, the sellers of rotary mowers might risk selling to booted users if they were sure enough that selling only to them avoided accidents. They might even sell to unbooted users (at a substantially higher price) if the differential made the price high enough to justify the risk of fine, jail, water torture, or whatever the penalty was.[6]

Even where some such modification did occur, however, the decision about who should bear the risk of the penalty if an accident occurs would not be made on the basis of market guidelines, such as best briber, used in general deterrence. Those guidelines

6. See supra pp. 118–19.

were based on the assumption that *except for reducing accident costs,* we did not care who bore the loss of accidents and made no moral judgment among the parties. The guidelines were therefore designed to help the parties to minimize accident costs and maximize information and choices—to foster, in short, shifting of losses to the *cheapest* cost avoider.

But this assumption is the opposite of the assumption made by specific deterrence. Specific deterrence seeks to hold responsible not the acts or activities that would reduce accident costs most cheaply in terms of market valuations, but those that would do so best in terms of some collective valuation of nonmarket variables as well. As a result, any free market shifting that ultimately placed the loss on the cheapest cost avoider would tend to run counter to the specific deterrence aim, and so would guidelines designed to aid such shifting.[7]

Specific deterrence cannot always avoid such shifting. At times great shifting is inevitable, and some shifting will almost always occur. The best that can be done from the standpoint of specific deterrence is to consider, in making a collective decision to penalize an activity, that the result may be to put pressure on another activity as well. But the best briber guidelines are of no use under specific deterrence, since they would only be relevant if we wanted the market to find the cheapest cost avoider, and *ex hypothesis* we do not. It follows that the more we use specific deterrence, the more

---

7. If we decide collectively that speeding should be limited in some way because of its accident propensity and its general undesirability, we will not welcome a market effect that—through bargaining—causes our specific deterrence limitations on speeding to be shifted from speeders to cars made in a certain way. This might occur (1) if speeders were usually caught only if they were involved in accidents; (2) if many people wished to speed; and (3) if cars made differently had very few accidents due to speed. Such an effect would simply show that in market terms, cars made differently could avoid those costs more cheaply than a change in driving speed could. But the collective decision presumably meant that regardless of this fact, it was *speeding* we wanted controlled because collectively we thought it was the *best* avoider, even if changing the construction of automobiles were, in some purely monetary and market sense, a cheaper way of avoiding accidents.

it is inevitable that the decision as to who should be penalized must be a hard choice decision, since to use the market guidelines would be to admit that the decision should be made in individualistic, market terms and not on the basis of our collective decision. It would, in short, be an admission that we wanted general and not specific deterrence.

THE HARD CASE

The specific deterrence hard choice is, as I have suggested, very much like the specific deterrence rough guess. A balance must be struck between collective judgments of an activity's desirability and the effect that barring or restricting that activity would have on accidents. In striking this balance, we must take into account whether a decision to restrict the activity would be externalized (i.e. whether it would merely result in discouragement of a broader activity), and whether the sanctions necessary to impose restrictions on the activity are acceptable. Because the activities that clearly should not be held responsible for accidents will have been ruled out in the earlier rough guess and externalization judgments, the hard case will be more difficult than the earlier decisions. And as we have seen, the possibility of transactions does not make the hard case decision easier under the pure specific deterrence approach.

What devices can collective deciders employ to decide which acts or activities should be barred because of their accident costs?[8] There are three relatively pure collective ways: trial and error, the use of actuarial science, and what I call "sheer politics." There is also a fourth way, which deviates from pure specific deterrence; it is to make a decision, enforce it through impure specific deterrence devices such as limitations and involvement penalties, and then revise the collective decision on the basis of the data that is made

8. A currently popular way of approaching collective decisions is through the analytical framework known as systems analysis. An interesting application of this approach to accidents indicating the difficulties which are involved is David M. Boodman, "Safety and Systems Analysis, With Applications to Traffic Safety," 33 *L. & Cont. Probs.* 488 (1968).

available by watching how people react in the market to the limitation or involvement penalties.

The first two of these devices can never, by themselves, be ways of evaluating an activity's overall desirability. They are principally ways of determining the activity's causal relationship to accident costs, a factor that under specific deterrence must be balanced collectively against the activity's desirability, aside from accidents, in determining the appropriate degree of control. Political reactions to a temporary prohibition or market reactions to impure enforcement devices may, however, give significant indications of the mass of people's notions of the desirability of the activity, either in a market or a nonmarket sense. Evaluation of the activity's *overall* desirability, however, because it involves countless variables such as society's estimation of the moral worth of the activity, must be made through some rough counting of votes and influence, that is, through the political process.

Determination of the relationship an activity or act bears to accident costs must always be made empirically, whether by individuals under general deterrence or by collective deciders under specific deterrence. In either case, those who are attempting to make such a determination will make use of two closely related but distinguishable empirical methods: trial and error, and actuarial science. Under general deterrence we do not usually worry much about how the determination is made by individuals or how accurate it is unless an incorrect determination causes externalization or too great secondary costs. The assumption is that leaving these other considerations aside, those individuals who make the determination most accurately will benefit most in the market, while those who err will learn from their mistakes, and that over time this will be sufficient incentive for accurate determinations. This is, in fact, the great advantage of the market; it is often a very effective trial-and-error device. But when the determination is made collectively it must be accurate, for an activity collectively deemed responsible for accidents will immediately be affected, and if the collective deciders make a mistake, it will not be corrected unless another, more accurate collective determination is made.

The types of trial and error that can be used under specific deterrence are of course far too numerous to discuss here. They range from narrow, laboratory-type experimentation to broad experiments affecting the behavior of the entire population. In theory, any type of trial and error used by individuals under general deterrence can also be utilized in a collective decision. Even in practice, trial and error under the two approaches is likely to be quite similar in the preliminary gathering of information. There will be substantial differences between the two approaches, however, when an accident cost reduction device, which looks good in preliminary testing, is tried in the field. When an individual under general deterrence puts an accident reduction device into practice, he does so only for himself, and he (and all others engaged in the same or a similar activity) can compare his results with those of others who use different devices. But when collective decision-makers judge a way of reducing accident costs good enough to try in practice, they are likely to try it on a large scale. The problems involved in putting the device into practice for just one part of the country and comparing the accident records there with the accident records elsewhere would be considerable, if for no other reason than that we tend to reject wholesale collective experiments where human life is at stake.[9]

Such trial and error in the field, moreover, would not occur automatically, as it would under general deterrence. For example, if preliminary testing led one rotary mower manufacturer to believe that installation of a guard might be an effective device for reducing accident costs, under general deterrence he would install the guard on all his mowers, or he would offer the guard as an option. If the guard saved more in accident costs than it cost to install, this would become evident, at least in theory, through the market process of trial and error. Collective deciders under specific deterrence could run the same preliminary tests with mower

9. See Calabresi, "Reflections on Medical Experimentation in Humans."

guards, but their decision to try the guards would not end the matter. They would have to decide whether to compel guards on all mowers, or just on mowers in a certain geographical area, etc. They would have to keep track of the accident records of all mowers with and without guards and then decide whether the reduction in accident costs when guards were used was sufficient to justify making them compulsory.

While a single experiment in the field such as the one just outlined would certainly be feasible, and while some trial and error under specific deterrence is obviously necessary, the possible ways of reducing accident costs are innumerable, and *collective* trial and error even for the majority of them would be impossible. In contrast, under general deterrence the market could evaluate countless accident reduction devices through constant trial and error.[10]

A second significant way of determining the relationship of acts and activities to accident costs is the use of actuarial science. Through the evaluation of statistics on accident involvement the extent to which an activity is involved in accidents more than it should may be ascertained.[11] No attempt need be made to isolate causes in any particular accident; we only need to note which factors are present to a greater degree than we would statistically expect when a given type of accident with a given type of damage occurs.

Such statistics can be helpful, however, only to the extent that we subcategorize when gathering the information. For example, if the proportion of small cars involved in accidents to small cars on the road is much less than the proportion of large cars involved in accidents to large cars on the road, actuarial science will reflect

10. Some experiments require the participation of the unwilling in order to be meaningful, and here direct governmental specific deterrence may be more efficient than the general deterrence approach buttressed by governmental compulsion.

11. "Involved" has a broader meaning here than elsewhere in this book. We could, roughly speaking, evaluate statistics for every variable of every accident, or, more likely, for all factors not excluded by the rough guess. See supra pp. 140–43, 176–78.

this only if in compiling the statistics we distinguish between large and small cars. And since a simple subcategorization between large and small may be misleading (perhaps the increase in accident involvement only occurs with extra-large Juggernaut cars and they should be in a subcategory of their own), we are once again best off if we subcategorize to the greatest possible extent within the limits imposed by the costs of subcategorization.

The fact that our actuarial statistics are only as good as our subcategorization has another important consequence. Actuarial information on an activity or subcategory which is inherently vague will be correspondingly imprecise. It would be impossible, for example, to compile actuarial statistics on the extent to which faulty conduct results in accidents because of the problems involved in gathering information on the incidence of faulty conduct in the population. Even if it were possible to define "fault" specifically enough to determine whether faulty conduct was involved in any accident situation, the incidence of faulty conduct *not* resulting in accidents could not be measured.

In a system of accident law that mixes the general and specific deterrence approaches, actuarial science can be especially useful in evaluating the trial and error that occurs in the market. Thus if we are confident that individuals are confronted with sufficiently high accident costs to encourage them to seek ways or devices for avoiding these costs but are not so sure that even the most effective devices will survive in the market, we may gather statistical information on the effectiveness of various devices tried through private initiative and then compel use of the device our statistics tell us is most effective (provided, of course, that the device is not unacceptable for reasons not related to accident cost reduction).

The third way of choosing among acts and activities I call "sheer politics." Sheer politics can be used to guess at the accident-proneness of various activities and is so used surprisingly often. But even if we have determined an activity's causal relationship to accidents through trial and error or actuarial science, there must be something of sheer politics in our judgment as to its overall desirability. While we can also use trial and error and even statistics to tell us something about the desirability of an activity in the market, or even the political desirability to an individual, this cannot suffice for specific deterrence. True specific deterrence requires collective desirability, and ultimately there is no way of evaluating the extent to which the body politic collectively desires a certain activity other than through political decisions, which may use market data on desirability but are not bound by it.[12]

Furthermore, the significance of market desirability in deciding overall desirability and the significance of expert evaluations of an activity's accident-proneness in determining its total desirability must be decided politically. One cannot compare expert or actuarial evidence on market worth and accident-proneness with collective judgments on moral worth in any other way. Thus there will be many instances in which the specific deterrence decision, like many of our decisions dealing with problems other than accidents, will be made politically in a way that ignores the experts even if their evaluations are relatively accurate. In other words, specific deterrence decisions, like all other collective decisions, will be greatly influenced by the political process of the society for which they are made.

MARKET MODIFICATIONS AND THE SPECIFIC DETERRENCE HARD CHOICE

One further general point relating to what-is-a-cost-of-what decisions under specific deterrence needs to be emphasized. Since individuals will react in the market as best they can to minimize

12. Dictatorships may ignore collective desires of the general public in their specific deterrence decision-making, but they may also be interested in ascertaining public views for the sake of order, contentment, and efficiency. Both the Soviet and Yugoslav governments have used sociological research and polls to discover what their people want in various fields. Such methods are imperfect but logical tools in such societies because their markets may not reflect people's desires to the degree markets in a free enterprise system do; moreover, public involvement in the decision-making through election of officials who have committed themselves to the decisions desired by the public is excluded by the very nature of dictatorships.

whatever burden is placed on them as a result of specific deterrence decisions, a specific deterrence decision to affect one or more activities will in all probability affect other activities. This will happen even if an activity is effectively forbidden, because substitute and complementary activities will be affected. It will happen in more ways when an activity, while not forbidden altogether, is limited through monetary or other burdens, because then the possibility of shifting part of the burden to other activities exists. It will happen even more dramatically whenever a penalty is imposed on an accident involvement basis or on any other basis that does not result in assessment of the penalty each time the proscribed act occurs, for then the shifting will occur specifically as a means of avoiding being caught and penalized. The shifting in this last case will result in avoidance of accidents if that is what results in being caught and in the penalty being imposed. If some other event such as being "squealed on" triggers the penalty, then avoidance of that event, rather than of accidents, will result.

All this means that in deciding whether to hold an act or activity responsible as the best accident avoider, the collective deciders must consider the effects their decision will have not only on that act or activity but also on other activities that will be affected through market-type reactions to the decision. They must also consider how much pressure will remain on the act or activity they originally sought to control after these market-type reactions have occurred.

Such questions are by and large empirical. Needless to say, they do not make the specific deterrence hard choice any easier, for they imply that the choice must consider not only which acts or activities should be controlled in view of their accident costs and which devices for controlling these activities are most desirable (e.g. torture is not acceptable, especially if we are not 100 percent sure that we want to forbid the particular activity), but also which control devices will bring about that combination of market reactions which we collectively desire. In other words, since the control devices chosen will in practice influence which activities are affected (besides the ones initially held responsible), the choice of activities we wish to control through specific deterrence also implies a difficult choice among control devices, and vice versa.

The significance of this relationship can be seen by considering the complex effect of two attitudes we probably all have toward specific deterrence controls. First, the more we believe (for both accident and other reasons) that the activity we are trying to prohibit is undesirable, the more likely we are to use harsh penalties to enforce our decision. Thus a balance must be struck between the desirability of the activity under consideration and the desirability of the practical means available for regulating it. As less harsh penalties are used, people will take a chance more frequently and engage in the prohibited activity, and the effect of the penalty on activities other than the one we wish to control will become more complex. In other words, as less severe penalties are used, more market-type modifications of the original specific deterrence judgment are inevitable. This necessarily means less pure specific deterrence.

Second, as we have already seen, we are more likely to want to bar narrowly defined activities than broad ones, i.e. rather than prohibiting activities we are more likely to want to *restrict* them by barring subcategories. But as we define activities more closely and prohibition seems more desirable, it becomes both more difficult to detect the occurrence of the act or activity and more difficult for people to control their behavior so as to avoid doing it.

These last two factors make pure specific deterrence difficult. The first increases the chance that people will not be caught and hence increases the market-type modifications of the prohibition. The tendency will be to avoid doing the act in ways that result in getting caught, rather than to avoid doing the act. The second makes pure specific deterrence difficult because the harder it is for people to avoid doing the act or activity we have barred, the less

effective our attempt to bar it will be, and the less comfortable we
will feel in imposing grave penalties when the proscribed act or
activity does take place. Indeed, the main effect of grave penalties
in such cases would be to induce people to avoid broader activities
that could result in the proscribed act or subactivity occurring. This
in effect is a market modification of our collective decision to affect
an activity into a decision affecting a broader activity instead.

The role of the market under specific deterrence and its effect
on those who would make collective decisions is even more complicated, moreover, than these two examples seem to suggest. This
is because of the residue of general deterrence which, as we have
already seen, is bound to remain even under a pure specific deterrence approach. I mentioned earlier that specific deterrence
would not avoid all accident costs and that those accident costs
that were not avoided would cause some general deterrence effects
If they are left on the victims, there will be a market movement
away from those activities which tend to be the principal sources
of victims. If they are allocated to other activities, these activities
will react in the market by trying to minimize the burden imposed
on them.

The collective deciders can react in several ways. First, they can
try to allocate the remaining accident costs to those acts or activities (involved in accidents) which they deem undesirable. The size
and preaccident uncertainty of accident costs, however, would
probably make this move counterproductive, at least if the intention was to deter narrow activities or acts.[13] The full extent of the

13. It would be counterproductive because the practice of allocating acci
dent costs to narrow activities or acts after the accident will usually only
serve to deter broader activities. If people insure against postaccident-cos
bearing, the insurance categories are not likely to be so narrow that the
insurance premium will attach the cost to the narrow act or activity sought to
be deterred. If people are forbidden from insuring, the unpredictable nature
of the costs and the danger that they may be enormous is likely to cause peo
ple to abstain from a broader activity if they are deterred at all. For example
people might substantially reduce the amount they drive if they could no
insure against the damages they might cause by some semicontrollable wrongfu
act (such as speeding) which might occur if they drove. This once again deter

difficulty and undesirability of this allocation will be seen most clearly later, when the fault system is examined directly. Here it is enough to say that such an allocation implies an unhappy and expensive compromise between general and specific deterrence.

Second, the collective deciders can allocate the remaining costs according to general deterrence standards. This means using a particular type of mixed system in which specific deterrence sanctions are applied up to a point beyond which accident cost deterrence is left up to purely market methods even if this results in modification of the original specific deterrence goal. This may not be a bad system, but it suggests a lack of certainty with the original collective decisions which may cast some doubt on the specific deterrence measures already taken.[14]

Third, the collective deciders can seek to neutralize the remaining costs through externalization. This requires further discussion. If the collective deciders are convinced that the mix of accident costs and activities achieved through the specific deterrence penalties they imposed is as close to what they want as possible, they will want to counteract any market effects coming from those accident costs that still occur. They may do this by placing such costs on activities that will not be affected (changed) by bearing these costs, either because they have no substitutes or because these costs represent so small a burden on these activities as to be negligible. A search for such activities may be limited to the parties involved in the accident or may go beyond them.

The first of these measures implies finding as the best loss bearer the very opposite of the general deterrence optimal loss bearer. If pedestrianism is thought to be fixed, those accident costs which still occur (after all specific deterrence penalties have been assessed

_____

broad activity rather than the narrow one sought to be deterred. (Cf. supra pp. 109–10.) General deterrence has analogous difficulties in reaching narrow acts, see supra pp. 103–05.

14. It would seem more efficient to reverse the process: let the market work to whatever extent thought necessary or desirable, and then modify the results collectively.

on "bad" cars and "bad" drivers) would be left on or shifted to pedestrians. This allocation, though fine from a specific deterrence standpoint, might be catastrophic in terms of secondary cost avoidance.

The second, going beyond the parties involved, implies direct externalization. Victims would be compensated, penalties would be levied, and costs would be shifted to an "inert" third party.[15] In practice, this would probably be the government. Accident costs would be externalized and met out of general taxes. The assumption would be that by meeting these costs through general taxation, the smallest effect on people's behavior that is consistent with our notions of justice and spreading could be achieved. Whether the taxes levied would maximize spreading or employ some form of deep pocket device would of course depend on more general societal goals.

These ways of handling the general deterrence residue by externalization have one fact in common: they require an allocation of accident costs by criteria unrelated to accident-proneness. Accident-proneness would, of course, be relevant to the specific deterrence penalties previously imposed. But as far as allocation of accident costs were concerned, maximum inertness consistent with spreading and justice would be the key factor because any additional effects on behavior would alter the result already judged most desirable.[16] No matter who bears these costs, however, the "danger" (in this context it is a danger) of transactions and bribes to minimize the size of these costs would exist nonetheless. It

15. An inert party is one whose behavior will be substantially unaffected regardless of whether accident costs are allocated to it. Allocation of costs to such a party minimizes the market deviations from the specific deterrence optimum resulting from the residue of unavoided accident costs.

16. I have assumed we want inertness. Theoretically, though, these taxes could be placed on any activities we wished to discourage, including one totally unrelated to accidents, such as prostitution. But it would seem that measures to discourage such activities should take place regardless of whether there are residue costs to be paid.

would exist even if the government bore the costs.[17] As a result, externalization would almost inevitably involve a prohibition of any transactions designed to lessen accident costs. And this in turn brings us back to the general problem of market modifications of specific deterrence decisions. Once again, the effectiveness of these prohibitions will depend on the penalties chosen to enforce them. And, in deciding what they want regulated, the collective deciders will be forced to make accompanying decisions on how they plan to effectuate the regulation.

17. Whoever bore the costs would presumably attempt to reduce accident costs in whatever way he could, regardless of the prior collective decision as to which accident avoidance measures are desirable. This kind of attempt to override the specific deterrence decision might even be made by a government agency made to bear the residue costs when there was a lack of coordination in the government's efforts to achieve society's goals; such lack of coordination is, of course, far from unknown.

CHAPTER 9

What Is the Cost?

Since any system of primary accident cost reduction is ultimately a system for determining the desired level of accident costs—i.e. how much we want to limit or restrict otherwise desirable activities because of the accident costs they cause—any system of primary accident cost reduction must face not only the question of which acts or activities "cause" accident costs but also the double-edged question of what value to give to the accident costs they cause and who in our society should be empowered to make that determination.

Actually, the same questions must also be faced, though somewhat differently, by systems of spreading or secondary cost reduction. To the extent that we wish to spread *all* costs of accidents, we must decide the value to be spread. To the extent we wish to spread only part, we cannot avoid deciding who should bear the remaining part and what its value is; shifting a part involves first valuing it. Leaving it on the injured party implies the decision that he should bear it and implies giving it the value the injured party and others similarly situated give to the injury. Since this question is posed most dramatically when primary cost avoidance is involved, however, I shall discuss it principally in terms of different approaches to primary cost avoidance.

The question of which acts or activities "cause" which accident costs, discussed in Chapters 7 and 8, I call what-is-a-cost-of-what; the second question, what value to give to accident costs, I call what-is-the-cost. While this second question must be posed to any system of primary accident cost reduction and therefore for specific no less than for general deterrence, the form the question takes and the answers to it will differ depending on which approach is taken and how closely we wish, or are able, to stick to either of the pure approaches. Accordingly, I will discuss separately how the question would be approached under each method.

THE GENERAL DETERRENCE APPROACH

The aim of general deterrence is to let individuals acting through the marketplace decide which acts or activities to forgo because of the accident costs they cause. As noted earlier, the ideal general deterrence solution to the what-is-the-cost question would be to have a market in accident victims. If people were willing to offer their persons and properties to be injured or destroyed for a price, we would have a pure market determination of the value of accident costs. Such a market does not, of course, exist in any meaningful sense. There is, to be sure, a "demand" for accident victims. Different activities are willing to compensate victims instead of introducing more expensive safety measures or reducing the extent of the activity. But as we have seen in our earlier discussion, there is no proper supply side to the accident market, and without this no pure market valuation of accident costs can be made.

As a result, some nonmarket valuation of accident costs is necessary even under a general deterrence approach. General deterrence will not, however, approach this problem of collective valuation in the same way specific deterrence would. The aim of general deterrence will be to value accident costs in a way that is as near to the market way as possible; collective decisions under general deterrence will therefore take account of individual valuations as much as possible. Such decisions will make as much use as possible of the limited supply side of accident victims that does exist, but they will attempt to cure that supply side of the undervaluations which seem to inhere in it. Similarly, general deterrence cost valuations will rely on what market valuations exist elsewhere (especially where property is involved) to give a value where no market valuations are available.

Above all, such valuations will seek to decide the value of the costs independently of what caused them. In other words, they will leave to the market, as much as possible, determination of the desirability of the activities causing accident costs and will not, simply because no adequate supply side of accident victims exists, seek to determine the amount of the demand.[1] In short, once the question of what different injuries are worth is resolved independently of what caused them, the decisions for or against accidents and for or against accident-cost causing activities would be left to the market.

The uncertainty inherent in this process should be obvious. We should not be surprised, therefore, if even in societies committed mainly to a general deterrence approach the result of the process occasionally proves to be collectively undesirable. In such cases, collective decisions to encourage or bar activities despite the market are likely. Such *ex post* modifications of market results on the basis of collective judgments, however, differ substantially from *ex ante* collective determinations of which activities we want and how we want them engaged in, and even from collective determinations of what value to give to injuries in terms of which activities caused them and hence in terms of which activities are collectively desirable. There is still a difference, in short, between even a highly modified general deterrence approach and various specific deterrence approaches, though at some point, if each approach is sufficiently modified, the distinction will not be worth making.

Since the problem of determining what-is-the-cost under general deterrence is very different for damage to things that have a clearly ascertainable market value and damage to those that do not, I shall discuss them separately, dealing first with damage to things that have a market value, then with physical injuries, and then with pain and suffering and injuries to what we term "sentimental"

1. The fact that the costs must be collectively determined under general deterrence does not mean that the levels of the activities which will be demanded are also being determined collectively. The level of the activity will be determined by individual reactions to the prices charged as a result of the costs the activity is made to bear. And individual reactions and desires are quite likely to vary even when the collectively determined accident costs remain the same.

or even "fanciful" interests. I shall then briefly consider the problems involved in valuing administrative costs, and finally deal with how the presence of possible transactions may alter our determinations of what-is-the-cost.

Objects with a Market Value

The easiest general deterrence cost valuation deals with damage to those objects that have a fairly definite market value. Generally speaking, this is the area of property damage. Since cars are bought and sold on the open market, the lack of a supply of cars to be given as "victims" of accidents does not especially bother us, for we can be fairly confident of our ability to extrapolate from the value given to cars in market transactions to their value in accident situations. And so it is whenever we deal with property that is not in some sense unique.

The object of general deterrence valuation of costs is to arrive at a close approximation of the value the market would give to the damaged object. The value the market gives to the destroyed object in a free buy-and-sell transaction and the value the market gives to repair of damage are usually adequate for this purpose. There may be some specific situations where this will not work well, and I shall discuss these later. Since our concern under general deterrence is not with compensating the owner but rather with reaching correct market decisions as to what accident-cost causing activities we want, specific instances of incorrect valuation will be unimportant. What matters is that the value given to the accident cost—to the damaged object—is, on the average, the value individuals in the free market would assign to it.[2]

---

2. Since the concern is not with compensation, individual instances of overvaluation and undervaluation of costs will not matter so long as the average valuation has the proper overall deterrent effect. This would seem likely if potential injurers and victims see that cost valuations are on the average correct and assume that on the average they will be paid or made to bear the correct losses. But in reality, it is not necessarily true that cost valuations that are, on average, correct will have the proper deterrent effect, because the use of averages entails a risk factor for each potential cost bearer.

If more information is needed, data derived from bargaining situations can be used. The psychological reasons which make people incapable of properly evaluating the risk of injury to themselves probably count much less with respect to property damage. The more something has a market equivalent, the more we can rationally contemplate its destruction. Furthermore, when property is involved, the damaged object is likely to have a constant value in bargains, regardless of the risk of damage to it. The results of free bargains based on risk of damage to objects would still not be an infallible guide because of such factors as lack of information on risk. But if all the parties could be made aware of the statistical risk figures involved, there would be little reason to doubt the bargaining results on psychological grounds except to the extent that in practice, risk of damage to objects often cannot be separated from risk of personal injury. It would be difficult to isolate the values given on the bargaining market to things which bear risk of damage from the values attached to the risk of personal injuries arrived at in the same bargains. It is worthwhile mentioning the theoretical use of bargaining values, however, because it is the very fact that the objects *have* a market equivalent which tends to protect such bargaining valuations from underestimation due to psychological attitudes. In effect, therefore, we are justified in returning to the initial premise that the value such objects have in the market is a fair indication of their value if damaged or destroyed in an accident.

Assuming that we seek to extrapolate property damage costs from market values, the question remains: should these valuations be made on a case-by-case basis or through schedules of damages? From the standpoint of general deterrence, the question is simply one of expediency. Is the added accuracy gained by examining the

---

Any individual might bear more or less than the appropriate cost. This risk may attract gamblers to the activity but repel the cautious, and if we do not have a balance between both types, the use of averages will influence the deterrence result in an improper way.

specific accident worth the added cost of doing so? Where it is, the use of individual valuations, allowing evidence of special market analogies, would be worthwhile. Where it is not, scheduled damages derived from current market valuations of similar objects (by classes) would be preferable. It would be essential that these schedules be kept up to date, since one of the most important possible reasons for greater accuracy of case-by-case determinations is the tendency for schedules to lag behind price changes. Out-of-date schedules cause poor damage valuations in the aggregate, not just in particular cases. And this, as we have seen, is crucial since the aim of general deterrence is not proper compensation of particular victims but proper valuation of categories of accident costs so that proper market decisions can be made with respect to accident-causing activities. Thus individual misvaluations are of relatively little importance, so long as on the average the costs are properly estimated, but general misvaluations, such as would be caused by out-of-date schedules, would be serious.

I have indicated that damage to objects with market value coincides with property damage. This is not fully true. A physical injury that has no sequelae, causes no pain and suffering, and results only in a forced vacation can be given a pretty good market valuation. Conversely, damage to some property interests may involve difficulties in market valuation.

Some of these difficulties are purely technical: how does one get an adequate market valuation for used underwear? Such technical problems, where uniqueness is simply a product of use, need not detain us, as we can extrapolate pretty closely from the marketable (new underwear) to the unique (used underwear) by means of depreciation figures.

Other difficulties may stem from individual attachments to specific items of property. To put it differently, extrapolation from values of things on the market to values of things damaged may not be accurate simply because the latter would not be sold by their owner at the market price. They are in some sense worth more to him than they are on the market. Our society does not attach much importance to this fact. We do not, for instance, take it into account in eminent domain valuations. It is not irrelevant, however, and it gives rise to an important specific deterrence type of limitation on our use of market valuations. It is, in fact, the reason why we do not allow *intentional* damage to property unless the equivalent of an eminent domain public purpose is shown.

In the law of nuisance, for instance, this takes the form of balancing the equities to decide whether an injunction (a relatively pure specific deterrence remedy) or damages (a general deterrence control) will be used.[3] Similarly, we forbid some activities that are statistically likely to cause property damage because they are "useless," even though those who would like to engage in them would be willing to pay damages. Both of these policies, like the public purpose requirement in eminent domain, reflect our inability to value with complete accuracy property that has not been placed on the market. The fact, however, that individual attachments to property are often ignored as fanciful or sentimental values suggests that where an act or activity which injures property meets certain minimal standards of usefulness and where the property damaged is not especially unique, we believe extrapolation from things on the market to equivalent things not on the market is sufficiently accurate. Indeed, it suggests a judgment that any attempt to take such fanciful values into account would be either too expensive to be worth its cost or more likely to distort the choice for or against accidents than ignoring these values would.[4]

Finally, some difficulties in property damage valuation result from the fact that some types of property are generally accepted as

3. If torts is difficult to define precisely, see supra note 14, Chapter 1, that branch of torts known as nuisance is even harder. As I use the term here, it refers to causes of action arising from damage, usually to property, caused by an activity not in itself illegal, where the harm is sufficiently repetitive to support the assumption that it will continue if it is not enjoined. A classic example would be noxious fumes from a factory rendering the neighboring houses uninhabitable.

4. The effect of ignoring them is to allocate the burden to the victims—which may well be desirable for the reasons given, infra pp. 214–15, 221–25.

unique. The difference between the damaged object and similar objects on the market is simply too great to trust any extrapolation. The problems in such situations obviously cannot be properly discussed in this section. They are, instead, closely analogous to the problems that arise when we discuss physical injuries generally, particularly to the problems of pain and suffering.

Physical Injuries

The problem of finding an adequate general deterrence valuation for physical injuries is a complex one. There are, to be sure, elements in most physical injury situations that can be valued reasonably well by extrapolating from market values determined in noninjury situations, e.g. working hours lost. There are also elements that can be valued in a market way because they can be satisfactorily repaired. And the costs of repairs (such as medical expenses and retraining expenses[5]) are, on the whole, pretty good market indications of their minimum value. Once again, from a general deterrence standpoint the importance of these valuations is not that they compensate the victim (indeed, the what-is-a-cost-of-what decision might leave some of the costs on the victim), but that on the average they reflect an accurate market valuation of that part of the cost of accidents which they represent, and hence can be the basis for market decisions for or against accident-causing activities. Here too, then, individual misvaluations are not too important as long as on the average the valuations do represent the cost of these injuries to society.[6]

Virtually all physical injury situations, however, also include elements for which there is no ready market value. One such element is pain and suffering; another is the "loss of dignity" caused

5. Conard, "Automobile Injuries," discusses the importance of such rehabilitative services and the extent to which they are presently available to most accident victims. See especially id. at 294–98.

6. Cost valuations which are on the average correct do not foreclose misvaluations in individual instances, and hence entail a risk factor. See supra note 2. And, of course, instances of individual misvaluations may give rise to secondary cost problems.

by such things as a scar or missing limb, even where the loss involves no physical pain. Similar problems are involved in attempting to value a life that is lost. If a fully appropriate general deterrence market judgment for or against accidents is to be made, these elements must be valued in some way regardless of whether or not part of the loss is ultimately left on the victim. The problem here is that since general deterrence operates through the market, it must seek to give things money values, but money values are not necessarily adequate representations of these types of injuries. This fact should be obvious and is the core of the statement that there is no adequate supply side to the accident victim market.

Use of Bargaining Data. How then do we go about valuing these elements? The first possibility is to derive from bargaining situations market valuations of the risk of physical injuries which could then be applied in nonbargaining situations. If it were known, for instance, that workers in two given industries did exactly the same type of work and that in one 20 out of 100,000 people were killed each year while in the other no one was killed, and if the workers had perfect mobility, one could assume that any wage differential between the two industries was due to the difference in risk of death. From the different risk figures and the wage differential, the market value given in that bargaining situation to a human life for activities with the same actuarial chance of taking a life could be derived. If enough such situations existed, we could get market figures for the value of various human lives under many different risk conditions, and these could then be applied in nonbargaining accidents involving human lives.

Obviously there are overwhelming difficulties with such an approach. First, as I have already mentioned, individuals consistently underestimate the risk of death or injury to themselves, so that the bargaining figures would not be accurate representations of actual injury costs. They would have to be discounted by the underestimation of the risk of the injury occurring, and an adequate value could not be given to this understatement. It can be argued that this difficulty is less significant where the bargaining is done by groups and carried out by individuals who are not likely to be injured themselves. Where unions are strong, for instance, it can be said that the risk factor is probably pretty well known and can be properly evaluated by both sides to the bargain because each views it as the risk of the injury occurring to someone else.

Second, even if this were substantially true (and there is reason to doubt it),[7] extrapolation from bargaining to nonbargaining situations would still not be an adequate solution to valuing physical damages. The other conditions necessary for it simply are not realistic. There would not, for example, be enough situations where the work was truly comparable. There would never be perfect mobility, and the greater the imperfection, the less adequate the wage differential would be as a guide to valuation of injury costs. Moreover, the wage differential would not simply reflect a difference in mortality, because not all accidents kill or kill cleanly. It would reflect instead an amalgam of differences in rates of mortality, pain and suffering, days lost, medical costs, disfigurement, etc., and it would be almost impossible to isolate a market value for one of these, such as an arm or a life, which could be used in a nonbargaining situation.

Third, even if such a value could be isolated, it would be very difficult to find a nonbargaining situation where it could be applied properly. At best the value given would be for an arm of the average worker at the given type of factory where a given probability of injury existed. But the person injured in the nonbargaining case

7. Since the pressure on the union representatives who negotiate with management about the value to be placed on the risks comes ultimately from the members' evaluations of the risks to themselves, it may be that underestimation would occur here too. A union may, however, be better able to contemplate and evaluate risks because with a sufficient number of members it will regularly see *actual* injuries to the people for whom it bargains. Thus a union representing 2,000 men in a situation where on average one in 500 is seriously injured every year will face a statistical certainty that its members will have several such accidents each year, while the average worker may never have or even see an accident and therefore be more likely to underestimate the risk.

would not be that average worker, and he would have been injured by an activity whose "risk of injury" is often unknown and unknowable. Thus, even if a great number of arm valuations could be derived from a great number of different bargaining situations, the problems of placing an arm lost in the nonbargaining situation on the scale of values given to arms in bargaining cases would be virtually insurmountable. And what is unrealistic in an employment context becomes absurd in the context of other bargaining situations, such as purchasing lawn mowers or traveling by bus instead of by plane. There are simply too many *nonaccident* differences for a valuation of the risk of accidents to be established.

Collective Determinations of Market Cost Valuations in General. The second approach to valuing physical injury accident costs under general deterrence is more frankly collectivistic. It recognizes that no adequate direct extrapolation can be made from those few market values available and therefore seeks to make, by a collective judgment, a guess as to what value a true market would give to various injuries. Such a method would use what indications could be gotten from the figures derived from bargaining situations. This approach might view these figures as suggesting minimum values (in view of the assumed underestimation of risk) or as starting points (in view of the fact that they were average figures for activities having a given accident risk, and reflected a conglomerate of different accidents). It would then proceed to use them, together with what monetizable elements could be isolated, to derive money values for various injuries. The aim would still be to approximate the market; in theory it would be to arrive at the amount that the actual injured party, had he been properly and fully aware of the risk people in his risk category bore, would have received in exchange for bearing that risk.[8] The value of the

8. We want to arrive at the figure the injured party would have received, rather than the figure he would have demanded, because the market value of the risk would presumably reflect an agreement on a figure somewhere between the offer initially made by whoever engages in the activity and the initial demands made by the risk-taker.

actual injury (the accident cost) would technically be this figure multiplied by the odds against the injury occurring. The desirability of the activity that caused the injury would not, of course, be considered or be relevant to such a general deterrence computation. The object would be to monetize the nonmonetizable, thus enabling market choices for or against accident-causing activities to be made. Individual errors would again be insignificant if on the average the valuations were reasonably accurate.

Obviously, such a collective estimate of hypothetical individual valuations is bound to be far from satisfactory. It may, however, be the best we can do. If so, the first question is what methods are likely to result in the best estimate, and the second question is what adjustments can be made later to alleviate our initial dissatisfaction.

Collective Determinations of Market Cost Valuations—Means and Their Relation to the What-Is-a-Cost-of-What Decision. There are two basic ways in which these collective valuations can be made. The first is by schedules of injury which go into more or less detail; the second is on a case-by-case, injury-by-injury basis. Here, as with property damages, the relative merits of the two methods depend on relative accuracy (in terms of the general deterrence aim) and relative cost. Clearly, the more particularized the guess, the more it can be an accurate reflection of what the injured party would have required to bear the risk of the injury occurring if he had been fully aware *ex ante* of what that risk was. If nothing else, the inevitable lag between schedules of values and current values should make this clear. But just as clearly, the more particularized the guess, the more expensive it is likely to be. Furthermore, since compensation is not the goal at this stage, the issue is not whether any particular injury is valued better through a case-by-case approach but whether the increased accuracy of this approach on the whole warrants the expense.

There is, moreover, a certain danger of inaccuracy if too much particularization is attempted. If we examine accident injuries

210

on too much of a case-by-case basis (especially if we use a jury), we may be affected by matters that are essentially irrelevant to general deterrence, such as the worthiness, from a collective point of view, of what the particular injurer or particular victim was doing. These may be perfectly relevant under other approaches. Indeed, under specific deterrence they would necessarily be considered in valuing costs of injuries. But under general deterrence they are irrelevant, for the market will decide the worth of the activities involved, once cost figures are determined independently of such notions of worth. It would be unrealistic to assume, however, that any valuer of costs of injuries who faced a particular accident situation would be able to keep from being influenced by a relative worthiness judgment in his valuation. And while this influence might not be undesirable in a mixed system, it would be in a pure general deterrence approach.

The degree of particularization that is desirable in deciding what-is-the-cost depends in part on the degree of particularization needed to decide what-is-a-cost-of-what, for it depends in part on the added accuracy it brings, and in part on its expense. And the expense involved in particularizing cost figures will depend in part on whether the what-is-a-cost-of-what hard choice is made on an individual or a category basis.

If it is made on an individual basis, some of the facts on which particularized cost valuations are to be based will probably have to be gathered anyway, and much of the apparatus for deciding each accident case individually will already be in use and paid for. Conversely, if we decide that such individualized what-is-a-cost-of-what decisions are not desirable, we are more likely to find that individualized cost decisions are prohibitive. One could start the other way, first considering the expense of valuing costs in individual instances and then considering the added expense of making individualized what-is-a-cost-of-what decisions relative to any added accuracy such case-by-case decisions might bring. But since it is unlikely that a general deterrence approach would find such case-by-case decisions regarding what-is-a-cost-of-what to be more accurate than category decisions, the general deterrence approach is likely to view the expenses of case-by-case decisions regarding what-is-the-cost as being justifiable only in terms of the added accuracy they might give to such cost valuations.[9]

In practice, the decision on the degree of particularization of cost valuations that is worthwhile will have to be based on empirical data which will vary in different types of accident situations. Such data would include the degree of similarity of injuries and injured parties; the expense of valuation in the particular accident context; the likelihood of misvaluation through too much particularization in the particular context (i.e. the likelihood of nongeneral deterrence judgments if a case-by-case approach is used); the likelihood of lags between schedules of values and current values; and the need for and cost of particularization in the specific context in view of the level of generality at which what-is-a-cost-of-what decisions were made in the area.

A discussion of ways to value costs cannot end with schedules versus case-by-case valuations. Some mention must be made of the institution making the valuation, regardless of the level at which valuations are made. Since general deterrence seeks to approximate individualized market decisions, it would in theory seek the institution that is most individualistic, i.e. the agency that on the whole would most closely approximate valuations individuals would make in the market. Again in theory, this would probably be a jury, instructed to value the damages in terms of what the injured party would have required *ex ante* to bear the risk of his injury, multiplied by the odds against that injury occurring to

9. What-is-the-cost information must, of course, be sufficiently particularized to make worthwhile the breakdown into subcategories in the what-is-a-cost-of-what decision. Unless we have a figure for the costs of accidents in which teen-age driving is involved, it will be fruitless to make a what-is-a-cost-of-what decision dividing driving into teen-age driving and adult driving. This works both ways, of course: in deciding how far to subcategorize in determining what-is-a-cost-of-what, we must take into account the extent to which it is worthwhile (in terms of tertiary costs) to break down our what-is-the-cost determinations.

someone in his risk category. In practice, this may reduce itself
to each member of the jury deciding how much he would require
for bearing the risk and multiplying that by those odds. Over a
mass of cases, this might not be too bad an estimate of what we
want under general deterrence.

The less we individualize cost valuations, however, the less
adequately a jury verdict would reflect the amount individuals
would require to bear the risk. A series of juries may serve to make
a reasonably good approximation of the mass of such individual
valuations because such a series may well be more representative
of total individual attitudes than virtually any other collective
body. But this is far from saying that one jury would be the best
representative of individual attitudes if the issue were the drawing
up of a generalized schedule of personal injury damages. In fact,
it should be obvious that as we move toward schedules of damages,
even highly particularized ones, the best estimate of the average
of individual valuations is not going to be made by a body like
a jury, but probably by other institutions with a broader popular
base.

Discussion of what combinations of bodies with expert knowledge and representative (perhaps legislative) bodies are likely to
be best in view of the dangers of lags and lobbying is well beyond
my scope. It is sufficient to point out that the current practice of
using juries in areas where damages are not scheduled and using
representative or expert bodies to create schedules in areas where
schedules are used is consistent with what might be done under a
general deterrence approach. Of course, the problems of expenses
and lags in our present systems might also find analogies in a system based primarily on general deterrence, though they could
probably be handled better than they are today.

*Specific Deterrence Modifications of General Deterrence Cost
Valuations.* Regardless of the means used to make collective cost
valuations that are as close to individualized market ones as possible, the valuations will never be totally satisfactory. As a result,
the second question I posed arises: what adjustments can be made

to alleviate our initial dissatisfaction? Actually, we cannot be fully satisfied with any way of valuing physical injuries because such injuries involve elements not fully convertible into money; thus any device which converts them into money will not be fully adequate. And yet in practice we do say that at some point, the cost of avoiding such injuries is greater than the cost of the injuries; at some point, we do make a decision *for* accidents which implies that the injuries are not priceless. This means that some valuation of their costs is inevitable.

Pure specific deterrence, as we shall see, would make this valuation entirely collectively, considering both the cost of the injury and the value of the injuring activity. General deterrence, as we have seen, tries instead to approximate market values of costs and then to let the market decide which acts or activities are worthwhile. The difficulties involved in valuing costs (i.e. in making such approximations of market values) under general deterrence suggest, however, that not all decisions for or against accidents that would result from the workings of the market would be acceptable collectively. Indeed, even the most avid backers of the free market are likely to want a collective review of the decisions for and against accidents reached through the market.

For example, it might be decided, after looking at the results accomplished by a general deterrence market approach, to bar 16- to 18-year-old drivers, or conversely to subsidize drivers over 65. The first of these decisions would be analogous to an eminent domain decision. We would be saying that no sufficient public purpose existed to justify the taking of lives and limbs by 16- to 18-year-old drivers. The second would be analogous to a decision to subsidize certain buyers of property to enable more of them to buy. Just as we demand more than a willingness to pay money value before we let individuals or groups take property (because we know that this money value is just an approximation), so we would demand more before we would allow them to engage in activities that might take lives or limbs.[10] Similarly, just as we

10. See supra note 25, Chapter 5.

decide that certain social benefits not reflected in the market may result from letting individuals take property they cannot, on the market, "afford," so we may make the same decision as to letting them take part in activities which, in effect, use up lives. Of course, since the nonmarket elements involved in valuing lives are likely to be much more significant than they are in valuing property, we may expect more restrictions and regulations in the accident field than in the field of eminent domain. And as the inaccuracy of market valuation increases, so will the likelihood of collective revisions of market decisions.

All this implies that we can never rely solely on general deterrence. It does not suggest that the general and specific deterrence approaches are similar. Valuing costs of injuries as objectively and in as near a market way as we can, viewing the results of such valuations on the market, and then modifying them through specific deterrence decisions is far different from making the type of all-inclusive value judgment at the cost valuation stage which, as we shall see, a pure specific deterrence approach would imply.

Relation of General Deterrence Cost Valuations Generally and the What-Is-a-Cost-of-What Decision. Thus far we have treated the question of cost valuations separately from the question of what-is-a-cost-of-what, except to note that the degree of individualization demanded for one of these decisions will affect the expense involved and therefore the desirability of individualization for the other. We should not, however, overlook the fact that a failure to recognize an item as a cost in a physical injury (or indeed in any accident) situation necessarily implies a decision regarding what-is-a-cost-of-what. *To the extent that the victim thinks of that item as a real cost to him,* failure explicitly to value the item means that he is left bearing that cost, and this implies that a what-is-a-cost-of-what decision has been made. The value of the cost item allocated in this manner will be its value to the injured party—that is, to the party left bearing it. Its general deterrence effect will depend on the ability of other parties that have the same risk potential with respect to such a cost item to take that risk into account in their market decisions.

This problem of ignored costs is important, and I discuss it at length in the following section on pain and suffering and sentimental damages, as it is there that it is most clearly significant. I mention it here to highlight the fact that any misvaluation of costs implies a decision regarding what-is-a-cost-of-what and as such has a possible general deterrence effect.[11] The question is more important under pain and suffering only because it is there that such misvaluations are most likely and that the general deterrence effect of misvaluations becomes most problematical and hence most interesting.

Pain and Suffering and Sentimental Damages

In essence, the problem of valuing pain and suffering is no different from that of valuing other nonmonetizable damages.[12] The same issues arise in theory. The possibility of using bargaining situations as guidelines exists, the same issues with respect to case-by-case and scheduled damages can be isolated, and the same questions as to jury versus nonjury determinations may be posed. The principal differences are in degree. Although the techniques are the same, the result of using them is more doubtful since almost *ex hypothesis* such items are only very inaccurately converted into money terms. And greater uncertainty creates greater expense.

In the first place, uncertainty means that average or scheduled damages are less likely to be reasonable approximations. This is not only because of individual differences in reactions to pain and suffering. (Here too, individual differences would be relatively in-

11. If the party left bearing a cost because of such an undervaluation has a bargaining relationship with an activity that can avoid that cost more cheaply that he can, the effect of the undervaluation will be ameliorated, but only in part. Conversely, if the cost is overvalued, and the party to whom it has been allocated has a bargaining relationship with potential victims, a partial correction may also take place. See infra pp. 227–29.

12. Here I am discussing real pain and suffering costs, not pain and suffering damages awarded to cover legal fees, which are discussed infra pp. 225–26.

significant for general deterrence if we could obtain figures that accurately reflected the average pain and suffering borne by categories that were significant in terms of what-is-a-cost-of-what decisions.) It is also because even average or scheduled figures on pain and suffering are not likely to be accurate unless they are derived from a sum of individual cases, for few guides to pain and suffering by categories exist. The practical effect of this is to militate for individual determinations, and these are expensive.

In the second place, uncertainty means that, even among the issues that might be decided on a case-by-case basis, valuation of items like pain and suffering is clearly more expensive than valuations of other cost items. More evidence is needed, more widely diverging claims can be made, and more time is required of all concerned.[13]

My principal interest in pain and suffering and other non-monetizable items does not, however, stem from the expense of valuing them as such. It stems rather from a consequence both of this expense and of the doubt which attaches to such valuations when they are attempted. This consequence is the tendency to call some of these items fanciful or sentimental damages and exclude them from cost computations altogether. The effect of such exclusion has some interesting implications for general deterrence which are paralleled to a greater or lesser degree whenever accident costs are misvalued. The questions are, what happens to accident costs that are not valued, or are not valued properly; whom do they affect from a general deterrence standpoint; and how do they do this? In this sense, pain and suffering and sentimental damages highlight a more general problem that deserves some attention.

As I have mentioned, failure to value a cost such as pain and suffering means leaving it on the party that originally bears it. This in turn has two implications: (1) a decision that he ought

13. *AACP,* at 214–15 indicates that only the basic question of the presence or absence of fault is a more frequent cause of contention between the opposing sides in an automobile accident tort action than pain and suffering.

to bear it (a pure what-is-a-cost-of-what decision), and (2) a decision that the value we want to give to the part left unvalued is the value the bearer himself gives to it (a what-is-the-cost decision). But the effect on general deterrence is not based on the value the party bearing the injury would give this burden after the injury. It is based instead on the value he and others bearing the same risk of being burdened with similar pain and suffering will give to the risk of bearing such uncompensated pain and suffering. This opens the considerable question of the degree to which the prospect of compensation for pain and suffering and similar injuries will affect people's behavior. This question is crucial because its answer will greatly affect the desirability of leaving such costs on the victim.

Attempting to compensate people who engage in activities that may result in pain and suffering (or other damages not easily monetizable) has some rather peculiar general deterrence effects if their behavior is affected solely by the fear of suffering such injuries and *not* by whether they will be compensated for the injuries. Let us assume, for example, that blasting operations cause a certain number of injuries per year to people who live in a certain area. Let us also assume that these injuries all involve *only* pain and suffering (or other damages that are hard to monetize) and that before accidents the behavior of the people in the area was totally unaffected by whether they would be compensated in money for such suffering, although they worried a great deal about the prospect of bearing the suffering. On these assumptions, a certain number of people would tend, other things being equal, to move away from the area. The degree of pressure to move would depend on how aware the people were of the risk of suffering injury. If the risk were properly valued, it would result in the exact equivalent of a general deterrence economic pressure being put on the activity of living in the area. The pressure would vary with each resident's likelihood of being injured and his evaluation of the cost of the pain and suffering to him. Thus, if we assume perfect risk awareness on the part of the residents and that the what-is-a-cost-of-what decision was to put *none* of the burden on the blasters, an optimal general deterrence pressure would exist.[14]

Moreover, given our assumption that it is the prospect of the suffering and not at all the prospect of *uncompensated* suffering which matters for the householders, that same pressure on them to move will exist regardless of whether compensation is paid or not. The man who fears losing his head and does not care whether he would be paid for it will move regardless.[15] Thus under this assumption, taken together with the assumption that householders are perfectly aware of the risk they bear, compensation by the blasting companies might seem to cause a deleterious general deterrence effect. Householders would reduce or alter their activity to the extent they deemed justified by the risk of pain and suffering, but in addition the blasting companies would alter *their* activities to an extent commensurate with the risk they bore of having to pay for such pain an suffering. In effect, the householders could not be compensated in a general deterrence sense since the prospect of compensation would not change their behavior. But the blasting companies, since paying compensation would affect their behavior, would also be bearing the loss (in a general deterrence way). Thus the burden of pain and suffering would be borne by both parties. Pain and suffering would be unshiftable from the victims, and the attempt to shift it would cause it to affect the blasters as well.

At first glance, this would seem to be undesirable from a gen-

14. This optimal general deterrence pressure would not, most likely eliminate all accidents or all pain and suffering, and society might wish to spread the cost of such pain and suffering by compensating the victims. Since we have assumed that potential victims would be unaffected in their choices by whether there would be compensation for pain and suffering, the spreading would not remove the general deterrence pressure from the potential victims.

15. That pressure to move might be reduced, however, if the householder could choose to be paid for the *risk* of losing his head in exchange for forgoing compensation if he does lose it and if he is willing to take such a risk for a price, for then he may benefit without losing his head. Compare infra pp 227–29.

eral deterrence point of view, since the costs would be fully allocated to each of the parties. Clearly this would be undesirable if
the victims were the optimal loss bearers (easiest loss avoiders)
as to the whole burden. Whether it would be undesirable in other
cases would depend, even in theory, on the answer to the following question. Assuming that the what-is-a-cost-of-what decision
would put some or all of the pain and suffering costs on the blasters
(as the easiest cost avoider with regard to that portion of the costs),
would a greater misallocation result from leaving this portion of
the burden on the victim, or from placing some money equivalent
of this burden on the blasters, knowing that this would not serve
to alleviate the burden on the victims? In other words, given that
perfect general deterrence pressure is impossible under our assumptions that pain and suffering costs are not shiftable from the victim
and that the blaster is the cheapest cost avoider,[16] would a
greater misallocation result from leaving part of the burden on
the less-than-optimal loss bearer (the victim) or from allocating
it both to him and to the optimal loss bearer (the blaster)? The
answer will obviously depend on how much better a loss bearer
(in terms of easiest cost avoidance) the blaster is than the victim.

This question need not detain us unduly, however, as there are
several objections, both theoretical and practical, to the basic assumptions that give rise to the problem. In the first place, in a
perfect and purely theoretical world the householders would always be affected by whether compensation would be paid. Before
the injury they would be able to borrow against the compensation
that would occur if the injury took place. Since they do not care
about postaccident compensation, they would always contract away
their rights to such compensation in exchange for payments for
bearing the risk before the accident. And if the householders were
unaffected in their behavior by the prospect of compensation after
the accident, they would inevitably be affected by the availability

16. Perfect general deterrence pressure is possible in the extreme case
where the potential victims are so inert that fear of pain and suffering will no
more move them than lack of compensation.

of preaccident compensation. This insurance in reverse would be used to bring about reduction of the risk of injury in the cheapest way possible. In our example it would help some to move, some to build storm cellars, and some to bribe the blasters to change their conduct. All these attempts to reduce the risk would occur in the short run regardless of whether compensation were paid, but their long-run effect might be quite different depending on whether the financial costs of the attempts were paid by the blasters (i.e. compensation for pain and suffering was allowed) or the householders (i.e. compensation did not take place).

This theoretical objection is, of course, unrealistic. Such reverse insurance does not really exist, and neither do such simple transactions. But it is worth mentioning because some of the assumptions under which it seems that pain and suffering type costs are unshiftable are theoretical, and it is of interest to know that to the extent we are in a world of pure theory, pain and suffering costs *can* in fact be shifted.

As we move nearer the real world, more practical reasons why it may matter whether pain and suffering costs are converted into money and allocated come to the fore. Again the principal one is the fact that people are likely to underestimate the risk of injury to themselves for psychological reasons, so that unless part of the cost (equivalent to the underestimation by the injured) is put on the injurers, some of these costs will, in effect, be placed on neither party. The householders would only be affected to the extent of their awareness of the risk, which we have just assumed is less than its actual value. The blasters would be unaffected, because they were not liable. In this sense, placing some of these costs on blasters would not result in a twofold effect, but merely in recognition of a cost which would otherwise affect neither party.[17] This

17. Another way of bringing about recognition of the cost would be to compel the householders to insure against the risk, thus making them aware of its actual value. Whether this is better than placing some of the costs on the blasters would depend on who the cheapest cost avoider is.

is all very well and good if we have some acceptable way of valuing the costs of pain and suffering, for then we can try to determine what costs should be put on blasters to make up for the under-valuation of risk by the householders. If, however, we have no confidence in our valuations, it is difficult to find the error in the householders' valuations, even though we are pretty sure that they are understated. Obviously, our tendency to approach the problem in this skeptical way will increase as we move to more and more personal and thus less and less monetizable damages—as we move, in effect, from personal injury generally to pain and suffering to sentimental values.

The situation is quite different if *in practice* people are affected by the fear of *uncompensated* pain and suffering rather than pain and suffering itself. To the extent that they are, it is fair to say that the cost item *can* be monetized, since the fact that people will behave differently when they know they will be paid if they are made to suffer itself reflects some monetization of the pain and suffering.

Any such all-or-nothing assumptions are probably unrealistic, however, and this is what makes the problem of pain and suffer-ing damages so difficult. It is probably fair to say: (1) that most people's behavior will be somewhat affected by whether pain and suffering is in fact compensated; (2) that the fear of the suffering itself, regardless of compensation, will be a significant factor for most people and a crucial one for some; (3) that despite this fear —or perhaps because of it—individual valuations of the risk of pain and suffering will be substantially inaccurate; (4) that collec-tive estimates of what individuals would require to bear the risk of pain and suffering if they were totally aware of the risk category to which they belong are often no more than wild guesses; and (5) that these difficulties increase as one moves away from simple, physical injury toward more personal damages such as psychologi-cal injury, pain and suffering, and finally, sentimental damages.

How then should we handle pain and suffering costs, especially

in view of the fact that a failure to value them or even an undervaluation of them, far from avoiding a decision, implies a what-
is-a-cost-of-what decision to leave the burden on the originally injured party? I would conclude that to the extent that some such
costs are relatively nonindividual, i.e. shared by most potential victims, collective valuations are feasible and people are likely to be
affected by whether they receive compensation or not. Valuations
can be arrived at for these costs (the most monetizable of the un-
monetizable), and a normal what-is-a-cost-of-what decision can
then be made. Such valuations will always be expensive and may
not be worthwhile because the tertiary costs may be greater than
the expected general deterrence benefits. But for this type of pain
and suffering costs, it may be possible to use average or scheduled
figures, making valuations feasible from the standpoint of administrative expense.

As we move closer to sentimental damages, both the feasibility
of collective valuations and the usefulness of the result for general
deterrence purposes become more doubtful. In addition, the expense of making such valuations, involving, as they would, more
and more individualization, becomes greater. At some point, we
must do better if we leave such costs on the victim and let him
value them, than if we compound the uncertainty and expense
of evaluating the costs collectively with the uncertainty of whether
the attempt to shift them will result in their being borne twice,
by both the victim and the injurer. This just means that at some
point compensation probably no longer affects victim behavior
and therefore implies a risk of assessing costs to both parties, and
it will be better to try to inform individuals of the risk they bear
than to determine the risk collectively in a reasonably correct
fashion and then make a wild collective guess regarding the cost
to the individual.[18] Most important of all, at some point the

18. It must be remembered, however, that in many instances it will be
virtually impossible, for psychological reasons, adequately to inform individuals of the risk so that they can properly evaluate it—they will simply refuse
to believe it.

what-is-a-cost-of-what decision implied in leaving these costs on the victim may turn out to be a pretty good one if the object is to burden the easiest cost avoider.

This may be so for two reasons. First, if costs are unshiftable because it is the fear of injury rather than of *uncompensated* injury which motivates victims, they cannot be externalized by transfer. Thus, if we wish some part of a blasting-householder accident to be left (on what-is-a-cost-of-what grounds) on the victim but fear that externalization by transfer will result, it is best to leave costs like sentimental damages which are difficult to externalize on the householders, and to shift easily monetizable and hence easily externalizable costs like work-hours lost to the blasters. Externalization due to inadequate knowledge can still occur, of course; in some ways it may seem to be an especially great danger with damages of this sort because the psychological inability to take in the risk may be strong. This can be alleviated to some extent by intelligent attempts to inform potential victims of the risk they do in fact bear. Nevertheless some psychological externalization by victims is probably inevitable. But regardless of how such costs are handled, externalization due to inadequate knowledge seems unavoidable because accurate valuations can no more be made collectively than they can individually. As a result, it may be best not to be too concerned about externalization by inadequate knowledge and to take advantage of the fact that externalization by transfer is difficult.

Second, to the extent that such nonmonetizable damages are highly individualized, it is likely that in such cases the victim is the cheapest cost avoider, if for no other reason than that he is more likely to be aware of the risk than anyone else. Thus a person who has particularly sensitive ears is probably the cheapest avoider of what blasting noise "costs" him. An average damage figure can —and perhaps should—be paid by the blasters to all inhabitants in the area, and this will affect the blasters' behavior. But if, despite such scheduled payments, noise occurs that hurts one person especially, it is likely that the cheapest way to avoid or reduce such a particularized cost is to have this individual wear earplugs or move away. The same analysis would of course hold for the person who is particularly subject to pain and suffering or sentimental damages.[19]

We may conclude, therefore, that as far as general deterrence is concerned, the problem of nonmonetizable costs, though substantial, is not unmanageable. Up to a point, valuations would be made in the same way physical injury damages are valued. Schedules of average or base pain and suffering and loss of dignity damages could be made, and allocations under the usual what-is-a-cost-of-what criteria could take place. Beyond that point, the costs could be left where they fell, in the knowledge that this implies allocating highly individualized damages to the victim.[20] This allocation would, of course, have to be taken into account in making an optimal what-is-a-cost-of-what decision with respect to the other costs, since one of the parties (the victim) will already have been allocated part of his possible share (the unvalued costs).

As I have noted elsewhere, the expense of making valuations (tertiary costs) and the desirability of spreading (secondary cost avoidance) will affect where the line between valuing and not valuing relatively nonmonetizable costs should be drawn, as will the possibility of modifying behavior through specific deterrence. To some extent these other goals and approaches would reinforce the general deterrence decision; to some extent they would alter it. But I am not, for the moment, concerned with that. At this stage, it is enough to see that under the general deterrence approach, in the imperfect world in which we live, we would refuse to recognize some highly individual and hard-to-value items of cost, there-

19. Those who are particularly sensitive in these respects can, of course, insure, and they are best suited to evaluate how much insurance against such items would be suitable. For this reason, we would probably not allow subrogation rights with respect to payment under such insurance, just as we do not allow subrogation to the proceeds of life insurance policies.

20. It is interesting that several of the recently proposed plans, e.g. the American Insurance Association proposal, in effect take this approach to "injuries which cannot be measured by economic loss." See *AIA Report*, at 5.

by deciding that they belong to the victims and that the victims can value them best.[21]

Administrative Expenses

Thus far I have discussed the problem of pain and suffering as though it involved only primary accident costs. In fact, it is well known that pain and suffering recoveries often represent payment of lawyers' fees, or, more generally, payment of some of the expenses of deciding liability and valuing damages. Whether this arrangement makes sense or not, a word needs to be said about these tertiary costs.

Once it is decided that a particular system of accident law will be used, the expenses of administering that system can be viewed simply as accident costs. We view them separately, as tertiary costs, in order to evaluate various systems, but once we have chosen a system they are as much and as primary an accident cost as a broken leg. General deterrence would thus require their valuation and allocation. There is nothing especially difficult about the valuation and allocation of these administrative costs, which in theory should be reducible to money. But while they do not involve many items that are theoretically nonmonetizable, they include some types of costs that in practice are very hard to value (e.g. what would be the cost of getting the judges needed to eliminate the court congestion that results from accident cases?). Nevertheless, most of what has been said about accident cost valuations is applicable here, including the relevance of the expense of valuing them and the relative merits of case-by-case as against group computations.

Similarly, their allocation is a fairly standard what-is-a-cost-of-what problem. However, since administrative costs are not necessarily avoided most cheaply by the same parties that could have avoided other accident costs most cheaply, it is not necessarily true

21. Specific deterrence modifications of the market results are possible, indeed likely, in view of the difficulty in valuing such costs. See supra pp. 212–14.

that such costs should be placed on the same activities that could have avoided the other accident costs most cheaply. Again, the fact that some activities can avoid some of the costs of an accident better than others is neither surprising nor limited to administrative costs. (Thus I have just suggested that there may be good what-is-a-cost-of-what reasons for putting sentimental costs on victims even if other more monetizable costs of an accident would be better allocated differently.) But while not uniquely applicable to administrative costs, this reasonably simple fact may be of particular importance to the general deterrence allocation of such costs.[22]

Obviously, general deterrence cannot be the only aim with regard to these costs. In practice, for example, the desire to avoid secondary costs may affect our allocation of administrative costs as much as it does other accident costs. The contrast between the English and American ways of handling administrative costs certainly indicates this.[23] But all this is beyond the scope of the present discussion. Here it is sufficient to point out that once we have decided on a system of accident law, the administrative costs of that system cannot be ignored, as they must be borne by someone. Accordingly, the general deterrence approach would require their valuation and allocation, along with other accident costs, in the way that would most effectively lead to intelligent market decisions for or against the activities that "cause" them.

22. In any given case it may appear that the cheapest avoider of the accidents is necessarily the cheapest tertiary cost avoider as well. But on a broader scale, since we will inevitably have some primary and secondary accident costs the question must be which activities can most cheaply reduce the tertiary cost of dealing with them.

23. The American practice of allowing attorneys' fees to be contingent upon recovery by the plaintiff probably avoids some of the secondary costs of accidents by allowing accident victims to pool the costs of suing for damages whereas the traditional English practice of allowing the winning party to recover legal costs from the losing party may very well have helped to hold down administrative costs but may have led to large secondary costs.

Revisions due to Transactions

I suggested earlier that a peculiar kind of market in accident victims does exist, at least in bargaining situations. The worker in a dangerous industry will, in theory, demand more pay if he is made to bear the cost of injuries than if he is not. We have seen that such transactions are of very doubtful usefulness in valuing accident costs. Since such a market does exist, however, one must ask what happens if costs of accidents are collectively given a value different from that which the parties to a bargain would have given them. What happens, that is, if we value a man's leg at $1,000 but the man himself would value it at $500 or $1,500?

In theory the answer is easy: the market would correct our error. If the man knew he would receive more than his leg was worth to him, he would be willing to work for less because of the possibility of the windfall. If he knew he would receive less than it was worth, he would demand higher wages because of the risk of uncompensated damage. In practice, such corrections would be highly limited, except where the damages involved are readily monetizable, i.e. except in those areas where there would be no reason for the collective valuations to be inaccurate. If collective valuations are inaccurate nonetheless, we may expect market corrections. This is, in fact, what has happened in many employment contexts where unions have bargained for higher disability payments than those given under outdated workmen's compensation schedules. In areas where damages are not readily monetizable, on the other hand, market corrections are unlikely to be significant. From the standpoint of general deterrence, however, those corrections that do occur will almost always improve matters and will only rarely suggest that it was a mistake to attempt a collective cost valuation in the first instance.

Consider the case of a worker who before an accident values his leg at less than the collectively determined market value. Theoretically it would seem that he stood to get a windfall if the accident occurred, and that he would therefore be willing to work for less. But the value the worker gives to his leg before the accident is based on the *preaccident* probability of the injury occurring. And as we have seen, the values given to such injury costs increase with the chance of the loss actually occurring. Accordingly, it is very unlikely that the worker who is injured will consider the money he receives for his leg to be a windfall, regardless of how little he valued the leg before. There is, therefore, virtually no chance that he will accept significantly lower wages before the accident, for the moment he realistically views himself as the victim of hard-to-monetize damages—as he would have to in order to consider himself as the possible windfall recipient—he will start to consider the payment inadequate rather than excessive.

This example leads to the conclusion that there is little danger that the chronic tendency of potential victims to undervalue risks would bring about a greater market correction than would be justified where the collective valuation overstated the value of the injury. The potential victim would underestimate the chances of compensation by as much as he would the risk of injury. And only if he could contract away his compensation rights for money *before* the accident could the market correction be deleterious. Only then could the accident costs be undervalued as a result of his wishful thinking once a collective valuation had been made. Unless such preaccident contracts to waive compensation were allowed, the collective valuation would set a floor on nonmonetizable injury costs. And such a floor would almost always be desirable in view of the tendency of potential victims to undervalue the risk of nonmonetizable injuries.

If we consider instead the case of a collective valuation that understates the cost of the leg to the victim, we can also conclude that the market effect is desirable, and that furthermore no harm is done by making a collective valuation in the first instance. In such a case the potential victim might demand higher wages because he deemed inadequate the compensation he would receive if an injury occurred. Any market correction of the collective valuation this might bring about would be to the good from the general deterrence standpoint. This correction, however, would probably not go far enough, for if the victim undervalued the risk of losing his leg, he would probably not demand enough in higher wages. But if this psychological disability existed, it would follow that without the original collective valuation, he would also have demanded too little. In other words, the market's failure to correct the collective error fully would be proof that valuation by individuals through bargaining—and without a collective valuation—would have erred by as much and probably even more.[24]

A great deal more can be said on this subject. One could, for instance, discuss the particular obstacles to market corrections of cost valuations which exist when such corrective transactions would have to be entered into by parties that are not already in a bargaining relationship with each other, i.e. where significant transaction costs are likely to exist. But all that is well beyond the needs of this discussion. From the standpoint of the general deterrence approach it is enough to conclude that while collective valuations of costs are virtually inevitable and only rarely harmful, placing liability on the party best aware of the risk of injury (in accordance with our earlier what-is-a-cost-of-what guidelines) is desirable, and the market corrections that may follow can only improve matters, regardless of whether the collective cost valuation was fully accurate or not (at least if preaccident waivers are barred).

THE SPECIFIC DETERRENCE APPROACH

The problem of determining what-is-the-cost is no easier under specific deterrence than it is under general deterrence. Indeed, in some ways it may be more difficult. Under specific deterrence we must decide what value to give to accident costs in order to decide collectively which acts and activities responsible for such costs to bar or limit. Because decisions to bar or limit acts or activities under specific deterrence are not made through the market but

24. This assumes, of course, a decision to put the collectively determined liability on the party most aware of the risk. See supra pp. 143–52.

are based on collective valuations of each activity's worth, there would be no separation of the valuation of the accident costs for which an activity is held responsible from the valuation of the activity itself. Thus, a characteristic fundamental to the general deterrence what-is-the-cost decision is irrelevant in the specific deterrence one. And in practice, a specific deterrence decision to bar or limit an act or activity always implies simultaneous, collective valuation of the accident costs and the desirability of the activity. In effect, it is a decision of how worthwhile the activity is, *given* its accident costs.

The first thing to note about this specific deterrence decision is that it does not initially involve the conversion into money terms of items not readily monetizable, or indeed even of readily monetizable items. This is true both of the activity and of its accident costs. Thus, not only would items like pain and suffering not be reduced into money values, but neither would nonaccident costs and benefits which the activity being examined might be thought to have and which the market might not reflect. As a result, the collective reexamination of market results which seemed likely in practice under any general deterrence system would have no equivalent under specific deterrence. The reexamination, which I analogized to the public purpose requirement in eminent domain, was designed to make collective corrections of misvaluations or nonvaluations of such nonmonetizable items on either the cost or the activity side, once the effect of the separate valuations could be seen in practice. Specific deterrence, since it would already have taken into account nonmarket values on the activity as well as on the accident cost side and viewed them together, would not need to make such a reevaluation.

The fact that nonmonetizable items do not need to be converted into money terms only gives the impression of making the what-is-the-cost decision easier. Thus, while it may not be necessary to convert pain and suffering into money terms, it is necessary to decide collectively how much various types of pain and suffering bother us in order to determine what to do about various types of acts or activities which we think are responsible for such pain and suffering. Converting nonmonetizables into money terms is, after all, simply a convenient way of reducing different items to the same scale of values so that we can compare them and choose among them. It is, in short, a way of enabling us to compare apples and pears. Monetization is necessary to any market choice among the different items, and while it is not explicitly necessary to a collective choice, a similar comparison of the different items must still be made if an intelligent collective decision is to be obtained. Ultimately, the difficulty of reducing nonmonetizables into money terms merely reflects the difficulty of this underlying comparison.

Thus, in order to decide collectively what kind of driving we want and when we want it, we must keep in mind the accident costs of driving as well as its benefits. Comparing these costs and benefits is just as difficult if they are *not* reduced to money as it is if they are. The more the costs become personal (as we move from property damage to physical injury, pain and suffering, and sentimental damage), the more the comparison of costs and benefits becomes problematical, just as it did under general deterrence. What is more, unless we are prepared to make an infinite number of collective evaluations of the costs and benefits of activities and in the light of these evaluations to examine collectively every activity separately and in infinite detail, we are going to have to consider costs in groupings, even for specific deterrence. And this immediately requires their reduction to some common measure. In other words, we are going to have to convert various accident costs into similar and comparable values. Once we arrive at this conclusion we face all the problems of monetization again, and virtually all the discussion of the problem under general deterrence becomes apposite, including the question of how individualized the valuation should be in relation to the expense of individualization.[25]

However, since specific deterrence does not accept market valua-

---

25. Market corrections will, however, be undesirable under specific deterrence; cf. supra pp. 191–97.

tions as the object of the what-is-the-cost decision, it is not useful
to divide the problem, as we did for general deterrence, into sections reflecting the relative availability of accurate market valuations of different types of accident costs. The fact that a pretty
good market valuation of property damages is available would not
end the matter for specific deterrence because the accuracy of that
particular market valuation—in terms of the broader goals of
specific deterrence—would have to be considered. Specific deterrence might well use such market valuations as a starting point.
But even this would simply imply the collective decision that the
market value happened to approximate the collective value for
the particular type of accident cost; it would not indicate that the
market valuation was best in general.

In practice, however, the very factors that tend to make property
valuations easy for general deterrence would probably militate,
under specific deterrence, for taking market values as a first approximation of accident costs when property damage is involved.
These values would then be combined in some way with the nonmoney costs and benefits attributed to the particular cost-activity
combination being considered and a collective decision would be
reached regarding what to do about accident costs in relation to
the activities involved. The decision would entail prohibiting certain acts or activities because collectively their value was deemed
less than their costs, and allowing others because their benefits
exceeded their costs.[26] The same type of decision would be made
in nonproperty areas, the only difference being that the market
valuations available would be less acceptable reflections of collective valuations. The choice would therefore be more openly
political, with all the difficulties this implies for making the decision as frequently as the large number of different possible accident-causing activities requires.

There is one further, important matter to consider in examining how the specific deterrence approach would decide what-is-

26. We might, of course, employ impure specific deterrence and limit some
acts or activities instead of prohibiting them. See supra pp. 114–19.

the-cost. This is the problem, already raised under what-is-a-cost-of-what, of handling those accident costs that would occur despite (or indeed in the wake of) our decisions to bar some acts and activities and not others. As mentioned before, no method of primary accident cost reduction will in practice abolish all accident costs, and specific deterrence, like general deterrence, is simply an approach to deciding which accident costs caused by which activities will not be eliminated. Some accident costs will therefore remain under a pure specific deterrence approach, and the question is how these are to be treated. If they are ignored, they are essentially being allocated to the victims. This implies (1) a decision that victims are responsible for these accident costs; (2) that we have collectively decided that the best way to reduce them further (after enforcement of our already adopted specific deterrence prohibitions) is through the market reactions of individuals who have to bear the risk of these losses; and (3) that the best value to be given to these losses is the value the victims themselves and others in the same risk category give to the loss and to the risk of its occurring. Clearly this is a highly individualistic or market tail on the collective, specific deterrence dog.

But to the extent that we decide that any less individualistic method of handling these costs is better, we must somehow shift the burden of the losses from the victims. And any shifting involves a valuation of *what* we are shifting. This is so whether we desire to shift the burden to the other party or parties to the accident (because we collectively feel their market reaction will bring about the best specific deterrence result), or whether we desire to shift the costs to parties totally unrelated to the accident (because we want no market reaction and therefore want externalization and allocation through general taxation). Regardless of whom we wish to burden, *so long as it is not the victim* we must somehow evaluate his loss in order to remove it from him, i.e. compensate him in the classical meaning of the word. This, of course, involves all the problems of monetizing nonmonetizables we encountered in the what-is-the-cost discussion under general deterrence. It also involves the problem of whether it is lack of compensation for certain injuries or the fear of the injury itself which motivates people. Once again, if we do not wish to cause potential victims to change their behavior because of the risk of accidents (except for the change prescribed by the prohibitions established by specific deterrence), we must compensate them fully if an accident occurs. And *ex hypothesis* this is impossible if no compensation makes up for the injuries suffered—if, in other words, it is fear of the injury and not of the monetarily uncompensated injury which motivates people.

The conclusion here, as under general deterrence, must be that to the extent people fear the injury and not the lack of compensation for it, it is virtually impossible to keep them from making market-type adjustments in their behavior. Accordingly, the specific deterrence approach must take these adjustments into account in deciding which steps to take to establish the best accident cost-activity mix. In addition, to the extent that lack of compensation for injuries rather than fear of the injury itself motivates people, specific deterrence must either arrange for compensation (and this implies monetization as far as possible of nonmonetizables), or expect victims to react through the market to the lack of compensation. In the former case, all the what-is-the-cost problems that I discussed for general deterrence become immediately applicable. In the latter case, the specific deterrence decision-makers must take into account and deal with a very substantial degree of free market individual decision-making in striving to establish the collectively determined best accident cost-activity mix.

All this analysis should not blur too greatly the differences between the general deterrence and specific deterrence approaches, even regarding valuation of accident costs. The difference between starting out with individualized market valuations as the aim and merely accepting some individualized market valuations as inevitable is considerable. The analysis should, however, serve to remind us that as soon as we abandon the hope of having a perfect world in which accident costs could be so particularized that general deterrence could infallibly price the acts or activities causing accidents out of the market, or specific deterrence could prohibit them with complete success, we necessarily move into a world where mixed approaches will prevail. The all-important question that remains, however, is which mixture accomplishes our mixed aims, not perfectly—as that is impossible—but best.

PART IV

The Fault System and Accident Cost Reduction

It is not my intention to discuss at any length most of the recent criticisms of the fault system, which are directed primarily at its excessive costs and at the inadequate loss spreading or compensation it gives. Most of these criticisms are familiar, and there is little point in reviewing them. My aim here is to examine the fault system in light of the analysis I have made of the various aims of accident law and to discuss whether or not it meets these aims in a satisfactory fashion. Thus, rather than stressing the fact that fault is expensive and results in inadequate spreading, I will discuss whether or not this expense and lack of spreading can be justified by the system's results in terms of primary accident cost reduction and in terms of justice.

The three most important things to realize about the fault system are (1) that it is essentially a mixed system—that is, a system that is not committed to just one goal or subgoal but attempts instead to achieve all the goals to some degree through mixed methods; (2) that it begins by viewing each accident as being the exclusive concern of the parties immediately involved and tries to allocate costs accordingly; and (3) that it allows insurance of both victim and injurer.

A result of the first characteristic is that most attacks on fault based on the notion that it does not achieve any single goal optimally are misleading. But those defenses of fault that attack its potential substitutes on the ground that *they* do not achieve a single goal perfectly are equally misleading, for implicit in such defenses is the notion that fault does achieve, or tries to achieve, a single goal.[1] Any comparison of different systems of accident law must focus instead on the question of which system accomplishes our mixed goals best. Moreover, in evaluating various systems we must remember that our goals, and the possibilities for accomplishing them, vary from one area to another. An analysis of how well various systems would be likely to work in particular areas

1. See Blum and Kalven, *Public Law Perspectives;* cf. Calabresi, "The Wonderful World," at 221.

would require much empirical research because our aims may differ in different areas and because the possibility of accomplishing well the different aims depends on the industries and market structures with which we are dealing in each area. Thus the best system for dealing with automobile accidents is not necessarily the best system for handling home accidents. This is why I do not propose to outline any total accident law system in this book. But a preliminary analysis of how well our present fault system is accomplishing the various aims of accident law—primary accident cost deterrence, spreading, efficiency, and justice—is, nonetheless, possible and definitely fruitful because it indicates the mode of analysis that can be used in evaluating other mixed systems, be they Keeton-O'Connell, the Blum and Kalven stopgap plan, or the Defense Research Institute approach.

The result of the second characteristic of the fault system— viewing each accident as the exclusive concern of the parties directly involved—is that the standards for allocating liability under fault tend to be those that would serve to accomplish the various aims of accident law if a division of costs among the parties to each individual accident were all that took place. Thus, under fault, deterrence tends to be viewed as a simple question of blaming individual faulty parties that have caused an accident. And the efficiency goal becomes no more than the cheapest way of dividing costs among parties to each accident, given our desire to deter. Even justice resolves itself into the simple and rather simple-minded issue of which of two parties to a given accident deserves to bear the burden. In such a narrow, bilateral view of accidents, secondary cost avoidance almost inevitably becomes a subordinate goal and is reduced either to pressures for comparative negligence or to an *ad hoc* hunt for the richest party in the particular accident.[2] The unsatisfactory nature of this is seen in pressures for

2. It may also lead to rules of liability that generally burden classes of relatively wealthy people. Some writers have attempted to explain *respondeat superior* liability of the employer for employment-connected torts committed by employees in this way. See, e.g., Young B. Smith, "Frolic and Detour," 23 *Col. L. Rev.* 444, 452–58 (1923).

compensation outside of accident law, e.g. social insurance, or through modifications of the bilateral universe such as those accomplished by voluntary or even compulsory insurance. But these are simply modifications tacked onto a system designed to deal with a bilateral universe. In fact, much of the current discussion of fault is misleading not only because it stresses single goals, but also because it tends to be limited to how our goals can best be met without abandoning this bilateral view of accidents.[3]

The fault system, in practice, does accomplish a mixture of goals and does, almost despite itself, because it allows insurance, effect an allocation of accident costs well beyond the specific parties involved in each accident. The goals it seems to center on are primary accident cost reduction, which is accomplished through a very particular mixture of the general and specific deterrence approaches, and justice. Some spreading and efficiency aims are considered, but only very incidentally.

Fault resolves the question of what-is-a-cost-of-what through case-by-case determinations made after the accident and generally made on an all-or-nothing basis. Since individuals are allowed to insure against responsibility, however, the deterrence pressure resulting from the allocation of costs affects the actuarial groups to which the party held responsible belongs. In other words, this pressure affects all those who bear the same risk *ex ante* of being held *ex post* responsible. This characteristic gives rise to some of the most significant criticisms of the system. Other equally severe criticisms could be made of any fault system which did not allow insurance. Since that is not the existing system, however, I will not emphasize them.

The criteria for determining responsibility in the fault system are not purely market ones. "Moral" evaluations of the activities involved enter into the decision, and the aim of the *ex post* decision is to find not the cheapest but the best cost avoider.[4] Yet, be-

3. Nowhere is this truer than where justice is considered. See, e.g., Blum and Kalven, "The Empty Cabinet," at 270. Cf. infra pp. 289–308.

4. "Best" is used in a narrow sense. It does not mean best in terms of secondary or tertiary cost avoidance, let alone in terms of fairness. The term

cause insurance is allowed, and because the determination of liability is usually made after the accident, deterrence is accomplished in large part through the market. The determination of
what-is-the-cost is, within certain collective guidelines, also made
on a case-by-case basis, by a series of juries (a *series* since ultimately
the decisions in individual cases get spread to actuarial groups)
which, properly or not, take into account the desirability of the
specific acts involved in valuing costs. Thus activities are made
more expensive through market pressure which varies both with
the accident costs the activities "cause" and in accordance with
jury evaluations of their desirability.

The fault system I have just described is buttressed in our accident law by a whole gamut of specific deterrence rules and regulations, such as safety legislation with criminal penalties.[5] I do not,
however, consider these part of the fault system, because the question before us is not whether these noninsurable penalties are
necessary or improve the fault system—clearly they do—but,
rather, whether the fault system as I have defined it adds anything
worthwhile to what could be accomplished directly by these specific
deterrence penalties and by a first-rate system of market control of
accidents. Only in this way can we approach the issue of whether
the fault system is worth keeping.

Leaving aside these specific rules and regulations, the question
is whether the particular characteristic of the fault system, i.e. the
ex post allocation of responsibility on a case-by-case basis despite
the knowledge that the costs will be spread to actuarial groups,
gives us enough in specific and general deterrence to justify the
secondary and tertiary costs of this peculiar mixture. I will argue

---

just implies that collective rather than only market judgments are introduced
into the primary accident cost avoidance decision.

5. Examples would be laws against driving through stop signs and red
lights, laws against drunken driving, laws requiring that certain vehicle maintenance standards be met, or laws providing criminal penalties for excessively
negligent behavior on the highways. The Defense Research Institute would
move to increase such regulations substantially. See infra note 20, Chapter 10.

that the answer is clearly no; but to justify this answer it will be necessary first to examine in detail the workings of fault as a system of primary accident cost control, and then to see whether the fault system can be made more efficient or into an adequate spreader. Since I will conclude that fault has grave shortcomings in terms of primary cost control and that it cannot be made efficient or into an adequate spreader without totally altering it, the final question will be whether fault can justify all these shortcomings on the basis of justice.

CHAPTER 10

The Fault System and General Deterrence

The fault system can be viewed as a way of generally deterring activities that are involved in accidents. Decisions are made regarding what-is-a-cost-of-what and what-is-the-cost. On the basis of these decisions, accident costs are allocated among parties involved in accidents. Third-party liability insurance serves to spread these costs to actuarially relevant activities, and these activities react through the market to seek to reduce the burden placed on them.

But this leaves open the questions: (1) to what extent does the fault system make its what-is-a-cost-of-what and what-is-the-cost decisions in accordance with general deterrence guidelines; and (2) to what extent does it (a) employ the forum and methods most suited for finding the cheapest cost avoider, (b) introduce factors that are irrelevant from the general deterrence standpoint, and (c) impose on itself limitations in making allocation decisions, which make finding the cheapest cost avoider more difficult?

THE FAULT SYSTEM AND THE GENERAL
DETERRENCE GUIDELINES

Externalization due to Inadequate Knowledge

The fault system does not adequately use any of the guidelines a general deterrence approach would employ. It ignores altogether most of the considerations relevant to the internalization guideline. In deciding who should be liable, the fault system pays little attention to which of the possible categories of cost bearers is most likely to be aware of the risk involved. As a result, although it may seem to choose a party that can avoid the accident cheaply, it actually often picks one that will bring about very little cost avoidance.

This is best seen by considering why workmen's compensation brought about such a change in industrial accident cost avoidance. In theory it should have made no difference whether the workers as a group or the employers as a group were held liable. As I have explained elsewhere, the same accident cost would have become a part of the employment contract no matter who bore the loss.[1] In reality it made an enormous difference because employees consistently underestimated the likelihood of injury and therefore did not take or demand safety precautions consonant with the risk. To employers, that same risk was a cold cost figure which could easily be compared with the cost of safety devices. The result was that many safety devices were adopted.[2] By concentrating on the theoretical cost avoidance abilities of the individual faulty workers, the fault system ignored the far more important fact that accident costs allocated to individual workers tended to exert little economic pressure for safety because workers not yet injured systematically underestimated the risks of injury. As a result, these costs were largely externalized from both of the two possible cheapest cost avoiders—faulty workers and nonfaulty employers. An allocation to nonfaulty employers could and did lead to cheaper cost avoidance because it resulted in adequate evaluation of the risk of injury

1. See, e.g., Calabresi, "The Wonderful World," at 223–24.

2. Some industries have undoubtedly reacted more than others. Thus, it is alleged that in the construction industry in Ohio and Michigan little account is taken by contractors of the fact that fewer injuries mean lower workmen's compensation charges. See Paul E. Sands, "How Effective Is Safety Legislation?" 11 *J.L. & Econ.* 165, 177–78 (1968). The article suggests, however, that this may be due to the peculiarities of the industry which make it difficult to show management that accident payments may cost more than accident prevention. The article does not deal with this problem at length. Its main thrust is that one cannot show that substantial safety legislation (specific deterrence controls) in Ohio has led to better safety records than in Michigan, which at the time of the study had no comprehensive safety code. This conclusion, of course, casts some doubt on the effectiveness of specific deterrence controls. It says nothing about the desirability of market incentives.

and in its full retention as an economic factor internal to the employment contract. Workmen's compensation thus eased the problem in one area. But it made no change in the fault system, which still largely ignores the question of which category of possible loss bearer is most likely to be adequately informed of the costs involved.

Externalization due to Transfer

The fault system ignores altogether the effect of externalization by transfer. In allocating losses between the faulty pedestrian and the nonfaulty driver, it may seem to consider the cost avoidance potential of each. But it never asks who really pays. If the effect of putting the cost on the pedestrian is that the tab is paid by social insurance raised from general tax revenues, behavior by pedestrians will not be affected at all. It would be far better to put the cost on the driver, making it a cost of driving and thus retaining it on the pedestrian-driver nexus, than to have it be externalized to taxpayers generally. The point would be the same, though the opposite conclusion would be drawn, if faulty drivers generally were judgment-proof and injured victims of judgment-proof drivers were compensated from general tax revenues. On this hypothesis, the issue of whether car-pedestrian accidents are most cheaply avoided by charging faulty drivers or by charging nonfaulty pedestrians would ignore the real issue, namely, whether they would be avoided more cheaply by charging taxpayers generally or nonfaulty pedestrians.

These hypotheses, of course, are not meant to represent the real world. They are meant to point out that the fault system is not very likely to pick the cheapest cost avoider because it never looks beyond the particular accident to who really pays.

Externalization due to Insufficient Subcategorization

The same concentration on the particular makes the fault system ignore the danger of externalization due to insufficient subcategorization.[3] At first glance this may seem strange, for what greater

3. But see Blum and Kalven, "The Empty Cabinet," at 244.

subcategorization can there be than to choose the individual driver or pedestrian in the particular accident? It may not be worth the cost to subcategorize that far, but surely the fault system cannot be faulted for failure to subcategorize enough. Unfortunately, the facts of accident cost allocation are such that the fault system, while incurring massive administrative costs in order to subcategorize to the last degree, ends up failing to subcategorize adequately. This failure is really a product of externalization due to both transfer and inadequate knowledge.

One could view the fault system as seeking the cheapest cost avoider in each accident.[4] The particular driver or pedestrian held liable[5] appears to be the smallest subcategory of driving or walking possible. The theory is that by holding the smallest subcategory liable one builds up relevant larger categories which bear their appropriate costs. Thus if 25-year-old and 35-year-old drivers had equal accident propensities, it would not matter, except in terms of administrative costs, that we bothered to differentiate them into separate subcategories. The sum of the cases would show an equal burden on both subcategories and the allocation by age would have been harmless. If instead it turned out that they had different accident records, the difference would be reflected in the sum of accident costs charged to each, and a potentially significant subcategory difference would have been made.

The problem is that categories are not built up that way; they are built up on the basis of insurance companies' estimates of what the relevant differences are and how expensive it is to recognize them. As walking is not an organized activity, it may be far more expensive to sell insurance by category of pedestrian than by cate-

4. In fact, the fault system probably does not even seek the cheapest cost avoider among the litigants in each particular accident situation. If nothing else, the intentional introduction of moral judgments into the liability decision should suffice to make inaccurate any such simplified statement of what the fault system attempts to do. If despite this we evaluate fault as a market control system, the best that can be said for it is that it may be trying to identify the cheapest cost avoider among the litigants. Cf. Blum and Kalven, *Public Law Perspectives,* at 63, 69.

5. For a definition of "held liable," see supra note 26, Chapter 7.

gory of driver. As a result, allocation of a particular accident cost to a faulty pedestrian in the belief that this will result in distinguishing a subcategory of pedestrians who are particularly accident prone may be doomed to failure. The costs of establishing such a subcategory may be so great that the result of this allocation would be to place the cost on pedestrianism generally or, even more likely, on living generally (through general accident insurance). This might be a less adequate subcategorization than if the nonfaulty driver had been held liable, since the costs of insurance categorization for driving might be such that this allocation would result in burdening that subcategory of drivers who are most likely to hit pedestrians.

The point is simply this: the fault system's concentration on whether the particular pedestrian or driver could avoid the accident most cheaply ignores the fact that because of insurance, neither will actually bear the accident costs. And the breadth of the insurance categories that will actually bear the costs and therefore affect behavior depends not only on the difference in accident-cost causing potential of the members of the category, but also on the cost of differentiating these members into subcategories and selling insurance to such differentiated groups. This in turn depends on whether the loss is placed on an organized activity such as driving or on an unorganized activity such as walking, and on whether it is placed in a way that stimulates first- or third-party insurance. If what we are looking for, in other words, is the feasible insurance category that can avoid the accident costs most cheaply (i.e. which subcategorizes as much as possible), we will do far better to look for it directly rather than to look for a totally hypothetical individual cheapest cost avoider and hope that charging him will result in the best insurance category possible.

It may be said, however, that this is simply a bad effect of insurance and that the fault system would successfully subcategorize if insurance were forbidden. Then, it might be claimed, each individual would bear his own losses and the greatest degree of subcategorization possible would be achieved. But this is not what would happen. Just as externalization by transfer (through insurance) causes the fault system's case-by-case allocation of accident costs to result in broader categories than are necessary, so externalization due to inadequate knowledge causes the same thing when there is no insurance. Without insurance, allocation of accident costs to individuals involved in specific accidents affects behavior only to the extent that other individuals correctly identify with those who are charged with the costs. To the extent that individuals fail to appreciate adequately the risk of an accident cost burden falling on them, the cost allocation will fail in its objective. Similarly, to the extent that individuals overestimate the risk to themselves, they will overreact to the cost allocation. Moreover, if individuals associate the risk with a broader activity than the one that would actually bear the cost if there were insurance, they may well abstain from a broader activity than they should, and once again inadequate subcategorization will have resulted.

Assume car-pedestrian accidents occur mainly to young drivers driving at night. Allocation of the costs to them, insurance being forbidden, may well result in externalization, even assuming that they are not judgment-proof. If young drivers who drive at night systematically underestimate the risk of such accidents, they will not modify their behavior. If older drivers overestimate the risk, they may unnecessarily (and uselessly) stop driving at night. Even worse, they may stop driving altogether because they do not realize the extent to which the risk is night-associated. In all these cases, the appropriate subcategory would not be affected.[6] Clearly, prohibiting insurance would not make the fault system an adequate system for internalizing costs.[7]

---

6. An equally undesirable result would occur even if drivers estimate the risk of accidents accurately but give that risk a greater value than they would if they could insure against it. This would happen if they believed—probably quite rightly—that an unspread burden would hurt them more than a spread burden. In this situation, prohibiting insurance would cause a larger than optimal burden to be placed on the activity.

7. This discussion leaves out other reasons why prohibiting insurance may result in externalization. If the result of barring insurance is that too many people are crushed by unspread accident burdens, the demand for some government compensation scheme is likely to arise. Such a scheme, if paid out of

Externalization and Fault—A Summary

The whole discussion of externalization can be summarized in the following way. It may be that the fault system seeks to allocate accident costs to the *individual* party to an accident who could have avoided the accident costs most cheaply. But such individual allocation fails to find the true cheapest cost avoider, because the individual who is picked often will not ultimately bear the costs charged to him, and even in those cases where he does, there is substantial danger that the allocation will not affect those who are, in fact, prone to the same accident costs as he. The costs in all these cases will be externalized to other groups of people.

Rather than centering on the individual, a system designed to find the cheapest cost avoider should therefore look to the groups that will actually bear the loss. By doing this, the system maximizes the chances of charging costs to the group that can avoid them most cheaply. It is useless to charge a pedestrian with the costs of car-pedestrian accidents, even though in theory he could avoid them more cheaply than the driver, if the effect of charging him is that income taxes go up by an infinitesimal amount and injured pedestrians are compensated from the general coffers. It would be appropriate to consider instead whether the category of drivers that would bear this loss if it were allocated to the driver could avoid the accident more cheaply than the state could. In my example it would be they, and not the individual litigants, who would be the cost avoiders among whom we must identify the cheapest.

Relationship between Avoidance and Administrative Costs

If the fault system does a poor job of keeping accident costs from being externalized for any given level of administrative costs,

---

general taxes, would have the effect of externalizing the cost of accidents from the people held liable to taxpayers generally. Even with insurance, demands for this kind of political externalization by transfer are great under the fault system. Without insurance the demands would probably be overwhelming.

it does a terrible job of achieving an optimal relationship between avoidance costs and administrative costs. The most expensive aspect of the fault system is its case-by-case jury determination of who should bear losses. And yet, as we have seen in the discussion of externalization, it is precisely that case-by-case approach which seems to lead to unnecessary externalization.

Perhaps this is not a necessary result. Perhaps one could devise a system of case-by-case allocation of costs that could consider the factors relevant to externalization. But at best this would be a harmless though costly exercise, walking uphill simply to walk down again. If the aim is to find the cheapest cost avoider categories, the burden must surely rest on case-by-case allocation of costs to prove that it adds something worthwhile. So far that has not been shown. I do not mean by this that records of individual cases ought not to be kept and used to decide which categories are relevant. I mean that the fault system's method of allocating damages is an extremely expensive way to build up a statistic, quite apart from the fact that the resulting statistic is likely to be misleading. We have already seen why it is misleading to the extent that it ignores externalization. As we shall soon see, such a case-by-case attempt to find cheapest cost avoiders is misleading for other reasons as well. Here it is enough to say that it is a very expensive way of being misled.[8]

Besides requiring what may be unnecessary administrative costs of case-by-case determination, the fault system fails to achieve an optimal level of administrative costs for another reason. In allocating accident costs, it fails to consider which of the parties is the cheapest spreader or insurance buyer. I am not concerned here with the failure of the fault system to spread accident costs adequately from society's point of view. This problem, which causes

8. The most efficient way of building statistics is to use scientific samplings of accidents. The fault system's samplings are anything but scientific. At best they are haphazard, and at worst they are biased toward those cases that reach the courts. In addition, they probably involve a much larger number of samples than would be needed if scientific sampling were used, entailing needless expense.

the fault system to be unstable, will be discussed later. I am concerned here with its failure to give weight to the fact that it costs different parties to an accident different amounts to spread the accident costs, even though they may be equally prone to that particular accident. The effect of allocating costs to parties that can spread only by paying relatively high insurance premiums is that unnecessary costs of spreading are introduced into the system, which can be avoided only by failing to insure. But then an unnecessary burden of unspread accident costs is introduced. Either way we have an inefficient system.

This problem only arises because of the existence of transaction costs. Without such costs, parties having equal risk of accidents would always face equal premiums. With transaction costs this often is not true. Industrial accidents may again be a good example. It may well have been true that workers could only get insurance for themselves at relatively high rates, whether they went to insurance companies or made individual contracts with employers to indemnify them. But employers, if held initially liable, could insure far more cheaply against precisely the same risks, indeed the same accidents. Yet the fault system deemed this irrelevant to liability.

As we have already seen, this weakness has an important connection with externalization. If the desire to spread accident costs is sufficiently great and if the cost of insurance to one party is sufficiently high, the result of holding that party responsible may be to cause him to insure anyway but at a very broad category level where insurance can be obtained more cheaply. The effect of this would be to avoid the unnecessary spreading cost but at the price of incurring less adequate accident cost avoidance because of externalization. In essence, this is what was involved in the example of the fault system's externalization by inadequate subcategorization.

If drivers and pedestrians were equally good avoiders of car-pedestrian accident costs but insurance against such accidents was much more expensive for pedestrians than for drivers (since walking is not an organized activity), making the pedestrian liable would present the following choices: (1) The pedestrian might not insure. (This would result in unspread accident costs and unnecessary losses; externalization due to inadequate knowledge might also occur.) (2) The pedestrian might buy pedestrian insurance. (This would accomplish the desired accident cost avoidance at an unnecessary cost because, *ex hypothesis,* an equally good accident-cost avoider, the driver, could buy insurance at lower rates.) (3) The pedestrian might find it cheapest to buy insurance that covered all accidents. (Spreading would be accomplished, but the cost of car-pedestrian accidents would have been made a general cost of living and not kept on either of the two subcategories of living that could avoid the accident costs most cheaply, driving and walking.)

Each of these results would be less desirable than what would occur if the cost were placed on driving originally. Indeed, even if drivers could avoid accident costs somewhat less easily than pedestrians (because all drivers were free from fault and all pedestrians were somewhat faulty), the same result might still hold true. The choices facing pedestrians would be the same. Both pedestrian noninsurance and pedestrian insurance might still cost society so much as to be less desirable than driver insurance, even though drivers could only avoid the accidents somewhat less cheaply than pedestrians. And externalization of the cost by pedestrians to living in general through comprehensive accident insurance would surely be less desirable than driver insurance because drivers could avoid car-pedestrian accidents more cheaply than citizens could in general.[9]

9. This general weakness of the fault system may come about simply because in ignoring who can insure most cheaply, the system seeks the cheapest cost avoider among the litigants in an incomplete way. It may seek the cheapest avoider of primary costs. But by ignoring which of the litigants is the cheapest avoider of secondary costs, it may burden a litigant who is not the cheapest avoider of the sum of primary and secondary costs. And this ultimately results in unnecessary costs being borne.

The Best Briber

The fault system does not even purport to take into account the third guideline I suggested for finding the cheapest cost avoider: when we are unsure who the cheapest cost avoider is, we should allocate the cost so that the market has the greatest chance of correcting possible errors. This amounts to saying: when in doubt, allocate the cost to the party that can most cheaply enter into transactions to rectify an error. There is no point in discussing this criterion at length. The manner in which transactions can be entered into in order to rectify allocation errors has been discussed in R. H. Coase's celebrated article;[10] I have tried to expand on his analysis in a recent article.[11]

The thrust of the argument can be readily shown by an example. Suppose the location of a factory near a residential area results in an air pollution problem. Suppose also that there are two possible methods of reducing the costs of pollution substantially. The first involves the factory building a higher smokestack with a smoke control device on it. The second consists of homeowners installing a new type of glass in their windows. Finally, make the unlikely assumption that we do not know which of the two methods would avoid the cost of pollution most cheaply. If it cost nothing to bribe, the market would always find and establish the cheaper method. But bribing costs money, and since it is almost certainly cheaper for the factory to bribe homeowners than it is for homeowners to unite to bribe the factory, liability of the factory would be justified. This is not because we know which method of cost avoidance is cheapest, but because by making the factory liable we have diminished the obstacles to corrective market action.

The contrast between this approach and that of the fault system is manifest. If there is "fault," the allocation would be placed on the faulty party, regardless of how doubtful it is that the existence of fault makes that party the cheapest cost avoider and regardless

10. Coase, "The Problem of Social Cost."
11. Calabresi, "Transaction Costs."

of which party can most cheaply bargain with the other to correct an error. If there is no fault, the fault system lets it lie where it falls and makes no attempt to charge the party that can find the cheapest cost avoider most cheaply. My example is an overly simplified one, and its very simplicity may help explain why the fault system is not often used in the area of factory pollution problems. But this does not alter the fact that the failure of the fault system to concern itself with the question of finding the best briber suggests pretty strongly that the fault system is not, by any means, a good system of market control of accidents.

THE FAULT SYSTEM: FORUM AND METHOD

If the fault system ignores the guidelines for finding the cheapest cost avoider, does it at least use a forum and method which can intuitively make the best judgment as to who the cheapest cost avoider is likely to be? The fault system uses a jury, a case-by-case allocation of losses, and adopts a series of limitations such as "all-or-nothing damages" and "no recovery if neither party is at fault." It also encourages the introduction of moral factors into the decision. Leaving the last point aside—for it obviously suggests that the fault system is meant to be a mixed system of accident control rather than a market system, and I am not yet discussing how effective a mixed system it is—both the forum chosen and the limitations which fault imposes on itself make selection of the cheapest cost avoider far less likely than need be.

Case-by-Case versus Category Determinations

The first point is that a case-by-case determination of who ought to bear losses is not particularly desirable if the object is to find the cheapest cost avoider. We have already seen that case-by-case decisions (1) make it difficult to take externalization into account, (2) make it difficult to consider what category can bribe most easily, and (3) entail substantial administrative expense.

There are, however, other reasons why case-by-case determinations are likely to be misleading in finding the cheapest cost avoid-

er. The effect of case-by-case decisions is to center on the particular
or unusual cause of an accident. If one asks, as case-by-case determinations tend to do, "What went wrong in this case?" the answer
will most likely center on the peculiar cause. Yet there is a very
good argument for the notion that the cheapest way of avoiding
accident costs is not to attempt to control the *unusual* event but
rather to modify a recurring event. It may be that absentmindedness is a cause of one particular accident, too much whiskey the
cause of another, and drowsiness the cause of a third. But it may
also be that a badly designed curve or inadequate tires are causes
of each of these as well. The fault system, because it centers on
the possible *particular* cost avoider, is very likely to ignore the
recurring cost avoider and hence fail altogether to consider some
potential cheapest cost avoiders such as highway builders or tire-
makers.

This weakness is compounded by the fact that concentration
on particular accidents inevitably means concentration on *accident*
avoidance. What we should be concerned with instead, in terms
of market control, is accident *cost* avoidance. It may be very expensive to avoid many car accidents altogether, and yet their costs
could be reduced substantially by designing cars differently. The
alternative approach, a system that assessed liability to categories
on the basis of broad accident cost statistics derived from individual
cases and did not seek to determine a single liable party in each
case,[12] would be much more likely than the fault system to give
accident *cost* avoidance the importance it deserves.

There are, of course, disadvantages to such a category-by-category
device for allocating losses. First, category-by-category allocation
makes the introduction of individualized moral judgments into the
allocation decision harder. This explains why category allocation

12. It may be that the doctrine placing liability without fault on ultrahazardous activities represented a rudimentary attempt to take such an approach—rudimentary partly because it assessed liability totally to one category, whereas a division of the burden might give cheaper cost avoidance.
See further infra note 19.

cannot be used in the fault system. Whether the impossibility of introducing individualized moral judgments in the cost allocation is serious will be considered later, when I examine mixed systems of primary cost control, since such judgments are unnecessary to market controls. Second, it is less flexible than case-by-case allocations and may therefore result in lags in recognizing changes in who could avoid costs most cheaply. Finally, just because it can concentrate on general or recurring causes of accidents, it might result in overlooking some very cheaply avoided particular causes of very high accident costs. But these last two disadvantages do not seem as likely as the errors that case-by-case decisions make likely. This is especially so since the statistics on which allocations of liability by categories would be based would continue to be compiled from investigation of particular cases.

Such a method of compiling statistics, moreover, though costly, is bound to be cheaper than the fault system's case-by-case allocation of losses, because the description of what happened given by the parties in a compilation-of-statistics method is inherently more credible than the description of the same events given by the parties to a tort action. This would be especially true if the description given for purposes of statistics were immune from subsequent use in criminal cases. The point is that in the fault system the victim has every reason to lie, or at least exaggerate, in order to establish the injurer's fault. This would not be so in compiling statistics if the right to compensation did not depend on the facts of the particular case and the statistics merely affected which categories of activities paid what amounts into the fund from which compensation would be sought.[13]

At first glance it might appear that this lack of incentive to exaggerate would already be the case with the insured injurer under the fault system. After all, he has already paid his premiums, so

---

13. Cf. Franklin, "Replacing the Negligence Lottery: Compensation and Selective Reimbursement," at 798–802. For another reason why such a method of compiling statistics would be cheaper, see supra note 8.

why should he lie about what happened?[14] But this conclusion ignores both the requirements of the insurance contract and the psychology of litigants. Insurance contracts normally require, on pain of nonpayment in case of liability, that the insured cooperate with the company in defending any suit. This is not meant to encourage exaggeration or misstatements on the part of the injurer, but it certainly puts him in the position of an adversary to the victim. Unreliability of the statements he makes follows as a matter of course. The effect is compounded by the fact of litigation. However little pressure to act safely the injurer may have felt before the accident because he was insured, once litigation is started he feels that, at least in part, he is on trial and that a verdict of liability impugns his behavior. Again the unreliability of his statements follows. A very different attitude and considerably greater reliability seem likely if, after each accident, facts are gathered only for the purpose of deciding which category of activities will pay what costs into a general compensation fund.

When the tendency of case-by-case jury decisions to miss relevant cost avoiders is added to the expense incurred and to the disadvantages of case-by-case determinations already discussed, it becomes pretty clear that a system seeking to allocate accident costs so as to maximize the degree of market control would not use case-by-case determinations. If this is so, use of case-by-case jury decisions in the fault system must find whatever justification it may have either in far better what-is-the-cost decisions or in aims unrelated to market control of accidents.

I think a fair conclusion to my earlier discussion of case-by-case decisions regarding what-is-the-cost would be that they are not worth their expense unless that expense is required anyway for what-is-a-cost-of-what decisions. And even if they were not too

14. The fact that he has already paid his premiums has other consequence. too. It renders the fault system ineffective as a system of collective control o faulty conduct (see infra pp. 269–72).

Because of externalization by inadequate knowledge (see supra pp. 148–50) the general absence of victim insurance does not suffice to put adequate pres sure on potential victims.

expensive, it is far from certain that they would be more accurate than cost evaluations made by categories of damages. Thus we may conclude that the case-by-case jury determinations used by the fault system can only be justified by aims and approaches other than the general deterrence of primary accident costs. To put the same thing slightly differently, a system that sought to accomplish a high degree of market control of accidents could, in theory, use jury and case-by-case decisions, but it is pretty clear that use of such a forum and method would be both wasteful and inaccurate in terms of that system's avowed goal.

Self-Imposed Limitations

The second point about the method the fault system uses to allocate accident losses deals with the limitations it imposes on itself. These are primarily (1) little or no quantitative division of damages, (2) little or no qualitative division of damages, and (3) allocation of damages to the victim where no fault is found. These limitations may not be as crucial to the fault system as case-by-case decisions; they could be modified and the system would still remain essentially a fault system.[15] At the moment, however, they are very much a part of the fault system and certainly hamper the search for the cheapest cost avoider.

Normally the fault system does not divide damages among involved parties. In terms of market control of accident costs, this implies that in every accident the cheapest way of avoiding costs involves altering the behavior of only one party. But this is clearly not the case. Often the cheapest way of avoiding accident costs is for several parties or activities to alter their behavior somewhat. The cheapest way of avoiding car-pedestrian accident costs may be for cars to use spongy bumpers and for pedestrians to wear

15. A general shift to comparative negligence is, of course, the most obvious example of such a modification. Greater emphasis than is now allowed on which individual litigant could control which types of damages most easily would be another. A shift to a division of damages on some nonfault basis where neither party is at fault would be a bigger change. But cf. Larsen v. General Motors Corporation, 391 F.2d 495, 503–04 (8th Cir. 1968).

fluorescent buttons rather than either to have cars adopt pedestrian-spotting radar or to have pedestrians wear armor-plated underwear. If this is true, an allocation of accident costs that divides the costs between drivers and pedestrians would be better than one that charges all costs to one group. I do not claim that this will always be the case. I do not even claim *here* that, in the absence of any indication as to who in fact is the cheapest cost avoider, a division of costs is better than lumping all costs on one party, although I have so argued earlier and although there are some reasons for believing this to be true. I merely argue that a system which, at least in theory, *excludes* division of damages is unnecessarily limiting itself in the search for the cheapest way of avoiding accident costs, because sometimes the cheapest way requires dividing accident costs among several parties.

As we saw when what-is-the-cost was discussed, qualitative division of damages may be even more significant than quantitative division of damages in terms of cheap accident cost avoidance. The activity that can most cheaply avoid certain types of costs is often not the activity that can most cheaply avoid others. Rules under the fault system requiring victims to take steps to mitigate damages once they have occurred can be viewed as halting steps to deal with this problem. So can the occasional cases allocating to victims damages that are totally atypical of the risk on the basis of which the injurer was deemed at fault.[16] But certainly the fault system does not make qualitative divisions of damages according to ease of cost avoidance as a matter of course. Typically damages for pain and suffering are readily given when recovery is allowed for physical and economic damage. Also typically, the exceptional

16. See, e.g., Fowler V. Harper and Fleming James, Jr., *The Law of Torts,* 2 (Boston, Little Brown, 1956), at 1136–37: "And carelessness in giving a gun to a young child is not negligence with respect to injury caused by dropping the gun on plaintiff's foot, since the risk of the child's dropping a fairly heavy object was not (we assume) so fraught with the chance of injury as to make the entrustment unreasonable." If the injured party was a hemophiliac and the party who gave the gun did not know it, the example would be especially apt.

value of a great violinist's hand is assessed to a faulty injurer because "one takes one's victim as one finds him." Yet there are good arguments to support the idea that in whole categories of cases, such as industrial accidents and car-pedestrian accidents, the injurer is likely to be the cheapest cost avoider with respect to normal physical and economic costs, while the victim may be the cheapest cost avoider with respect to pain and suffering and highly individualized economic damage like the violinist's hand. These arguments are far from conclusive, and there is no need to resolve the issues here. It is sufficient to point out that the fault system seems oblivious even to the possible relevance of widespread qualitative division of accident costs. Therefore, it must fail too frequently to allocate costs in a way that would maximize the chances of causing their cheapest possible avoidance.

The last and perhaps most important self-imposed limitation of the fault system is the rule that in the absence of fault, costs remain where they fall. Holmes gave the best justification for this rule when he wrote that where no benefit accrues to society from shifting a loss, there is no reason to incur the administrative costs of shifting it.[17] That statement is unexceptionable in itself, but as applied to the faultless accident it contains invalid premises.

First, it assumes that administrative costs are saved by not shifting the loss in faultless accidents. But this is true only if the distinction between faultless and faulty accidents is so clear that, on the one hand, a great number of costly attempts to shift losses are precluded by the rule and, on the other, those losses that are shifted under the rule do not cost substantially more to shift because of the existence of the rule. A little reflection on how the fault system operates today should suggest that this is a dubious assumption. How often do people fail to sue because absence of fault is obvious? How much more expensive than necessary is accident litigation because fault is an issue in each particular case?

17. See Oliver Wendell Holmes, Jr., *The Common Law* (Howe ed. Cambridge, Belknap Press, 1963) at 76–77.

Second, Holmes' statement also requires that no societal benefit accrue from a shifting of the loss. He did not, of course, consider spreading as a possible societal benefit, and for the present, neither do I. But is it so clear that in the absence of fault, spreading would be the only reason to shift some accident losses? Is it clear, that is, that in such a case it would make no difference in the search for the cheapest cost avoider who bore the loss? I think enough has been said to suggest that the opposite is true. By no means does the absence of fault eliminate the possibility of making an allocation to the cheapest cost avoider, thereby maximizing market control of accidents and minimizing the sum of costs of accidents and of their avoidance.

Most obviously, if in the absence of any indication that one party is a cheaper cost avoider than the other, an even split maximizes the chances of allocating costs to the cheapest cost avoider, letting costs lie where they fall is bound to be wrong. In addition, one party may be a better briber than the other where neither is at fault. As we have seen, other things being equal, allocation of costs to the best briber maximizes the chances of optimal market control of accident costs.

Finally, even if we assume that absence of fault means that the individual parties to the accident are precisely equal in terms of ease of accident cost avoidance, the possibility of externalization might make one party a far cheaper loss avoider than the other. Once again, in concentrating on the individual parties and being indifferent to who bears the loss (in terms of fault or even in terms of cost avoidance), the fault system fails to look to who really pays, therefore failing to consider whether indifference still exists when the choice is between the parties who really pay. A pedestrian and a driver involved in an accident may be faultless, and we may therefore think it makes no difference who pays. But allocation of the loss to the pedestrian may result in the cost becoming a general cost of living, while allocation to the driver may make it a cost of driving for a particularly accident-prone group. If these two allocations are compared, we may find that we are no longer indifferent.

There may be other, quite complex reasons why a cheapest cost avoider can often be found even between two faultless parties, even viewing fault in terms of its best definition (Learned Hand's classic negligence calculus),[18] and even leaving aside externalization, best briber and so on. These involve the relevance of foreseeability to, and the effect of moral elements on, the negligence calculus. But they are too lengthy to outline here and are not essential to the point that a system seeking to burden the cheapest cost avoider would often shift losses even in the absence of fault. Indeed, the best answer to Holmes is that there are many areas in torts today where the shifting of losses in absence of fault has clearly resulted in a reduction of the sum of the costs of accidents and their avoidance and therefore in a benefit to society quite apart from possible spreading benefits.[19]

INSTABILITY OF THE FAULT SYSTEM'S MARKET DETERRENCE

There is still another reason why the fault system is a poor system of market control of primary costs. The reason is grounded in the fault system's failure to meet either the primary cost avoidance aim or the other aims of accident law satisfactorily. To the extent that the fault system fails to accomplish the spreading we desire, for example, it gives rise to demands for allocations of accident

18. See, e.g., Conway v. O'Brien, 111 F.2d 611, 612 (2d Cir. 1940), rev'd. on other grounds, 312 U.S. 492 (1941).

19. The effect on the development of safety devices caused by workmen's compensation and strict liability for ultrahazardous activities are two obvious examples. Cf. supra note 2. Another example might be the use of assumption of risk (in those few situations where the doctrine is used properly) to deter certain kinds of ultrahazardous plaintiff activity by denying liability where the behavior of the plaintiff was in no sense faulty, but where he (or the category to which he belonged) could, in fact, avoid the accident costs most cheaply, as he knew the risks involved as well as anyone and could avoid them more cheaply than anyone else.

costs on the basis of the best spreader and even to demands for social insurance. Similarly, to the extent that the fault system fails to deter adequately primary accident costs, it gives rise to demands for more specific regulations.[20] As a result of these and similar demands, modifications may be made in the fault system which in effect take us further from the general deterrence goal than is necessary.

If the desire to spread accident costs more widely than can be done under the current fault system leads to even partial social insurance, as in the Blum and Kalven stopgap plan, for example, the costs of accidents will be externalized to parties even less likely to be cheap cost avoiders than the "faulty" party. This may be desirable if it is the only way to achieve the amount of spreading we want. Clearly it is not desirable if allocation of costs on some basis other than that employed by the fault system could achieve the desired spreading and yet keep the accident costs on parties who are relatively cheap cost avoiders, as might perhaps occur under the Keeton-O'Connell or the American Insurance Association proposals.

Thus even the market deterrence that the fault system does accomplish is threatened by the system's instability, for many of the systems proposed to correct the faults of the fault system are ones that ignore the requirements of general deterrence altogether. The fact that there do exist other systems of liability that can be at least as effective (and probably more effective) from a general deterrence point of view and yet more secure against criticism on spreading and even on specific deterrence grounds suggest that

20. A prime example of this is the recent development of federal safety standards for automobiles. The fault system apparently did very little to encourage automobile manufacturers to make their cars accident-proof.

The Defense Research Institute has called for a program of detailed regulation and criminal penalties to prevent car accidents, "A Program for Highway Accident Prevention," 9 *For the Defense* 65 (November 1968); and for directives from state and local governments to their employees to wear seat belts, "Board Seeks Directives to Wear Safety Belts," 9 *For the Defense* 17 (March 1968).

an overall evaluation of fault as a system of general deterrence must result in a pretty low rating. Fault does accomplish some general deterrence, but it does so more expensively than necessary, with no systematic attempt to improve its general deterrence results, and with enough other defects to seem to be just a stepping stone to systems involving little or no general deterrence at all.

CHAPTER 11

The Fault System and Specific Deterrence

Thus far in this part I have attempted to establish that the fault system is not the system we would use if our aim were the establishment of an optimal system of market control of accident costs. I have tried to show that we would not allocate costs on the basis of fault if our object was to allocate accident costs to the party, category, or activity that can best make the choice between avoiding and incurring accident costs and thereby bring about the minimization of the sum of the costs of avoiding and having accidents. Finally, I have tried to show that the fault system is a poor system of market control even disregarding the fact that it decides who should bear losses partly on the basis of moral considerations antithetical to pure market control of accident costs.

It can be argued, however, that the fault system has no such market control aims in mind, and that the very fact that it introduces moral elements suggests that it is a different type of system which must be judged on a different basis—namely, its effectiveness as a system of collective control of accidents. I agree, but only in part. Some of the recent arguments in favor of fault are quite unclear on the issue. For example, Blum and Kalven imply at times that the perfect justification for the fault system is its efficacy as a system of market control of accidents.[1] Elsewhere in the same pieces, they imply that the system is justified by the purity of the justice it doles out (something I fail to see but will consider later). Finally, they sometimes seem to defend fault as an effective system of collective control.[2] I have argued that the fault system

1. See, e.g., Blum and Kalven, "The Empty Cabinet," at 244, 257; Blum and Kalven, *Public Law Perspectives,* at 63, 69.

2. See Blum and Kalven, "The Empty Cabinet," at 254–56, 268–72; Blum and Kalven, *Public Law Perspectives,* at 12–13, 83–84.

must be judged on all these bases—that it, like all real systems, is a mixed system which combines all these goals. Accordingly, I shall first consider the success of the fault system as a system of collective control of accidents and then evaluate how well it mixes market and collective elements.

The crucial difference between market deterrence and collective deterrence is that in the former we let individuals decide whether an act or activity is worth its cost to society, while in the latter we make the same decision collectively for individuals. It is not difficult to show that the fault system does nothing by way of collective deterrence that could not be done more effectively by a system of rules and regulations enforced by appropriate penalties, ranging from criminal nonmonetary penalties, such as jail, to civil monetary ones, such as noninsurable tort fines.

To see why the fault system is an inefficient system of collective control, we must first restate the two basic types of situations that most often seem to justify collective control. The clearest type is where the act or activity involved raises enough moral issues for us to be unwilling to let individuals decide for themselves whether the activity is worth its cost to society. In such cases it is irrelevant whether or not the origin of our moral attitudes rests on cost evaluations made long ago. The crucial point is that now, individual decisions are deemed undesirable. Murder is one obvious example; suicide is another.

In the second type of situation, the basic element is not morality but cost; here collective controls are more efficient than market controls. Early in this book I suggested that while it was inefficient to try to decide everything collectively, it could also be enormously expensive to put the cost of certain closely defined activities, or acts, on individuals in such a way that they could choose whether or not the act was worth its cost. Where we can be reasonably sure that most individuals given the choice between abstaining from a specific act and paying its costs would abstain, we are usually justified in barring the act altogether. The savings in administrative costs resulting from using collective controls would usually outweigh the loss to those few who would, if permitted, pay for the right to perform the act.[3] In both these situations it can be shown that use of noninsurable penalties would be far more effective than the fault system.

It may be well to underscore that when I refer to the fault system I am *not* talking about collectively determined noninsurable penalties based on fault or other wrongdoing. The question is: given the knowledge that the costs will be spread to actuarial groups, does postaccident allocation of responsibility on a case-by-case basis add anything desirable in the way of specific deterrence that we would not get under a system of noninsurable fines, penalties, and limitations? Do any situations exist where the fault system accomplishes specific deterrence better than appropriate noninsurable penalties?

SITUATIONS INVOLVING MORAL ISSUES

No accident situation can raise moral issues unless the individual can know before the accident, when he is still in control of his behavior, that the act or activity he wants to engage in is considered wrong or faulty, whether or not it leads to an accident. This follows from the meaning of the word "moral." Such wrongful acts or activities cannot always be described *precisely* before a specific event such as an accident. But they must at least be sufficiently definable and defined so that a normal individual can, if he wishes, apply the definition to the particular situation in which he finds himself.

Consider, for example, the distinction between drunken driving and careless driving. Drunken driving can be described clearly enough for individuals to know what is considered wrongful totally aside from the occurrence of any accident. Careless driving is another matter. It too may be considered wrongful, but it is difficult to give it an all-inclusive definition in the abstract. Still, we might be justified in classifying it as wrongful if individuals can apply our general notions about careless driving to real situations. But

3. Cf. Calabresi, "Transaction Costs," at 69–73.

practically speaking, this would only be meaningful—even in terms of the fault system's definitions—if individuals could apply them in time to avoid the socially unacceptable act. This fact is crucial to the fault system's ineffectiveness as a system of collective control.[4]

It should be readily apparent that whenever we are dealing with activities that can be defined independently of accidents, such as drunken driving, a system of appropriate noninsurable penalties is more likely to be an effective deterrent than the fault system, which allows a substantial part of the penalty to be both shifted and prepaid through insurance. The effectiveness of the collective deterrent is bound to be greater if the drunken driver must bear the penalty himself and if he faces the prospect of the full penalty at the time he chooses to drink and drive. In theory, collective deterrence would fine drunken drivers regardless of accidents. But noninsurable penalties remain more effective than the fault system even if in most cases drunken drivers are caught only if they have an accident. Indeed, the sole reason for catching drunken drivers only if they have an accident is one of economy. It costs too much to check if all drivers are sober, so we penalize drunken drivers only when an event such as an accident calls their drunkenness to our attention.

The case of careless driving is similar, but here there is even more reason for bringing collective controls to bear only when an accident has occurred. It is often impossible to label the act or activity careless except in the context of a potential accident situation. Therefore it is even more expensive, indeed impossible, to catch and penalize some types of careless driving unless an accident occurs. But the fact that much careless driving can only be caught after an accident does not alter the basic fact that we would not call it wrongful unless we believed that the driver could judge his behavior improper early enough to change it. Whenever this is so, whenever normal individuals can choose whether or not to engage in wrongful conduct before an accident, an appropriate

4. See supra pp. 119–28.

noninsurable penalty is necessarily a more effective deterrent than an already paid insurance premium.

I have emphasized the appropriateness of the penalty for several reasons. First, we may not always be correct in gauging whether the conduct was wrongful, i.e. whether the individual could identify it as such and abstain from it before an accident. Too large a fine or criminal penalty in an area where errors are likely may, as we have already seen, result in individuals abstaining from conduct we do not wish to affect, such as driving in general, for fear that if they drive at all they may occasionally be incorrectly condemned and penalized. Similarly, as we also saw, too small a penalty will simply be taken as an invitation to take a chance. These difficulties are, of course, unavoidable, but they do not alter the fact that a rational system of fines and penalties is bound to be more effective in dealing with this type of conduct than insurable fault payments, in which the only financial deterrent that can be effective at the time of the choice between doing or not doing a wrongful act is the possibility of higher premiums in the future[5] —a possibility that exists even when an accident is not due to a wrongful act by the insured.[6]

5. None of this discussion, of course, precludes making the noninsurable penalty greater if serious harm results than if it does not. As I noted earlier, supra note 22, Chapter 6, this might be done if the collective deciders believe that the degree of preaccident wrongdoing can to some extent be gauged by the seriousness of the resulting damages. Such a judgment represents, however, only one part of what is involved in choosing an appropriate size and type of penalty. In addition to the considerations mentioned in the text, another factor affecting the appropriate size of a noninsurable penalty is the income level of the wrongdoer, at least if the collective deciders seek to deter all individuals equally regardless of income size. See supra note 25, Chapter 6. Thus only by the merest coincidence would the appropriate penalty be equal to the damages caused, let alone to the increase in the injurer's insurance premiums resulting from his having had an accident.

6. It is often said, and as often denied, that insurance premiums are based not on the fault record of drivers, but rather on the record of their involvement in fault-caused accidents. The reason only fault-caused accidents are used is that only these involve payments by insurance companies, and therefore only these become part of insurance company actuarial tables. The reason

One may well ask if there is not a category of acts or activities that can be deemed wrongful only *after* an accident has occurred, or at least after it is too late to avoid them. And if there is such a category, is not this precisely the category the fault system attempts to deter collectively?

The answer is no, there is no such category, and even if there were the rubric of the fault system (its foreseeability requirements, etc.) would seem to make such a category irrelevant to a defense of the fault system.

After an accident we may all agree that certain acts were undesirable and regrettable. Nonetheless we could not properly call such acts wrongful when they occurred. Indeed, the most that can be said about acts that are deemed undesirable only when it is too late to avoid them is that they may cause us to judge undesirable some activities in which they tend to occur too frequently. If that is so, we may decide collectively that these activities are wrongful and should be controlled by fines, taxes, or penalties; or we may decide to let the market determine how much of each of the dangerous activities is wanted. In neither instance does a case for the fault system exist.

Situations in Which Collective Deterrence Is Economically Desirable

If the fault system cannot be justified when collective deterrence is sought because of the moral undesirability of certain acts, can it be justified where collective deterrence is sought on economic

---

involvement in such accidents may be used rather than *fault* is hard to understand if fault is a viable concept. The reason would seem to be that even if fault is a somewhat better indicator of who will be involved in future accidents, it is not sufficiently better to make categorization by fault worth its costs, *even after the expense of assessing fault has already been borne!* If this is so, it should by itself serve to damn fault irreparably. In any event, the manner in which insurance rates change as a result of accidents clearly is so haphazard and arbitrary under the fault system that the possibility of rate increases cannot conceivably be as good a collective deterrent as an intelligently fixed noninsurable fine.

grounds? Is there a place for the fault system where market controls are too expensive?

The answer is no. The typical case where market controls are too expensive involves the control of individual acts. It is much too expensive to put on the man who would run a red light the actual cost to society (in terms of risk of accident costs) of his running that light. The most a market system of controls can do efficiently is to assess higher rates—reflecting higher accident costs —to those who perform activities in which the temptation to run red lights is great. But a market system will do this only if charging such a risk category more is the cheapest way to avoid the costs of running red lights. A fault-insurance system can do no better; it will charge the same category of "possible red light runners." Indeed, it will charge that category *even if charging another category would do more to diminish these particular accident costs* (therein lies its difference from the market system).

But another way is available which we believe to be more effective than either the market or the fault system, and that is direct collective prohibition of running red lights and noninsurable punishment of violators. Such a noninsurable penalty represents the collective opinion that if individuals were made to pay the true costs of running red lights each time they ran one, they would usually find the cost greater than the need to run the light. Because the fault system, like the market system, must work primarily through raising the cost to categories of individuals rather than affecting the individual at the time of decision, it is necessarily as ineffective as the market system in dealing with such acts, and considerably less effective than a system of penalties.

I submit that the kind of reasoning applied to these two major areas where collective deterrence offers the best control system can be applied equally well to other areas. Moreover, the inadequate and inefficient collective control of accident costs that the fault system does achieve is threatened by the same instability that threatens the inadequate market control given by the fault system. If the result of the fault system's insufficient spreading and undue expense is that accident costs get handled through social insurance, the specific deterrence elements in the fault system will be lost.[7] Thus it should be clear from the criticisms leveled at the fault system that it seeks the best cost avoider only in the narrowest of terms. Many collective goals are ignored by the fault system; this explains its current instability. Implicit in this statement is my belief that other systems can be established which would give better collective control of primary accident costs and still be better at secondary and tertiary cost avoidance than the fault system. Accordingly, I conclude that the fault system cannot be justified as a system of collective control of accident costs.

There is still the possibility, though, that even if the fault system does a bad job of both market control and collective control, it does an adequate job of mixing the two, or at least a better mixing job than other possible systems. Once again, what we are considering is the fault-insurance system itself, not the noninsurable penalties that go along with the system. The question is not whether we want to keep or add to noninsurable penalties, nor whether we want a system of market control of accidents, but whether, assuming we want a mixed system of accident cost control, the particular mixture that the fault system (as I have defined it) gives us is better than other possible mixtures.

7. Some specific deterrence will remain as a result of the criminal fines and penalties buttressing the fault system.

CHAPTER 12

The Fault System as a Mixed System of Primary Cost Control

There are two basic types of mixed systems of accident cost control that we may prefer to a pure system. We may wish to limit an activity or penalize it on an involvement basis; as we have seen, this calls for a combination of collective and market controls. Or we may wish to control some activities or subcategories of them collectively, while leaving other activities or subcategories of activities to market control. The question is, then, whether the fault system achieves our goals in either of these situations. Does it help us when we want a mixed control of one activity? Does it help us when we want to control different activities in different ways?

The answers to these questions depend on whether there is anything that prevents us from using the best market control devices together with the best collective control devices in either of these situations. If there is nothing to prevent us from using the best market and collective methods together, then the case for the fault system as a good compromise must fall.

Let us look first at activities we wish to control in a mixed way, ones we wish to limit rather than restrict. A simple example will show that there is nothing to keep us from using the best market and collective controls together. Suppose that for various collective reasons, moral or otherwise, we wish to *limit* cigarette smoking by adults, but that we do not care when or where adults smoke. (To the extent that we do care, we would use collective deterrence sanctions to control the situation, as, in fact, we do with respect to smoking in gas stations.) If this is our only aim, the easiest way would be either to limit the amount of cigarettes produced and let the price rise until the demand for cigarettes met the newly limited supply, or to tax cigarettes to the point where buyers would only demand the amount we collectively sought to have produced. Either way would be a simple combination of collective and market controls and would be more efficient than raising the price of smoking by considering all smokers involved in accidents to be faulty.

If our concern with smoking were broader, if we also worried about accident costs that smoking "caused," the situation would be somewhat more complex. In this situation we could use the fault system, allocating all accident costs where one party was smoking and where smoking turned out to be one of several contributing ("but for") causes of the accident to that party.[1] This would reduce accident costs to some extent and it would reduce smoking to some extent—but it would do neither optimally.

We would still do better to charge the *cheapest* cost avoider in accidents involving a smoker, whether this was the smoker or not, for this would reduce accident costs optimally—that is, most cheaply. To the extent that this allocation still left too many cigarettes being smoked (in terms of our collective judgment to limit smoking), we could further reduce smoking by an appropriate tax. If, in addition, smoking in some situations was now collectively thought to be too dangerous or wrongful because it caused too many accidents, we could control *that* type of smoking by directly imposed noninsurable penalties. We could, for ex-

---

1. Here and in the next several pages I do not use the term "contributing" or "but for" cause in the strict sense of a condition *sine qua non,* as Hart and Honoré define it in Chapter 5 of *Causation in the Law,* but rather to include all those factors they term "causally relevant." Thus, my term includes each of two smokers whose simultaneous, independent lighting of a match results in a gas explosion. I use the words "but for" despite the existence of such cases because, as Hart and Honoré say, once "we allow for these anomalies, and are careful to distinguish the merely analytic or incidental forms of condition *sine qua non* then we may treat a factor that survives the test question 'Would Y have happened if X had not?' [the strict "but for" test] as likely to be causally relevant in some one of the ways we have distinguished," and because the phrase "but for cause" is probably more generally understood than a term such as "causally relevant." Id. at 122.

ample, treat smoking while driving like smoking at gas stations. These moves would accomplish both our collective and our market aims better than the fault system because they would allow those individuals to smoke who enjoyed smoking most and who were harmless in the sense that their smoking (1) did not lead to accidents that could have been avoided most cheaply by their refraining from smoking, and (2) did not take place in circumstances in which smoking was collectively deemed to be wrongful. Indeed, only if we wanted to reduce accidents in which smoking was one of several "but for" causes, regardless of whether this was the best way of reducing the amount either of smoking in general, or of dangerous or wrongful smoking, could we justify a system that made all accident-involved smokers liable. To abstract from the particular to the general, this means that the fault system can only be justified if what we wish to minimize is *neither the sum of the costs of accidents and their avoidance (the market goal), nor "faulty" or wrongful behavior (the collective goal), nor both of these (the mixed goal), but rather only those accidents in which "faulty" behavior is a "but for" cause.* The more one examines this proposition, the more absurd the fault system becomes.

This conclusion is the direct result of the fact that optimal methods of market control can be used consistently with optimal methods of collective control, whether the aim is to limit an activity, or to control some activities (or parts of activities) through the market and other activities (or parts of activities) collectively. We can control driving by minors by establishing rules and penalties, while at the same time controlling driving in higher age groups strictly through market devices. In fact, we would usually want to use considerably more complex mixtures. For instance, we can: (1) control driving by certain categories (e.g. driving by minors under 16, or driving by convicted speeders, or drunken driving) through collective prohibition; (2) control driving by other categories (e.g. people over 18 and under 70) solely through the market; and (3) control driving by other categories (e.g. people between 16 and 18, whom we will license only with parental permission and only if they can pay their potential accident costs, or people over 70, whom we may license if they pass a physical examination and can afford the insurance) by various mixed market and collective devices.

The combination of optimal collective and market devices can become as complicated as the societal aim demands.[2] The crucial point is that there is no reason to use the particular combination embodied in the fault system simply because we require a complex mixture.[3] Therefore the fault system cannot find justification in the fact that it is a system of mixed market and collective control. It can only find justification either if the one mixed goal it accomplishes well (i.e. the peculiar goal of minimizing neither accident costs, nor wrongful behavior, nor both, but, rather, only those accident costs in which wrongful behavior is a "but for" cause) is what we desire, or if there is something about its case-by-case jury determination of both moral and causal elements that, despite its weaknesses in terms of primary, secondary and tertiary costs, meets our justice requirements far better than any other mixed system. Before we turn to a consideration of justice, however, we must see whether the fault system can be made into a better avoider of secondary and tertiary accident costs than it is today.

2. See Calabresi, "The Fault System," at 460, n. 44.
3. The very fact that we supplement the fault system with many criminal penalties in order to obtain better collective control than it would otherwise afford is the best possible evidence that there is no inconsistency in mixing some direct collective prohibitions with other devices. If we can use non-insurable penalties to supplement civil liability based on fault, we can certainly use them to supplement civil liability based on market control.

CHAPTER 13

The Fault System and Secondary Cost Avoidance—Possible Modifications

One of the principal failings that is attributed to the fault system, and one that accounts for its present instability, is its alleged failure to spread the costs of accidents adequately, creating unnecessary secondary social and economic costs. I need not elaborate on the charges that fault leaves some victims destitute, overcompensates others, and does both with such enormous delays that it creates yet another source of secondary costs based on the delay itself.[1] All these charges have become part of the required reading of the most elementary tort courses by now. Nor should we be unduly detained by the defense of the fault system based on the notion that it does not intend to spread accident costs,[2] for the issue is not the supposed intent of the fault system, but rather what we want from a system of accident law. I submit that it is reasonably clear that— for better or worse—we want more spreading than the fault system currently gives us.

Given the inefficacy of fault as a system for achieving primary accident cost control, it is doubtful whether any modifications designed to promote spreading can make it an acceptable system of accident law.[3] But since much of the hue and cry about fault has centered on its poor spreading, such modifications deserve dis-

---

1. See Morris and Paul, "Financial Impact," at 923–24.

2. Cf. Blum and Kalven, *Public Law Perspectives,* at 37–38, 71, 74, 81. Compare Louis L. Jaffe, review of Blum and Kalven, 39 *So. Cal. L. Rev.* 331, 332–33 (1966).

3. If the fault system was considered to be so just by its very nature that no fundamentally different system could match it in this regard, then fault modified to accomplish some spreading might well be the optimal system. But see infra pp. 289–308.

cussion. Several have already been suggested. The first is adoption of comparative negligence.[4] The second is to establish compulsory insurance, which I shall consider for both injurers and victims. The third is to include consideration of who the best risk spreader is in determining fault. The fourth is to supplement the fault system with a system of social insurance.

COMPARATIVE NEGLIGENCE

Comparative negligence is fully consistent with the fault system. Indeed, it has become almost traditional to note that, if carried to its logical conclusion, the concept of fault would require comparative negligence. I would go even further and say that if fault were a system of either general or specific deterrence, it would have to provide for division of damages even among two non-negligent parties. Comparative fault, comparative ease of cost avoidance, or, under specific deterrence, comparative worthiness, would be desirable even in those cases.

But it is hard to see how comparative negligence would help very much to promote spreading. It would, of course, tend to divide damages more evenly among the parties to each accident. But unless it were administered with a fine eye to who the best loss spreader was, many heavy unspread losses would remain, as would many of the secondary costs of delay. In fact, those who advocate comparative negligence and comparative non-negligence to improve spreading in the fault system appear to assume that in practice, such a system would be administered so as to put loss burdens on the best spreader.[5] Most cases would get to juries, and

4. Traditionally, American law bars recovery to an injured party whose fault contributed to the injury even though the injurer was at fault. This doctrine, which is full of exceptions, is known as contributory negligence. Several jurisdictions have abandoned the doctrine and adopted one that allows recovery despite some fault in the plaintiff, but takes that fault into account in the award of damages. Most variants of this approach are called comparative negligence.

5. Compare, e.g., James' attitude toward comparative negligence with his attitude toward contribution among tort feasors. See Harper and James, *The Law of Torts*, 2, at 1203, 1207; James, "Contribution Among Joint Tort-

juries would inevitably be affected by this factor. In addition, the proponents could argue that the very fact that a jury would decide each case would make settlements more frequent and thereby mitigate the secondary costs of delay.[6]

All this is true, of course, but in a sense it is irrelevant, for these arguments are premised on the notion that adoption of comparative fault would tend to negate fault. That is, it is based on the assumption that comparative negligence would not refine the determination of fault, but would cause the bulk of liability burdens to be placed on the best spreader regardless of fault. This may not be a bad result, but it is disingenuous to consider it to be no more than the spreading effect that the fault system would have if carried to its logical conclusion. This effect must indeed be considered, but it should be discussed together with other existing tendencies to allocate responsibility to the best loss spreader while paying lip service to the fault system (the third modification of fault I listed), not in a discussion of comparative negligence.

My conclusion is, therefore, that while comparative negligence is certainly desirable in terms of accepted objectives of fault, and

---

feasors: A Pragmatic Criticism," 54 *Harv. L. Rev.* 1156 (1941); Charles O. Gregory, "Contribution Among Joint Tortfeasors: A Defense," id. at 1170; James, "Replication," id. at 1178; Gregory, "Rejoinder," id. at 1184.

6. The argument would be that the knowledge that an all-or-nothing result is unlikely under comparative negligence, combined with the jury's tendency to divide the loss on the basis of who is the best spreader, will encourage a defendant to settle in a situation where his chances of escaping liability altogether under contributory negligence would discourage him from settling. This, as the text indicates, would be buying spreading at the cost of negating fault. A true reduction of secondary costs with no undercutting of the fault system would occur if the reason more settlements occurred under comparative negligence was not fear that the jury might consider the relative ability of the parties to spread, but simply that the all-or-nothing gamble of contributory negligence had been removed. This greater tendency to settle would occur to the extent that it is a preference for gambling that causes litigation under contributory negligence. If the opposite is true, settlements that occur in contributory negligence jurisdictions in order to avoid the gamble might be lost under comparative negligence. Plaintiffs and defendants probably differ in their desire to gamble.

while it might somewhat improve fault's record as a spreader of losses, it would satisfy our desire for spreading only if it were applied in a way that would place the bulk of liability on the best loss spreader rather than on the party most at fault. Therefore it can save the fault system only if we are willing to accept greater modifications in the system than the adoption of comparative negligence would seem to imply.

COMPULSORY INSURANCE

Compulsory insurance attacks the poor spreading record of the fault system directly. There is no need to restate the analysis of why individuals are unlikely to insure voluntarily to a degree that will adequately avoid secondary losses. The reasons are many and affect both injurers and victims. Clearly a system of complete compulsory insurance for potential victims as well as for potential injurers would go far toward mitigating the spreading deficiencies of fault. The question is (aside from any political objections to compulsory insurance) how this mitigation would affect fault as a system of primary accident cost control.

If we compel liability and victim insurance, we are no longer allocating accident costs to individual faulty parties at all. We are allocating the entire cost to groups made up of individuals subject to approximately the same actuarial risk of (1) having an accident and (2) being made to bear that accident's cost under the rules of the fault system. Thus at best we are dealing with situations where any possible benefits of the fault system, as compared with a non-case-by-case approach of either general or specific deterrence, are extremely dubious. In addition, total compulsory insurance, when combined with case-by-case determinations of fault, is bound to result in extreme externalization. Thus compulsory victim insurance would most likely occur through general accident insurance rather than through insurance for the specific activities of walking or being a passenger in a car. It is too difficult to structure insurance coverage to such unorganized activities as being a passenger in a car. But unless insurance were so structured, the practical effect of fault plus insurance would be not to discourage faulty walking or faulty passengerism, but to put a burden on living generally. And this would result in far less specific or general deterrence than would be achieved by a nonfault allocation of costs to the more organized or institutional activities, such as driving, involved in the accident.[7]

Thus the fault system combined with compulsory insurance may achieve adequate spreading but only at a greater cost in terms of deterrence than is necessary. This should not be surprising. A system originally designed to achieve both primary accident cost avoidance *and* spreading could pick out the cheapest or best cost avoidance category consistent with adequate spreading. The fault system begins by finding the theoretically best cost avoider in each particular case. Then, since it turns out that this allocation is intolerable from a spreading point of view, it may seek to remedy the matter by *requiring* these theoretical best cost avoiders to pool their risks through insurance. But there is no reason to expect that the ways of pooling these risks will result in any pressure remaining on cost avoiders who are any good at all from either a collective or a market standpoint. It is, instead, much more likely that where individual best cost avoiders (faulty parties) are members of unorganized activities, pooling will result in externalization of the burden to activities like living generally (through general accident insurance), which are terrible primary cost avoiders in either a collective or a market sense. In short, if we seek to burden not individual best cost avoiders but the category that can best avoid primary accident costs while giving adequate spreading as well, we should concentrate directly on finding and burdening that activity or group and not go through the expensive ritual of burdening an individual because this might, in theory, achieve the best cost avoidance if the burden were left on him.

If we wish to deter the individual, there are perfectly good ways of doing so directly. Fines, tort fines, penalties, etc. are available

7. See supra pp. 145–49. Cf. Blum and Kalven, *Public Law Perspectives,* at 85; and Jaffe, book review, at 335.

and can be adjusted so as to minimize conflict with the secondary cost avoidance aim. And as we have already seen, there is nothing to prevent us from mixing such individual deterrence devices with category deterrence devices that are not in conflict with adequate spreading. Pedestrians, for example, could be deterred by fines and tort fines, and drivers (the category that can most cheaply or best avoid car-pedestrian accidents consistently with our spreading aims) could be deterred by being charged with car-pedestrian accident costs. By contrast, charging faulty pedestrians involved in automobile accidents with the costs of such accidents would either violate our secondary cost avoidance goal, or violate our primary cost avoidance goal by causing us to require insurance of pedestrians as part of a general cost-of-living insurance. (Such insurance would remove the money incentive to be careful which the fault system sought to place on pedestrians without substituting for it any equivalent incentive on drivers).[8]

We can conclude that compulsory insurance, like comparative negligence, can be a satisfactory way of mitigating the bad spreading record of fault only for those who do not care whether fault serves to bring about adequate primary accident cost avoidance (i.e. for those who would prefer general social insurance to any other cost reduction system). Those concerned about primary accident cost deterrence would recognize that other systems, designed with both deterrence and spreading in mind, would be much more likely to give deterrence consistent with spreading than a patched-up fault system would.

CONSIDER SPREADING ABILITY IN DETERMINING FAULT

The third modification of fault proposed to achieve better spreading is to let the determination of the loss bearer be directly influenced by secondary cost considerations as well as by traditional criteria of fault. This could be done either explicitly or implicitly.[9] The principal difficulty with this modification is that

8. See Blum and Kalven, *Public Law Perspectives*, at 85.
9. It is sometimes claimed that juries do this now. But it is highly unlikely that they do it enough to satisfy our spreading goals.

it would be both erratic and expensive. Its erratic nature would tend, on the one hand, to diminish the effect of the fault system as a deterrent of primary accident costs and on the other, to allow occasional cases of outrageous secondary costs to exist nonetheless. Indeed, as the current fault system may in practice be relatively close to this modification, it might not be unfair to apply all the criticisms of the fault system as it works in practice (both as a deterrent of primary costs and as a spreader) to this third suggestion.

If, however, the thrust of this proposal is that the main aim in fixing liability should be to find the best spreader rather than the faulty party, a different criticism is in order. In that case, the difficulty would be that once again we would have completely subordinated our primary accident cost avoidance goal to that of spreading, and in a rather cumbersome and expensive way. Indeed, it is not surprising that those who view the current fault system as essentially a spreading system also view it as a stepping stone to a more efficient system of secondary cost avoidance—social insurance.

COMBINE SOCIAL INSURANCE WITH FAULT

At first glance, the fourth suggested modification of the fault system is the most promising. It involves keeping the fault system but supplementing it with a system of generalized social insurance to mitigate secondary costs. A little thought, however, must reveal that such a system, which is simply a rather less stingy version of the Blum and Kalven stopgap plan, would suffer from problems identical to those of a fault system supplemented by compulsory insurance.

Again, and for the same reasons, spreading would have been bought at the price of giving up too much primary cost deterrence. This result could be mitigated in turn by adding specific deterrence noninsurable fines and tort fines to the system. But then one would be sorely pressed to explain the relevance of the fault-determined allocations of accident costs to the system and to justify their expense, except perhaps as a necessary—though expensive—bow to our past. Under this mixture, fault would be a luxurious appendage which could be tolerated only because it did not affect, except in the most minor way, who actually bore accident costs and which acts or activities were deterred.

The problem with all these suggested modifications is the same: if our aim is to coordinate such ultimately inconsistent goals as primary and secondary accident cost avoidance, we are unlikely to do it best by operating within the framework of a system that developed without any rational design in mind. Indeed, the very fact that we are operating in such an irrational system is the reason we can hope to get closer to all of our inconsistent goals than we are today, for it is only because the fault system is irrational—in terms of all types of accident cost avoidance—and achieves none of our subgoals well, that we can hope to do better with respect to all of them.

CHAPTER 14

The Costs of the Fault System

In the preceding chapters I contended that fault is not a good system of specific or general deterrence and that it is a very poor system of loss spreading. These charges might not be so crucial if it were not for the tertiary costs of the fault system. The fault system does accomplish some specific and general deterrence and could be modified, though at the expense of primary cost avoidance, to achieve more spreading. But the question that inevitably arose in each of the previous sections was: does fault further these goals sufficiently to justify its expense? And the answer was inevitably no.

Since the costs of the fault system are the source of most of the criticisms, and since, as I pointed out at the beginning of this book, tertiary costs are always best discussed together with the aims in whose name they are incurred, I shall not spend much more time on the issue. It is sufficient to note that the costs of the fault system arise principally from its inherent characteristics and hence are not readily avoidable without getting rid of the system. To achieve what deterrence it does, the fault system must make individual case-by-case determinations, and this is a major source of its expense. Moreover, compensation depends on the facts found in each case, and this is another major source of expense because it means that the injured party cannot be relied on to describe accurately what happened.[1] Finally, to reach an acceptable estimate of the

1. It is instructive to compare workmen's compensation with Blue Cross on this issue. According to Conard, "Automobile Injuries," at 290, and *AACP*, at 52–60, Blue Cross insurance has a low operating cost ratio (under 10%) compared to workmen's compensation, where the ratio is over 50%. The ratio for workmen's compensation is still well under that of the fault system, in which the operating costs exceed the net benefits going to injury victims.

value of the costs it allocates and to achieve enough spreading to survive, fault must use a jury; this is a third source of expense.

Other systems might, of course, have the same characteristics and the same costs. I suggested earlier that both general and specific deterrence approaches might, in theory, employ case-by-case determinations and even juries. I think it was clear in those discussions, however, that such devices would not be essential to an adequate system of either specific or general deterrence. Nor are they essential to many of the various possible systems that mix the two approaches and combine them with the goal of adequate spreading. They are, however, essential to the fault system for the reasons already given, and because any possible claim to justice that the fault system may have depends on them. Fault implies individual stigma and therefore necessarily implies the whole individualized apparatus.[2]

2. A system of tort fines would be accompanied by the expense of case-by-case determinations, but the expense would not be nearly so great as that of the fault system because only one issue would have to be settled on a case-by-case basis. In addition, witnesses might be available whose statement of what happened would be relatively more reliable because their possible recovery for injuries suffered would not depend on the assessment of a tort fine on the defendant. The availability of such witnesses might result in guilty pleas or dropped prosecutions, either of which would lessen costs.

If the tort fine system were extended to cover parties whose conduct did not result in an accident, its administrative costs could well become greater than those of the current fault system. The extension would presumably add deterrence to that given either by the fault system or by a tort fine system that only covered parties whose conduct led to an accident. The question would then be whether this added deterrence was worth its costs.

PART V

Justice and the Fault System

None of my criticisms of the fault system, based as they are on its failure to reduce accident costs adequately, would be decisive if the fault system found substantial support in our notions of justice. The criticisms can be reduced to the statement that there are likely to be systems that accomplish primary, secondary, and tertiary accident cost avoidance better than the fault system does. The question that remains is whether such systems accomplish this cost avoidance in ways that meet the requirements of our sense of justice or fairness as well as or better than the fault system. As we asked earlier, does the particular way in which the fault system determines who pays for accidents (using a jury in a case-by-case process and allowing insurance) satisfy our sense of justice far better than other more efficient mixed systems could? If it were true that the only fair system for determining liability for accidents was the fault system, then it would follow that our sense of justice would require us to pursue the rather peculiar mixed goal that the fault system does accomplish, i.e. the minimization neither of accident costs, nor of wrongful behavior, nor of both, but rather of only those accident costs in which wrongful behavior is involved.[1]

Before we accept such an unlikely result, it would be well to examine briefly what the requirements of our sense of justice in this area seem to be. In doing this we must distinguish two uses of the phrase "sense of justice." The first is as a working approximation of what philosophers might define as justice. Such an approximation can be derived from what a community deems to be just but must be subject to rational criticism, since the object of the approximation is to enable us as critics to decide if a particular system is fair. This I call the critic's sense of justice. The second

1. It should be apparent that I am talking about the fairness of substituting another system of accident law for the existing fault-insurance system and not about the usefulness or fairness of fault as a criterion for responsibility. That is an entirely different question. Indeed, many of the devices, such as tort fines, discussed under specific deterrence, would make substantial use of wrongdoing or fault as a criterion for responsibility.

use treats the phrase as referring to a political fact, a datum to be dealt with like the climate. This datum, which I call the community's sense of justice, gives rise to tactical questions, such as what can make a change in accident law acceptable to the public at large. Often the two merge, but both uses of "sense of justice" must be examined in evaluating the fairness of the fault system.

In this examination, I do not pretend to consider what we mean by justice in any broad context. I will simply try to point out the factors critics and the public seem to focus on when they consider whether a system of accident law is fair. Then the fault system can be examined with these factors in mind.

CHAPTER 15

The Moral Framework—Consistency and History

Accident law is only a small segment of the legal world. Only a small minority of the problems with which we wish to cope through a legal framework arise from accidents. As a result, what seems just both to critics and to the public in accident law is inevitably affected by what is done and what is considered fair in related areas. If society were ever to reach the conclusion that murderers are not responsible for their acts and are never to be punished, it would require some explanation and some convincing before we could accept punishment of speeders who cause accidents. Similarly, even if accident costs could be reduced by 10 percent by beheading all people who knowingly run red lights, it would nevertheless be hard to accept or to sell it to the community. We would have to be convinced and be able to convince the public that things we had always considered similar were really different.

The moral context of accident law, however, does not arise only from what is considered fair in other fields of law. It also requires some consistency in what is done within the area of accident law itself. The same desire to deal with accidents with a regard for what happens outside of accident law also urges us to deal with similar accident situations in similar ways. And this involves not only consistency of legal rules but also consistency in the effect of those rules. Thus, the legal rule that affects the rich and the poor differently because of a delay in payment of damages may strike us as no less unfair than the existence of different rules for handling work accidents and automobile accidents.[1]

1. Cf. Jeremiah Smith, "Sequel to Workmen's Compensation Acts," 27 *Harv. L. Rev.* 235, 344, 363 (1914).

Moreover, our sense of fairness may be offended by procedural inconsistencies as well as by substantive ones. We will tend to demand procedures similar to those employed in criminal law if fines or stigmas are imposed civilly to reduce accident costs. We will also be reluctant to have juries in some accident situations and administrative tribunals in others unless we believe that there are real differences between the situations.

To the critic consistency, or apparent consistency, is not an absolute requirement either within accident law or in the relations between accident and nonaccident areas. For example, unjust pressures or undue costs might be necessary to achieve consistency. But apparently inconsistent treatment is not easily accepted by the public and must be explained both rationally and emotionally if a community sense of fairness is to be preserved. It does not necessarily help that the situations treated differently are in fact different if the public views them, for historical or other reasons, as the same. Conversely, when people view situations as dissimilar, both rational and emotional arguments may be necessary to win acceptance for similar treatment. We must always remember that the community's sense of justice is not, and never can be, simply a rational reaction, and that it must be reckoned with whether or not it is sensible. The critic can only hope that over time rational considerations will overcome irrational ones.

So far we have viewed justice mainly as a problem of consistency (or apparent consistency). Moral attitudes are far more complex. They involve, at the very least, whole categories of acts that have come to be considered "good" and whole categories that have come to be considered "evil." No system of accident law can operate unless it takes into account which acts are deemed good, which deemed evil, and which deemed neutral. Any system of accident law that encourages evil acts will seem unjust to critic and community even if economically it is very efficient indeed.

Any examination of evil, good, and neutral acts in relation to accident law should distinguish those which have come to be blamed or praised because of the accidents they were thought to cause or avoid from those which received their moral status regardless of their relation to accidents. Speeding is generally considered evil. A system of accident law that required people to go 90 miles per hour would not be readily accepted by the community even if it cut down accidents substantially. And yet the difficulties it would encounter would be minimal next to those that would meet a system of accident law urging free love (the fewer frustrations, the fewer accidents).

Speeding probably came to be considered bad because of the accidents it was believed to cause. If it were conclusively shown that speeding did not cause accidents, the public could not change its feelings about it immediately. Moreover, traditional moral attitudes toward speeding would make it very difficult to convince people completely that speeding did not cause accidents. If the proof were strong, however, we can predict that in time the attitude would change. The change would likely occur more quickly if it were also shown that slow driving caused accidents, as this would make it easier to believe the proof that speeding did not. In any event, speeding's ability to reduce accidents costs would be accepted more slowly than would the ability of a morally neutral device (such as a safer tire) or of a morally favored device (such as driver education).

Whatever the reasons why free love is not looked on with favor in our society, it is unlikely that they would be affected if it were found that free love reduced accidents. I do not mean to suggest that if it were shown that free love caused accident reduction there would be no effect on our attitudes toward fornication. But even massive accident reduction would only affect these attitudes slightly —much more slowly than similar evidence would affect attitudes toward speeding. And this might be true of the community's attitude even if the reasons why fornication was originally deemed immoral were no longer applicable.[2]

2. The critic's moral attitude would be minimally affected only if fornication was deemed immoral for valid reasons unrelated to accidents. To him the statement in text simply means that there often are goals apart from accident law which we lump together under justice and which will prevent us from

While my example may seem fanciful, I believe it emphasizes a point. We have, over time, stigmatized certain acts because of the accident costs we think they cause; we have stigmatized other acts for other reasons. Accident reduction plans involving acceptance of acts in the latter category will be considered just or fair by the community much less readily than plans involving the former category regardless of whether a critic could argue as to each category that the reasons why the acts were originally deemed wrongful no longer apply.

Even within the former category I have suggested that we must not anticipate that an expected reduction in accident costs will change the public's attitude quickly or even in some cases, ultimately. Moral attitudes develop and decay slowly. They become encrusted with significance that is often quite foreign to the situation that engendered them. The longer the history of a moral attitude toward an act, the more likely it is that the attitude will have become separated from its cause and the more difficult it will be to change the attitude even if the cause is no longer valid. All this is just a way of saying that, almost by definition, "moral" status has a strength of its own apart from the original source of the status.

What I have said of individual acts is also true of legal systems. Over time, they too become encrusted with moral imperatives. Even a superficial reading of the early cases in which courts attempted to deal with nonfault liability in the context of workmen's compensation should suffice to point this out.[3] It is, however, a fact that in the area of accident law dramatic change *has* occurred in the past, albeit over time, and seemingly in response to the demands of economic efficiency. This suggests that the moral imperatives that the public attaches to systems of accident law are directly related to cost avoidance and hence subject to change as what

---

taking steps to reduce accidents if these steps undercut those goals. See supra pp. 31–33.

3. See, e.g., Ives v. South Buffalo R. Co., 201 N.Y. 271, 94 N.E. 431 (1911). But see Kennerson v. Thames Towboat Co., 89 Conn. 367, 94 A. 372 (1915).

brings about cost avoidance changes. It remains true, however, that any change affecting the moral imperatives attached to a system of accident law will, at least at first, seem unjust to the community. The critic can argue that if the reasons for a system have ceased the law should change. But *cessante ratione cessat lex,* although a convincing enough epigram even for the public at large, does not imply speedy changes in systems when moral values are involved. This does not mean that the role of the iconoclast is to be scorned—only that here, as everywhere, the iconoclasts must expect resistance from the iconodules.

Among the traditional moral attitudes toward accidents is one that must be singled out for special attention. For centuries society has seemed to accept the notion that justice required a one-to-one relationship between the party that injures and the party that is injured (and his family).[4] This notion remains strong in accident law despite the fact that its importance has lessened in nonaccident areas. Thus relatives of a homicide victim no longer have the right to institute proceedings against the alleged murderer or to take matters into their own hands in a lawful trial by combat to punish him. In areas of sexual crimes or wrongdoings, the notion that the crime of passion was somehow excusable has declined. At the same time, compensation from the wrongdoer to the wronged party in heart balm cases has become increasingly disfavored.[5] Yet where accidents are concerned, the law still gives the equivalent of these early remedies.

There is, of course, no logical necessity for linking our treatment of victims, individually or as a group, to our treatment of injurers, individually or as a group. Indeed, I noted that one of the confusions existing in current discussions of accident law is

4. The Code of Hammurabi, compiled in Babylonia more than 4,000 years ago, reflects this notion, providing a long schedule of damages to be paid by the injurer to the injured or his family and in some cases requiring the injurer to pay medical expenses.

5. Heart balm cases include damage actions for alienation of affection, damage actions by parents for seduction of a minor daughter, and related causes of action.

the belief that there must be individualized relationships between injurers and injured.[6] Nevertheless, it may be that individualized treatment of accidents appeals strongly to either the critic's or the community's sense of justice despite the breakdown of similar attitudes in other areas. This is often claimed to be so as to the community's attitude, although the available empirical evidence suggests that it is much less important than most law professors believe.[7] I discuss the significance of this alleged community attitude in the next chapter.

As far as the critic is concerned, the notion that we need individualized treatment can be divided into two rather different attitudes. The first is that the victim—or his family—has the right to see that retribution is exacted. This concept may take the rather extreme form of giving the victim the right to exact retribution himself. (This is roughly analogous to the right of combat by a representative of a murdered or wronged party.) More often, it is limited to giving the victim the right to see to it that the injurer is brought to justice. (This is analogous to the ancient right of the homicide victim's family to indict the alleged murderer criminally.[8]) This "self-help" attitude, especially in its extreme form, smacks more of revenge than of deterrence or compensation. It stems, I would guess, from the not very healthy urge to get even. But in its more limited form, it may also involve an element of

6. *AACP*, at 99–102, contains a discussion of the more practical aspects of linking, its advantages and its disadvantages.

7. See *AACP*, at 106, indicating that there is a general feeling that failure to care for injuries is reprehensible, but that this feeling does not appear to be linked with the belief that it should necessarily be the "causers" of loss who should pay. There is instead a general, if vague, feeling that some sort of system should be set up to insure adequate compensation.

8. This right was not repealed in England until a famous murder case prompted reform in 1819. The previous year the right was claimed after years of disuse when a man earlier acquitted of murdering a girl was privately indicted by the dead girl's brother. Under the old law, one so accused could opt for trial by combat with the accuser. This the rather stout defendant did, thereby inducing his accuser to drop the charge. Ashford v. Thornton, 1 B & Ald 405, 106 Eng. Rep. 149 (1818), Sir John Richard Hall, *Trial of Abraham Thornton* (Edinburgh, William Hodge & Co., 1926).

doubt as to the ability of the government to handle the situation adequately. If so, the right to press charges against the injurer may originally have involved deterrence aspects as well. One can readily question whether the whole apparatus of the fault system is needed for this purpose today.

Somewhat different is the second attitude underlying individualized treatment. This holds that the injurer should pay damages according to the degree to which he wronged the victim. This is not really based on vengeance, but rather on the concept that between the two parties involved in an accident, it is better that the loss be borne by the one who has committed acts carrying moral stigma than by the one who has not. At its logical conclusion this notion would lead to a full comparative negligence system. The problems with this second attitude are treated in the next chapter, when we consider directly how the critic's and the community's notions of justice affect specific systems of accident law, such as the fault system.

These few pages cannot begin to enumerate all the ways in which generalized attitudes of justice or fairness affect our approach to accidents. Specifically, I have left out all the many attitudes toward accidents and the placing of accident losses that cause critic and community to hold fair and just those systems believed to reduce accident costs, be they costs of inadequate spreading or what I have described as primary costs. This is not because such approaches have not acquired moral status of their own. Many have, and seem fair now apart from their cost reduction origins. Thus, fairness has long been used to support approaches allocating accident costs to the activities that "cause" them or profit from them.[9] These approaches are left out because in a sense they have already been considered in relation to their cost reduction effects. The discussion of justice here was designed to point out some of the factors that influence our attitudes regardless of cost reduction and that impose

9. See, e.g., Fowler V. Harper, *A Treatise on the Law of Torts* (Indianapolis, Bobbs-Merrill, 1933), at 332–34, 413, and Harper and James, *The Law of Torts, 2,* at 731, 760, 785–87.

on us the vague but nonetheless imperious command that when we try to reduce accident costs, we do it fairly. We do it, in other words, in ways that do not involve decapitating speeders, that do not involve blessing fornicators, and that do not so greatly offend us for noncost reasons that we would rather bear the costs of accidents than be offended.

CHAPTER 16

The Fairness of the Fault System

There is no doubt that some possible justifications for the fault system can be found in rather undifferentiated notions of justice.[1] It strikes critic and community as unfair if a person injured by someone who has violated a moral code is not compensated, or if someone who violates a moral code and is hurt is compensated at the expense of an innocent party. It also strikes us as unfair if acts that we deem wrong and immoral go unpunished, quite apart from any issue of compensation of the possible victims of such acts. Such sentiments are often said to be the principal mainstays of the fault system.

From the critic's point of view, though these sentiments are valid they do not in reality support the fault system. They would only do so if the choice society faced was which of two or more parties directly involved in each accident should ultimately bear its costs. Then it would be true that if an injured party were not compensated by his faulty injurer, he would go uncompensated. It would also be true that any compensation of a faulty victim would in many cases have to come from the pocket of an innocent party. Such results would, of course, violate the critic's sense of justice. Similarly, it would seem unfair if in the absence of a fault system wrongdoers went unpunished. But to say that to avoid such results we must use the fault system is patent nonsense based on a simplistic bilateral view of the accident problem.

In reality, we live in a multilateral world with a whole population of injurers and victims. The degree of wrongdoing and the amount of damages vary throughout the population. In such a

1. But cf. *AACP*, at 105–07.

world, the question need not be whether it seems fair for an individual injurer to compensate an individual victim; in our society it can be how much all injurers should pay, in relation to their individual wrongdoing, into a fund to compensate all victims, in relation to their injuries and *their* wrongdoing. It is difficult to see why payments based on how faulty a particular injurer is in relation to *all* injurers would not seem fairer than payments depending only on his fault in relation to his victim's fault and to the injuries suffered by that particular victim.[2] It is equally difficult to see why recoveries by a victim should depend on how his conduct compares with that of the individual who injured him, rather than how it compares with that of all individuals involved in accidents. Certainly the broader comparison is much more consistent with how we treat wrongdoing in areas other than accident law. Indeed, one could go even further and suggest that the fortuity of involvement in an accident is not a fair manner of determining payments. Would it not seem fairer for compensation of relatively worthy victims to come from a fund made up of payments by all who are at fault (i.e. who violate society's code) according to their faultiness, whether they are involved in an accident or not? This may not be feasible. But if it were, would it not be more just?[3]

The moment one accepts the notion that justice does not require that an individual injurer compensate his individual victim —and the allowance of insurance for faulty parties is clear indication that this notion is accepted—and the moment one realizes that wrongdoers can be punished for wrongful acts quite apart

2. This comparison assumes at least a comparative negligence system and therefore gives the devil more than his due by considering the fault system as though it were modified in ways that would make it fairer than the present all-or-nothing system.

3. Once again, this would not rule out making a differentiation between wrongdoing that resulted in serious harm and wrongdoing that did not, where the fact of serious harm could be taken to be an indication that the injurer was particularly faulty. It should be obvious, however, that in gauging faultiness the fact of serious harm is at most one of many factors. See generally supra notes 22, Chapter 6 and 5, Chapter 11.

from whether they must compensate victims, it becomes very hard to see how the fault system can be supported on grounds of justice. Nevertheless, in a world that has abandoned the necessity of a one-to-one relationship between injurer and victim, attempts to support fault on grounds of justice have been made. They usually take the form of suggesting that individual determinations of fault in each accident situation result in the creation of actuarial insurance categories which reflect the risk of faulty conduct being undertaken by its members. This, it is argued, amounts to the same thing as making the least worthy pay for accident costs in relation to their blameworthiness.[4] Passing over the question of whether the fault system with all its defects actually gives rise to such fair insurance categories, one must still ask whether the categories it creates are the best possible ones in this sense, and whether the fault system is the best way of creating these categories.

I shall not spend much time on these questions; they have been answered earlier. Where conduct can be defined as undesirable with sufficient precision, the best way to make those who engage in it pay (and the way that is most consistent with other areas of law) is to assess them directly and individually—through noninsurable fines if they can be caught regardless of accidents, and through noninsurable tort fines if they cannot. Where conduct cannot be defined with sufficient precision before an accident (if it makes sense to speak of fault at all in this area), our moral imperatives can be worked into actuarial categories—i.e. we can charge different groups different amounts in relation to the relative desirability or blameworthiness of the activities in which they are engaged—more efficiently and effectively through means other than the case-by-case adversary determinations of fault. What I said before still holds: unless one considers the purpose of creating fair insurance categories to be not the deterrence of wrongful acts, nor the deterrence of accident costs, nor even the deterrence of

4. Compare and contrast Blum and Kalven, *Public Law Perspectives,* at 14, 66–67. Even if the fault system could be viewed as creating optimal insurance categories for injurers, it does not even pretend to do so for victims.

both, but rather the deterrence of those accidents in which wrongful acts are involved, the insurance categories the fault system creates cannot be thought of as required by fairness.

It may be argued, however, that I have been too quick to suggest that our sense of justice does not require payments by each individual injurer to his victim on the basis of their relative faultiness and the injuries that resulted. Logic is all very well, and it may affect the critic's sense of justice, it may be said, but the community's sense of justice depends on other things. People may require a one-to-one world of payment and compensation even if logic and economics make it unnecessary and even, in some sense, unjust. And it is not enough to point out what ought to satisfy the public's sense of justice if people simply do not view it that way. I would argue, however, that as a practical matter our society is quite ready to abandon the view that justice requires individual injurers to pay their victims on the basis of fault and that moreover, wherever an adequate alternative has been presented, people have tended to prefer it to the traditional fault system.[5]

One need only look at the general acceptance of workmen's compensation and at jury verdicts that seem to ignore negligence on the plaintiff's part and lack of negligence on the defendant's to get some sense of this.[6] Similarly, the general acceptance of

---

5. See *AACP* at 105–07. Whether people say they prefer fault may depend on what question is put to them, of course. When asked: "It has been suggested, when there is an accident involving two cars, that each driver be paid damages by his own insurance company without trying to determine if one driver was at fault. Does that sound like a good idea or a poor idea to you?" only 34% of those questioned in a Minnesota poll said the suggestion sounded like a good idea. "Minnesotans Reject Premises of Keeton-O'Connell Plan," 9 *For the Defense* 65 (November 1968).

6. See, e.g., Wilkerson v. McCarthy, 336 U.S. 53 (1949) and the Utah Supreme Court opinion it reversed, 112 Utah 300, 187 P.2d 188 (1947). Said Mr. Justice Jackson in dissent: "I am not unaware that even in this opinion the Court continues to pay lip service to the doctrine that liability in these cases is to be based only upon fault. But its standard of fault is such in this case as to indicate that the principle is without much practical meaning."

insurance strongly suggests that we do not worry too much about whether the individual faulty party pays his victim, so long as the victim is paid. Of course, we have not yet reached a point where we are willing lightheartedly to compensate a victim who is *really* faulty (i.e. "wanton and willful"), though we do—with some misgivings—generally allow insurance against liability for wanton and willful misconduct, which is close to the same thing. The source of our misgivings is that we sometimes fear that noninsurable fines proportionate to the wrongdoing and adequate to achieve deterrence will not in fact be placed on wanton and willful wrongdoers. If they were, we would not be troubled by the fact that liability beyond such fines could be insured against. Analogously, were a wanton and willful victim jailed or made to pay a noninsurable fine that was in some way commensurate with his wrongdoing and with the specific deterrence we wished to obtain, we would hardly be troubled if the excess of the damages to him (and inevitably to his family) were compensated, so long as it did not appear that the burden ultimately fell on individual innocent parties. (Such punishment would be totally in keeping with what was needed to destroy a one-to-one, victim-injurer combat right in criminal law.)

I think one can fairly conclude that the traditional defense of the fault system based on the notion that justice requires that the costs of a particular accident be divided according to the relative faultiness of the parties involved has been given more importance in scholarly writings than it deserves. The critic and the public have been concerned, and rightly so, that burdens should not rest heavily on the relatively innocent while the relatively guilty go unpunished. But both the logical and practical indications are that this concern does not necessitate the fault system. It requires only

---

336 U.S. at 76. It is, of course, often difficult to say whether public acceptance of a new approach such as workmen's compensation precedes or results from its institution.

that all parties involved in similar accidents divide all the injury costs according to a scale of relative guilt.

We could go further and perhaps do still better by fining wrongdoers, whether or not an accident occurs, to help pay for compensation of those who are injured, and even by taxing activities and people according to the likelihood of their involvement in accidents in which their conduct would be deemed blameworthy. The burden, whether called fine, tax, or insurance, would depend on the general wrongdoing or undesirability of the activity, not on the fortuity of an accident occurring to the particular parties. Once again, therefore, we return to the fact that the issue does not simply involve two parties to an accident, but involves, instead, how we establish insurance categories fairly and how we punish individual wrongdoers justly and effectively. And the fault system cannot deal with that issue as well as a system that mixes noninsurable fines and limitations on undesirable activities with market deterrence in a way that is consistent with our spreading demands.

The basic difficulty with supporting the fault system on grounds of justice can be stated simply. Our sense of justice is made up of history and tradition, but it is also highly dependent on consistency within a moral context. While the fault system may be consistent with our moral history in blaming the relatively guilty party in any given accident situation, it leads to results that are totally inconsistent with other existing penalties because it imposes a burden that is substantially unrelated to wrongdoing or to penalties inflicted on similar wrongdoing in other areas of law. It also leads to results that are totally inconsistent with what occurs in many situations within accident law. Workmen's compensation is the prime example of this inconsistency, but the fact that the fault system allows insurance, and therefore in practice allows faulty injurers to spread the burden more easily than faulty victims, is an equally good instance. Indeed, these basic inconsistencies are additional reasons for the fault system's current instability, since even if the fault system meets some requirements of our sense of justice, its inconsistencies violate still more pressing requirements of that goal.

In the end, justice will support the fault system only if there is no sensible alternative system presented, only if the choice is solely between crushing one relatively wrongful and one relatively innocent party. It will not support the fault system in a world where faulty or undesirable acts, activities, and actors (whether victims or injurers) can be penalized according to their undesirability, and injured parties can be compensated according to their injury. I do not suggest for a moment by this that compensation should predominate over deterrence, general or specific. I only suggest that the moral aims of our society, and even our undifferentiated sense of justice, can be better met through systems that concentrate on the deterrence and compensation we want than through an archaic system of liability that presumes an organization of society in which the best that can be done is to treat each accident instance as a universe unto itself.

The fault system may have arisen in a world where one injurer and one victim were the most that society could handle adequately, and in such a world it probably was a fairly good mixed system. It did a good job of meeting our combination of goals: general and specific deterrence, spreading, justice, and even efficiency.[7] But even assuming that such was the world in which the fault system grew, it is not today's world. Today accidents must be

---

7. *If* there are only the two parties to choose from, fault can be defended as a fair mixture of such relevant considerations as allotting costs to the activities causing them, spreading, and providing a just standard of foreseeability. Even in their earliest days juries may well have tempered, somewhat clumsily, the worst evils of fault by modifying the verdict called for under the premises of fault if it resulted in extreme visible hardship or social dislocation. Also, Holmes' argument that efficiency dictates letting costs lie where they fall in the absence of fault may make sense when only the two "involved" parties are considered.

An interesting view of the historical development of the law of torts is presented in Jørgensen, "The Decline and Fall of the Law of Torts," soon to be published in the *American Journal of Comparative Law*.

viewed not as incidental events linking one victim with one injurer, but as a more general societal problem. That is why the
fault system has become totally inadequate for *any* of our mixed
goals, even justice. It has become so inadequate, in fact, that other
mixed systems can improve our record as far as *each* of these goals
is concerned, even though at their extremes some of the goals are
inconsistent with one another.

PART VI

Toward a New System of Accident Law

I do not deny that there is an abstract attachment, often expressed in terms of justice, to the fault system. As I said earlier, systems no less than acts come to carry moral connotations, and these remain long after the reasons for the connotations are gone. This has undoubtedly happened with the fault system and serves to explain why the same individuals who are quite happy to allocate losses on a nonfault basis in individual cases can profess loyalty to the fault system in the abstract.

This abstract loyalty is strengthened by the fact that proposed changes often represent dangers to vested interests. It is not surprising that some of the staunchest defenders of the justice of the fault system are those lawyers who grow fat on the inefficiencies of fault.

On a rather higher moral level, the abstract loyalty is also strengthened by the fact that some of the systems suggested to replace the fault system are less effective than it is with regard to some of our goals. We need only consider a few of those discussed in the general introduction to see this. Systems of social insurance paid for out of general tax revenues are less effective than the fault system at primary accident cost avoidance. And a system of social insurance buttressed by many specific deterrence rules and regulations may still be less effective than the fault system in dealing with those acts or activities that cannot be well controlled collectively. Conversely, a system that attempts to allocate costs to cheapest cost avoider categories, i.e. to raise the social insurance fund by taxing these categories, not only might fail to control wrongful acts as adequately as fault does, but also might be as bad a spreader, or as administratively costly, as the fault system. In addition, a system (such as the Defense Research Institute approach) that relied primarily on specific deterrence penalties for primary accident cost avoidance and on payments from collateral sources (like Blue Cross and wage security plans) for secondary cost avoidance, even if it retained the fault system as an expensive appendage, might very well provide less market control of accidents than the fault system as it works today. Payments by the collateral sources would become primary under this approach, and very great externalization would occur, as the American Insurance Association report noted. Thus the defenders of the fault system are often able to argue that a particular system, though it does one thing well, is less adequate than the fault system at another.

It is for this reason that I have not attempted in this book to suggest a system to replace the fault system. In practice any system we are likely to want in any given area of accidents may well give more weight to one goal (e.g. spreading) than the fault system does. And if it does, we may well be willing to settle for less of another goal (e.g. primary cost avoidance) than even the fault system gives. What I have tried to demonstrate in this book is the more general proposition that a mixed system can be developed which does *all* the things we want in the way of accident cost reduction better than the fault system and does them consistently with our sense of justice.

Such a system could begin by allocating accident costs to those categories that can avoid accidents most cheaply but are sufficiently broad to spread the costs adequately enough to meet our secondary cost avoidance goals. It could be buttressed by an array of non-insurable fines, penalties, and taxes assessed so as to deter or limit further those particular acts and activities we collectively decided to punish or to deter beyond what the market could accomplish. Conversely, subsidies could be given to those categories we wished to encourage because they were collectively deemed especially desirable. The degree of collective as against market control, just like the degree of primary as against secondary cost avoidance, could be varied for each area of accidents.

At some point the mixture, in accomplishing more and more of some aims, will no longer accomplish other aims as well as the fault system. One object of this book has simply been to show that there are a variety of points possible where *all* of the aims except that represented by the desire to stay with the status quo, regardless of its faults, can be met better than under the fault system.

Another object of the book has been to indicate the questions we must ask in deciding whether one system is preferable to another. Sometimes these questions are essentially empirical. How much more primary accident cost avoidance in relation to the administrative costs entailed would we get by subcategorizing in an area? And how great would the burdens of unspread accident costs be in an area under a system that allocated accident costs to the cheapest cost avoidance categories? At other times the questions are political. Do we want a system of accident law based more on market control or more on collective control of accidents? Do we, in view of our current income distribution, prefer a system of accident law that minimizes the effects of accidents on the poor by emphasizing deep pocket secondary cost avoidance, or one that concentrates either on avoiding the secondary costs implicit in *changes* in income distribution or on minimizing the primary costs of accidents?

I have tried to indicate the questions not so much by raising them directly as by analyzing the implications of different approaches to accident law. In that light it may be well to examine in a cursory fashion a few of the systems discussed in the general introduction to see the answers they implicitly give to some of these questions. First-party insurance plans such as the Keeton-O'Connell and American Insurance Association plans can serve as good examples.

One basic assumption underlying these plans must be that in the area of automobile accidents market control is important. If not, the administrative efficiency of general-revenue based social insurance plans supplemented by direct, specific deterrence controls would make that approach clearly preferable. Thus the Keeton-O'Connell plan in effect answers positively the question of whether there is a sufficient gain in market deterrence to justify the costs of the categorization the plan implies. In addition, to the extent that these plans allocate most economic costs to car owners rather than victims, there is the basic assumption that categories of car owners are cheaper avoiders of economic losses than categories of victims. The assumptions that must underlie allocation of some pain and suffering losses to victims are more complex and need not be discussed here, but the earlier discussion of pain and suffering should serve to indicate what they are.

Another assumption these plans make is that the insurance categories that would result are sufficiently broad so that there would not be undue secondary costs. First-party insurance categorization, it is assumed, would not make driving so expensive for certain accident-prone groups that we would, as a society, prefer to have more accident costs than bear the secondary costs implied in excluding these groups from driving. This assumption may be only a tentative one, however, for it is still possible for first-party insurance plans to subsidize particular categories of car owners, e.g. the aged, should the plan result in too great a concentration of accident costs on them.

Perhaps more interesting are the answers implicit in the choice made for first-party rather than third-party insurance. Here the questions seem to deal with what kinds of subcategories are most important in terms of cheap accident cost avoidance. In effect, the Keeton-O'Connell and American Insurance Association plans seem to assume that it is more important, in terms of market control of accidents, to distinguish subcategories of car owner by the frailty and number of passengers they are likely to have and by the passenger protection (such as seat belts) their cars afford, than it is to distinguish car owners by subcategories that reflect their proneness to injure those who ride in other cars. From the standpoint of market control of accidents this is essentially an empirical question.

It would be an error in terms of our analysis, however, to suppose that only a choice as to optimal categorization for market control of accidents is implied in the decision for first-party insurance. The decision implies a great deal about what can be best accomplished through specific deterrence as well. Thus, third-party insurance systems are likely to lead to specific safety rules governing those car safety features affecting passenger safety. (It is not surprising in view of the fact that our current system is basically third-party that recent safety legislation has been especially of this kind.) Adoption of plans like Keeton-O'Connell would give rise to a demand for a totally different kind of collective rule, one that centered on third-party safety and distinguished, for instance, between the Safety Six which gives passenger safety without endangering third parties, and the Juggernaut Eight which does not. A choice for first-party plans must, therefore, imply answers regarding not only which subcategories can be controlled best through the market, but also which subcategories can be controlled best through collective measures. We may well choose to use market control of subcategories that are not quite the best suited to market control if the supplementary collective controls this market system requires are much more effective, or on moral grounds much more desirable, than the collective controls required by alternative market control systems. In short, the choice between first- and third-party insurance systems implies a choice as to the *comparative* advantage between controlling some subcategories of driving through the market and others collectively. And this is a political as well as an empirical question.

More than this is implied, however. It is possible, for instance, that first-party insurance categories are broader and result in fewer secondary costs than third-party categories. If this is so, plans like Keeton-O'Connell may seem preferable to third-party plans even if they cannot show that they would lead to better primary cost avoidance than third-party plans would. (Indeed, if the secondary cost avoidance they give is great enough, they might be preferable even if they were slightly less effective at primary accident cost avoidance.) Similarly, the administrative efficiency of one type of plan might justify it over its alternatives where we have insufficient information as to the relative advantages the competing systems have with respect to either primary or secondary cost avoidance.

One could go on and examine each plan and its alternatives in great detail, as in effect I have done with the fault system, but that is not my object. I have spent a little time on the implications of first-party versus third-party plans not to begin to choose between them, but to indicate the kinds of questions the analysis in this book would wish to have discussed in great detail in choosing between plans of all descriptions.

Some of these questions imply political choices and thus have no clearly discoverable answer; and even the empirical questions relevant to choosing among plans are rarely capable of precise answer. It would nonetheless be a grave error to conclude—as Blum and Kalven seem to—that we cannot shift from our current system until precise answers are available. In the first place, if good questions are asked, good guesses can be made where empirical data needed for precise answers is unavailable. In the second place, as has already been pointed out, the fault system is so ineffective that even if we cannot choose with total certainty among possible substitutes we can certainly do better than we are doing now. We can do better, that is, with regard to every goal of accident law except the goal of retaining the status quo.

In such a situation, change is virtually inevitable, whether it is made consciously or not. Thus it is instructive that Blum and Kalven themselves end up advocating a plan that is more radical than most because it involves total externalization of some accident costs. And the Defense Research Institute, while also seeming to advocate no change, supports moves that seem to lead inevitably to a largely social insurance type of system. The question is not, therefore, whether we will change. It is, rather, whether we can make changes consciously and intelligently, guessing where we must, seeking precise answers where we can, and making political judgments where they are implied; or whether we are required by the existence of opposition to change to accept changes, such as those implied in the ever increasing importance of collateral sources of compensation for accident victims, not because they seem to be the best, but because they can be made without ever meeting the current system head on.

A third possibility does exist, of course, and that is to make changes consciously but to retain enough of the current system to satisfy those who live off it or who would regret its passing for sentimental reasons. In this regard it is significant that two systems of accident law recently suggested as replacements for the fault system in the area of automobile accidents, Keeton-O'Connell and Alfred F. Conard's plan, have both contemplated retaining something of the fault system's determinations at the fringes.[1] In neither of these cases is the fault system expected to be crucial in allocating accident costs. On the contrary, it is retained as an appendage that is expected to wither over time, and that, although costly, can be put up with so long as it does not significantly affect the allocation of accident losses.

More significant, from my point of view, than the retention of this stump of a fault system is the fact that these two proposed systems take diametrically opposed views on the relative importance of primary market control of accidents as against secondary and tertiary cost avoidance.[2] As such, they pose in the most general way real alternatives which those who are concerned with systems of accident law must face. Indeed, a look at most of the systems proposed for the reform of accident law suggests that the real issue of the coming decades will not be the show battle over the fault system, but rather the quiet war between those who, by pushing various systems of so-called enterprise liability or first- or third-party nonfault insurance, seek to give primacy to primary cost avoidance and some market control over accidents and those who, by urging greater and greater social insurance paid for from general taxes, seek to give primacy to secondary cost avoidance, with perhaps some collective primary cost control attached. The

1. Compare *AACP* at 127–28 and Alfred F. Conard and J. Ethan Jacobs, "New Hope for Consensus in the Automobile Injury Impasse," 52 *A.B.A.J.* 533 (1966), with Keeton-O'Connell, at 274–76, 323–26.

2. The plans emphasizing secondary and tertiary cost avoidance can be taken to imply that specific deterrence types of penalties (fines, loss of driving privileges, criminal sanctions, etc.) should be used to give some primary cost avoidance and thereby buttress secondary and tertiary cost avoidance; Conard's is one of the few which discusses the issue explicitly, however.

fault system may remain nominally untouched as this war is fought, but it is already clear that the important allocations of accident losses will not be made in accordance with its criteria. How they will be made will depend in any given area of accident law on whether the enterprise liability or social insurance point of view prevails.

List of Works Cited

BOOKS

American Insurance Association, *Report of Special Committee to Study and Evaluate the Keeton-O'Connell Basic Protection Plan and Automobile Accident Reparations,* New York, American Inance Association, 1968.

Arrow, Kenneth J., *Social Choice and Individual Values,* 2d ed., New York, John Wiley & Sons, 1963.

Atiyah, P. S., *Vicarious Liability in the Law of Torts,* London, Butterworths, 1967.

———, *Accidents, Compensation and the Law,* London, Weidenfeld and Nicholson, 1970.

Blum, Walter J., and Kalven, Harry, Jr., *Public Law Perspectives on a Private Law Problem—Auto Compensation Plans,* Boston, Little, Brown and Co., 1965.

Cahn, Edmond N., *The Sense of Injustice,* Bloomington, Indiana University Press, 1964.

Comporti, Marco, *Esposizione al Pericolo e Responsabilità Civile,* Napoli, Morano, 1965.

Conard, Alfred F., et al., *Automobile Accident Costs and Payments: Studies in the Economics of Injury Reparation,* Ann Arbor, University of Michigan Press, 1964.

Duesenberry, James S., *Income, Saving and the Theory of Consumer Behavior,* Cambridge, Harvard University Press, 1959.

Elliott, Derek William, and Street, Harry, *Road Accidents,* London, Allen Lane, Penquin Press, 1968.

Fleming, John G., *An Introduction to the Law of Torts,* Oxford, Clarendon Press, 1967.

Gregory, Charles O., and Kalven, Harry, Jr., *Cases and Materials on Torts,* 2d ed. Boston, Little, Brown, and Co., 1969.

Hall, Sir John Richard, *Trial of Abraham Thornton,* Edinburgh, William Hodge & Co., 1926.

Harari, Abraham, *The Place of Negligence in the Law of Torts,* Melbourne, Law Book Co. of Australasia Pty Ltd., 1962.

Harper, Fowler V., *A Treatise on the Law of Torts,* Indianapolis, Bobbs-Merrill Co., Inc., 1933.

————, and James, Fleming, Jr., *The Law of Torts,* vol. 2, Boston, Little, Brown and Co., 1956.

Hart, H. L. A., and Honoré, A. M., *Causation in the Law,* Oxford, Clarendon Press, 1962.

Hippel, Eike von, *Schadensausgleich bei Verkehrsunfällen,* Berlin, Walter De Gruyter, 1968.

Holmes, Oliver Wendell, Jr., *The Common Law* (Howe ed.), Cambridge, Belknap Press, 1963.

Keeton, Robert, and O'Connell, Jeffrey, *Basic Protection for the Traffic Victim,* Boston, Little, Brown and Co., 1965.

Linden, Allen M., *The Report of the Osgoode Hall Study on Compensation for Victims of Automobile Accidents,* Toronto, Ryerson Press, 1965.

Little, I. M. D., *A Critique of Welfare Economics,* 2d ed. Oxford, Clarendon Press, 1957.

Marshall, Alfred, *Principles of Economics,* 8th ed. New York, Macmillan, 1920.

Pigou, A. C., *The Economics of Welfare,* 4th ed. London, Macmillan, 1932.

Revue Internationale de Droit Comparé, 19 (1967), 757.

Rodotà Stefano, *Il Problema della Responsabilità Civile,* Milano, Giuffrè, 1964.

Samuelson, Paul A., *Foundations of Economic Analysis,* Cambridge, Harvard University Press, 1953.

Stigler, George J., *The Theory of Price,* 3d ed. New York, Macmillan, 1967.

Trimarchi, Pietro, *Causalità e Danno,* Milano, Giuffrè, 1967.

————, *Rischio e Responsabilità Oggetiva,* Milano, Giuffrè, 1961.

Tunc, André, *La Sécurité Routière,* Paris, Librairie Dalloz, 1966.

ARTICLES

Andenaes, Johannes, "General Prevention—Illusion or Reality?" *Journal of Criminal Law, Criminology & Police Science,* 43 (1952), 176.

————, "The General Preventive Effects of Punishment," *University of Pennsylvania Law Review,* 114 (1966), 949.

Blum, Walter J., and Kalven, Harry, Jr., "The Empty Cabinet of Dr. Calabresi," *University of Chicago Law Review, 34* (1967), 239.

———, "A Stopgap Plan for Compensating Auto Accident Victims," *Insurance Law Journal* (1968), 661.

———, "The Uneasy Case for Progressive Taxation," *University of Chicago Law Review, 19* (1952), 417.

Bohm, P., "On The Theory of 'Second Best,'" *Review of Economic Studies, 34* (1967), 301.

Boodman, David M., "Safety and Systems Analysis, With Applications to Traffic Safety," *Law and Contemporary Problems, 33* (1968), 488.

Buchanan, James M., "In Defense of *Caveat Emptor,*" on file, Yale University Law Library.

Calabresi, Guido, "Fault, Accidents and the Wonderful World of Blum and Kalven," *Yale Law Journal, 75* (1965), 216.

———, "Views and Overviews," *University of Illinois Law Forum* (1967), 600.

———, "Does The Fault System Optimally Control Primary Accident Costs?" *Law and Contemporary Problems, 33* (1968), 429.

———, "Transaction Costs, Resource Allocation And Liability Rules —A Comment," *Journal of Law & Economics, 11* (1968), 67.

———, "The Decision for Accidents: An Approach to Nonfault Allocation of Costs," *Harvard Law Review, 78* (1965), 713.

———, "Reflections on Medical Experimentation in Humans," *Daedalus* (Spring 1969), 387.

———, "Some Thoughts on Risk Distribution and the Law of Torts," *Yale Law Journal, 70* (1961), 499.

———, and Bass, Kenneth C., III, "Right Approach, Wrong Implications: A Critique of McKean on Products Liability," on file, Yale University Law Library.

Clark, J. M., "Toward a Concept of Workable Competition," *American Economic Review, 30* (1940), 241.

Coase, R. H., "The Problem of Social Cost," *Journal of Law & Economics, 3* (1960), 1.

Conard, Alfred E., "The Economic Treatment of Automobile Injuries," *Michigan Law Review, 63* (1964), 279.

———, and Jacobs, J. Ethan, "New Hope for Consensus in the Automobile Injury Impasse," *American Bar Association Journal, 52* (1966), 533.

Cramton, Roger C., "Driver Behavior and Legal Sanctions," *Driver Behavior—Cause and Effect* (Proceedings of the Second Annual Traffic Safety Research Symposium of the Automobile Insurance Industry), Washington, Insurance Institute for Highway Safety, 1968.

Davis, O. A., and Whinston, A. B., "Piecemeal Policy in the Theory of Second Best," *Review of Economic Studies, 34* (1967), 323.

———, "Welfare Economics and the Theory of Second Best," *Review of Economic Studies, 32* (1965), 1.

Defense Research Institute, Inc., "Alleged Savings Under Keeton Plan Disputed," *For the Defense* (DRI Newsletter), 8 (1967), 73.

———, "Auto Compensation Plans Change—At Any Cost?" *For the Defense, 8* (1967), 73.

———, "Basic Protection—Diminished Justice At High Cost," *For the Defense, 8* (1967), 73.

———, "Board Seeks Directives To Wear Safety Belts," *For the Defense, 9* (1968), 17.

———, "Defense Memo—The Case Against the Collateral Source Rule," *For the Defense, 8* (1967), insert between pp. 60–61.

———, "DRI Board Opposes All No-Fault Plans," *For the Defense, 9* (1968), 73.

———, "Minnesotans Reject Premises of Keeton-O'Connell Plan," *For the Defense, 9* (1968), 65.

———, "A Program for Highway Accident Prevention," *For the Defense, 9* (1968), 65.

Dorfman, Robert, "Comments on Roland N. McKean, 'Products Liability: Trends and Implications,'" on file, Yale University Law Library.

Feezer, L. W., "Capacity to Bear Loss as a Factor in the Decision of Certain Types of Tort Cases," *University of Pennsylvania Law Review, 78* (1930), 805.

Fishlow, Albert, and David, Paul A., "Optimal Resource Allocation in an Imperfect Market Setting," *Journal of Political Economy, 69* (1961), 529.

Franklin, Marc A., "Replacing the Negligence Lottery: Compensation and Selective Reimbursement," *University of Virginia Law Review, 53* (1967), 774.

Friedman, Milton, and Savage, L. J., "The Utility Analysis of Choices Involving Risk," *Journal of Political Economy, 56* (1948), 279.

Fromm, Gary, "Aviation Safety," *Law and Contemporary Problems, 33* (1968), 590.

Gilmore, Grant, "Products Liability: A Commentary," on file, Yale University Law Library.

Gregory, Charles O., "Contribution Among Joint Tortfeasors: A Defense," *Harvard Law Review, 54* (1941), 1170.

————, "Rejoinder," *Harvard Law Review, 54* (1941), 1184.

Hand, Learned, "Have the Bench and Bar Anything to Contribute to the Teaching of Law?" *Michigan Law Review, 24* (1926), 466.

Harari, Abraham, book review, on file, Yale University Law Library. (Review of Fleming, *An Introduction to the Law of Torts*).

Hellner, Jan, "Tort Liability and Liability Insurance, *Scandinavian Studies in Law, 6* (1962), 129.

Jaffe, Louis L., book review, *Southern California Law Review, 39* (1966), 33. (Review of Blum and Kalven, *Public Law Perspectives on a Private Law Problem—Auto Compensation Plans*).

James, Fleming, Jr., "Contribution Among Joint Tortfeasors: A Pragmatic Criticism," *Harvard Law Review, 54* (1941), 1156.

————, "Replication," *Harvard Law Review, 54* (1941), 1178.

Jolowicz, J. A., "Liability for Accidents," *Cambridge Law Journal, 26* (1968), 50.

————, "The Protection of the Consumer and Purchaser of Goods under English Law," *Modern Law Review, 32* (1969), 1.

Jørgensen, Stig, "The Decline and Fall of the Law of Torts," forthcoming, *American Journal of Comparative Law*.

————, "Towards Strict Liability in Tort," *Scandinavian Studies in Law, 7* (1963), 25.

Lave, Lester B., "Safety in Transportation: The Role of Government," *Law and Contemporary Problems, 33* (1968), 512.

Linden, Allen M., "A Century of Tort Law in Canada: Whither Unusual Dangers, Products Liability and Automobile Accident Compensation?" *Canadian Bar Review, 45* (1967), 831.

Lipsey, R. G., and Lancaster, Kelvin, "The General Theory of Second Best," *Review of Economic Studies, 24* (1956), 11.

————, "McManus on Second Best," *Review of Economic Studies, 26* (1958–59), 225.

McKean, Roland, N., "Products Liability: Trends and Implications," on file, Yale University Law Library.

McManus, M., "Comments on the General Theory of Second Best," *Review of Economic Studies, 26* (1958–59), 209.

——, "Private and Social Costs in the Theory of Second Best," *Review of Economic Studies, 34* (1967), 317.

Morris, Clarence, and Paul, James C. N., "The Financial Impact of Automobile Accidents," *University of Pennsylvania Law Review, 110* (1962), 913.

Negishi, Takashi, "The Perceived Demand Curve in the Theory of Second Best," *Review of Economic Studies, 34* (1967), 315.

Nutter, G. Warren, "The Coase Theorem on Social Cost: A Footnote," *Journal of Law & Economics, 11* (1968), 503.

——, "The Extent and Growth of Enterprise Monopoly," in Grampp, William D., and Weiler, Emanuel T., eds., *Economic Policy,* Homewood, Ill., Richard D. Irwin, Inc., 1953.

O'Connell, Jeffrey, "Taming The Automobile," *Northwestern University Law Review, 58* (1963), 299.

Rottenberg, Simon, "On the Social Utility of Accidental Damage to Human Resources," in *Federal Programs for the Development of Human Resources* (papers submitted to the Subcommittee on Economic Progress of the Joint Economic Committee of the Congress of the United States, 90th Congress, 2d Session), Vol. 2, Washington, Government Printing Office, 1968.

Ruggles, Nancy, "Recent Developments in the Theory of Marginal Cost Pricing," *Review of Economic Studies, 17* (1949), 107.

Sands, Paul E., "How Effective Is Safety Legislation?" *Journal of Law & Economics, 11* (1968), 165.

Schelling, T. C., "The Life You Save May Be Your Own," in Chase, Samuel B., Jr., ed., *Problems in Public Expenditure Analysis,* Washington, Brookings Institution, 1968.

Smith, Jeremiah, "Sequel to Workmen's Compensation Acts," *Harvard Law Review, 27* (1914), 235, 344.

Smith, Young B., "Frolic and Detour," *Columbia Law Review, 23* (1923), 444.

Spengler, Joseph J., "The Economics of Safety," *Law and Contemporary Problems 33* (1968), 619.

Tunc, André, "Introduction," *Revue Internationale de Droit Comparé,* 19 (1967), 757.

Vickrey, William, "Automobile Accidents, Tort Law, Externalities, and Insurance: An Economist's Critique," *Law and Contemporary Problems, 33* (1968), 464.

Weiler, Paul C., "Defamation, Enterprise Liability and Freedom of Speech," *University of Toronto Law Journal, 17* (1967), 278.

Whitford, W. C., "Law and the Consumer Transaction: A Case Study of the Automobile Warranty," *Wisconsin Law Review* (1968), 1006.

————, "Strict Products Liability and the Automobile Industry: Much Ado About Nothing," *Wisconsin Law Review* (1968), 83.

Williamson, Oliver E., Olson, Douglas G., and Ralston, August, "Externalities, Insurance, and Disability Analysis," *Economica, 34* (1967), 235.

Analytical Table of Contents

Index

LAW

THE COSTS OF ACCIDENTS

A Legal and Economic Analysis

by Guido Calabresi

Accident law is currently under review throughout the United States, and indeed the world, as present systems prove increasingly inadequate to handle the mounting costs of automobile accidents. In this pioneering work, Guido Calabresi develops a framework for evaluating different systems of accident law.

Defining the goal of accident law as the maximum reduction of accident and accident avoidance costs that can be achieved fairly, he examines the political and economic choices implied in various approaches to reducing these costs. Calabresi then considers two fundamental problems all systems of accident law must face: who should be held responsible for accident costs, and how should they be valued? He analyzes the fault-insurance system now widely used and finds it wanting on grounds both of cost reduction objectives and fairness. In conclusion, he discusses recent proposals for reform of the law, points out questions they raise, and ends by indicating the two he thinks most likely to prevail and the fundamental conflict between them.

"Calabresi's book is most significant for its first-rate combination of modern economic analysis and legal policy. The methodology and underlying principles extend far beyond the particular subject matter of accident law to many other legal areas that could benefit from economic analysis. In turn, some economic analyses may become the richer for the discussion in this book. It is truly one of those rare important volumes."
—Gerald M. Meier.

Mr. Calabresi is John Thomas Smith Professor of Law at Yale University. He has served as law clerk to Mr. Justice Black, Supreme Court of the United States, and as a consultant to the federal Department of Transportation. $4.25

YALE UNIVERSITY PRESS, NEW HAVEN AND LONDON

ISBN 0-300-01115-6